Due
Diligence

Due Diligence

An M&A Value Creation Approach

WILLIAM J. GOLE
PAUL J. HILGER

WILEY

John Wiley & Sons, Inc.

For general information on our other products and services or for technical support, please contact our Customer Care Department within the United States at (800) 762-2974, outside the United States at (317) 572-3993 or fax (317) 572-4002.

Wiley also publishes its books in a variety of electronic formats. Some content that appears in print may not be available in electronic books. For more information about Wiley products, visit our web site at www.wiley.com.

Library of Congress Cataloging-in-Publication Data:

Gole, William J.
  Due diligence : an M&A value creation approach / William J. Gole, Paul J. Hilger.
    p. cm.
  Includes index.
  ISBN 978-0-470-37590-7 (cloth)
  1. Consolidation and merger of corporations.   2. Strategic planning.   3. Management.
I. Hilger, Paul J., 1959– II. Title.
  HD2746.5.G646   2009
  658.1′62—dc22   2009005651

Printed in the United States of America.

10 9 8 7 6 5 4 3 2 1

Contents

Preface   **xiii**
   Step-by-Step Guidance   xiii
   Organization   xiv
     Planning   xv
     Investigation   xvi
     Execution   xvii

About the Authors   **xix**

PART ONE

Planning   **1**

CHAPTER 1
Introduction   **3**
   Overview   3
     Mergers and Acquisitions: A Way of Corporate Life   3
     Mixed Results   6
     Acquisition Risk and Due Diligence   7
   Preventable Causes of Failure   10
     Myopic Approach to Due Diligence   11
     Reacting to Deals   11
     Compartmentalized Behavior   13
     Inactionable Findings   13
     Exclusive Focus on Risk Mitigation   14
   Key Success Factors   14
     Holistic View of Due Diligence   14
     Growth Strategy   15
     Integrated Management   15
     Purposeful Action   16
     Value Orientation   16

Due Diligence and Value Creation   16
Plan to Create Value   16
Strategic Purpose   17
Value Drivers   20
Key Risks   23
Purposeful Behavior   24
Key Points   25

CHAPTER 2

Planning for Value Creation: Growth Strategy   **27**
Introduction   27
Central Role of Strategic Planning   27
Chapter Focus   28
The Strategic Planning Process   29
Managing the Process   30
Characteristics of an Effective Planning Process   31
Process Overview   32
Strategic Assessment   32
Market Targeting Process   33
Investment Objectives   34
Market Expansion   35
Vertical Integration   37
Infrastructure Improvement   38
Investment Alternatives   38
Characteristics of Investment Types   39
Backup Planning   45
Plan Outputs   46
Conclusion   51
Key Points   51

CHAPTER 3

Implementing the Growth Strategy   **53**
From Identification to Pursuit   53
Choosing an Acquisition Strategy   53
Winnowing Process   54
Identification   58
Marketplace for Acquisitions   58
Identifying Prospects   59
Qualification   64
Strategic Fit   64
Availability   66
U.S. Antitrust Considerations   66

Engagement 67
  Proactive Engagement 68
    Role of Management versus Intermediaries 70
    Confidentiality of Information: Nondisclosure
      Agreement (NDA) 70
  Reactive Engagement 71
Assessment 73
  Notification/Approval Document 73
  Plan to Create Value 76
Pursuit 78
  Transaction Framework: Sellers' and Acquirers'
    Different Perspectives 79
  Taking Action: Assembling the Core Acquisition Team 81
Key Points 83

PART TWO

Investigation 85

CHAPTER 4

Preparing for Due Diligence 87

Introduction 87
  Due Diligence Reviews 88
  Chapter Focus 89
Environmental Factors 90
  External Constraints of the Sale Process 90
  Internal Limitations of the Acquirer 92
  Nature of the Target Company 92
  Impact of Environmental Factors on the Review 93
Creation of the Due Diligence Team 93
  Introduction 93
  Composition of the Due Diligence Team 94
  A Caveat 97
  Other Considerations 97
  Initial Preparation Measures 98
Development of the Due Diligence Program 99
  Program Development Process 99
  Key Aspects of the Due Diligence Program 100
  Objectives, Procedures and Findings, and
    Recommendations Illustrated 103
  A Due Diligence Mind-Set 105

Planning Due Diligence   106
    Finalize the Program   106
    Mechanisms for Team Coordination   107
    Resolve Issues of Overlap   107
    Maintain an Aggressive Posture   107
    Communicate Logistical Information   108
    Communicate Responsibility and Timing of Report
        Submissions   108
Key Points   108
Appendix 4A: Due Diligence Checklist   109
    I. Review Company Background and Organization
        and Proposed Transaction   109
    II. Financial   112
    III. Technology   114
    IV. Products   115
    V. Marketing and Sales   116
    VI. Legal   116
    VII. Insurance   119
    VIII. Human Resources   119

CHAPTER 5
Conducting the Due Diligence Review   **125**
    Introduction   125
    Overview of Transaction Types   125
        Auctions   126
            Auctions: The Buyer's Perspective   127
        Preemptive Bids   128
            Purchase Premium Preemption   129
            Price Preemption: The Buyer's Perspective   129
            Relationship-Based Preemption   130
            Relationship-Based Preemption: The Buyer's
                Perspective   130
        Summary of Transaction Characteristics   131
    Components of the Due Diligence Review   131
        Management Presentations   132
        Management Team Interviews   134
        Document Review   135
        Tour of the Facilities   136
        Technology Trade-Offs   137
    Due Diligence Reviews: An Objectives-Driven
        Approach   138

Overview 138
Due Diligence Objectives 139
Integration 140
Assessment by Function 141
   Finance and Accounting 142
   Human Resources 145
   Sales and Marketing 148
   Research and Development 150
   Information Technology Review 151
   Operations/Production Review 152
   Legal and Insurance Review 153
Cross-Functional Coordination and Analysis 154
Conclusion 159
Key Points 159
Appendix 5A: Illustrative Final Process Letter Outline 160
Invitation 160
Description of Transaction Process 160
Guidelines for Final Offers 161
Appendix 5B: Illustrative Data Room Information
Listing 161

CHAPTER 6
Reporting on Due Diligence: Deliverables and Decisions **165**

Introduction 165
Outcomes of the Due Diligence Review 165
The Importance of Backup Planning 166
Elimination in the Auction Process 167
Outputs/Reports 168
The No-Go Decision 170
No-Go Discoveries 171
   Strategic Issues 171
   Valuation Issues 172
   Risk Issues 173
Outputs/Reports 175
Renegotiations of Major Terms 175
Outputs/Reports 178
Decision to Proceed 179
Outputs/Reports 179
   Comprehensive Due Diligence Report 180
   Summary Due Diligence Report 180
   Corporate Approval Document 182

Integration Plan   186
Contingency Plan   188
Key Points   188

PART THREE

Execution   **191**

CHAPTER 7
Optimizing Value: Translating Due Diligence Findings into Action   **193**
Acting on Due Diligence Findings   193
Preacquisition vs. Postacquisition Issues   193
Revisiting the Valuation and Purchase Price   195
Reviewing the Acquisition Transaction Structure   199
Contingent Purchase Price   199
Acquiring Assets vs. Stock   200
Sharing Risk: Contractual Terms and Conditions   202
Marking Up the Draft Purchase Agreement   202
Contract Drafting and Revision   202
Key Sections of the Purchase Agreement   203
Purchase and Sale   203
Closing   205
Representations and Warranties of the Seller   206
Representations and Warranties of the Buyer   208
Covenants   208
Employment Matters   209
Conditions to Close   210
Termination   211
Indemnification   211
Tax Matters   212
General Provisions   212
Disclosure Schedules   213
Transition Services Agreement   213
Managing Contract Negotiations   215
Effective and Efficient Negotiations   215
Empowered Leadership   215
Support of Legal Counsel   216
Support by Experts   217
Review and Feedback   218
Commitment to Getting the Deal Done   220

Closing	220
Shepherding the Transaction toward Closing	220
Regulatory Approval	221
Hart-Scott-Rodino (HSR) Act	221
Buyer Financing	224
Third-Party Consents	224
Closing the Transaction	224
Key Points	225

CHAPTER 8
Integration: Extracting Value and Mitigating Risk   **227**

Dual Focus of the Integration Effort	227
Extracting Value	228
Mitigating Risk	229
Integration Team	231
Early Formation	231
Leadership	232
Structure and Composition	233
Integration Plan	234
Plan Components	234
First 90 Days vs. Longer Term	238
Management of the Integration Process	239
Communication	239
Reporting and Decision Making	242
Contingency Plan	245
Broader View of Risks	245
Plan Components	245
Human Factors	247
Culture	247
Knowledge Transfer	249
Recommendations for Postacquisition Management	250
Key Points	251

APPENDIX
What Is the Premerger Notification Program: An Overview   **253**

Index   **275**

Few corporate transactions rival mergers and acquisitions (M&A) for their magnitude, complexity, and risk. Prospective acquirers, acutely aware of M&A's mixed track record, seek to reduce risk by conducting a thorough examination of a business prior to closing a transaction, a process commonly known as a preacquisition due diligence review. Indeed, the words "due diligence" have become almost synonymous with risk mitigation.

Yet simply avoiding risk does not in itself ensure that an acquisition will succeed; many acquisitions of good companies still fail to create shareholder value for the acquirers. In our experience, we have found that acquirers are better served with a broader view of due diligence than traditionally held, one expanded to include both risk avoidance and value creation, and which guides the efforts of the acquiring organization throughout the entire transaction. We have based *Due Diligence: An M&A Value Creation Approach* on just such a holistic perspective, and believe that its application positions acquirers to optimally extract value from the transaction while avoiding preventable mistakes.

We are not seeking to minimize the importance of the risk assessment aspect of due diligence. Instead, we hope that the broader approach that this book advocates will allow those involved in the due diligence process to adopt the mind-set of investors as well as auditors, better aligning their organization's efforts with the transaction's underlying purpose: to create shareholder value for the acquirer.

STEP-BY-STEP GUIDANCE

We begin our discussion with a description of the strategic framework that should be in place prior to the initiation of a transaction; we then focus heavily on in-depth examination of the acquisition target prior to close; and, finally, we apply the results of that examination to the negotiation process and postclosing integration. Throughout the book, we emphasize and reinforce the following operating principles:

- *Holistic due diligence.* A cross-transactional perspective of risks and opportunities that spans the entire acquisition process, from pre-acquisition planning to postacquisition integration.
- *Sound strategic framework.* The fundamental basis and the touchstone for the acquirer's investment objectives and growth initiatives.
- *Integrated management.* Cohesive teamwork characterized by top-down objectives and cross-functional organizational coordination.
- *Purposeful behavior.* Planning and findings that determine actions before, during, and following the close of the transaction.
- *Explicit planning to create value.* An investor mind-set that looks at all actions through the lens of how they will mitigate risk or create value.

ORGANIZATION

The book is organized in a manner that places the due diligence review in the broader context of the acquisition transaction. It reflects our view that due diligence is most effective when it is a seamless overlay on the acquisition process—flowing out of its preparatory stages and influencing the team's subsequent behavior. We present the acquisition transaction as composed of the following stages:

- Establishing a growth strategy
- Screening and selecting candidates
- Establishing diligence objectives
- Validating value
- Developing actionable findings
- Negotiating and closing
- Integration
- Post-deal assessment

Holistic due diligence, in turn, is divided into three main activities, which define the book's three parts:

1. Planning
2. Investigation
3. Execution

Planning

Transaction planning includes activities that underpin the decision to acquire and inform the acquisition team's view of a prospective transaction's risks and opportunities, beginning with the development of a strategic growth plan and including the initial evaluation and screening of potential acquisition targets.

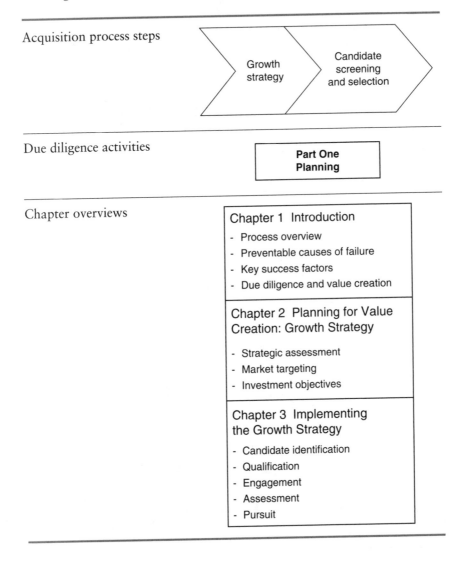

Acquisition process steps

Growth strategy

Candidate screening and selection

Due diligence activities

Part One Planning

Chapter overviews

Chapter 1 Introduction

- Process overview
- Preventable causes of failure
- Key success factors
- Due diligence and value creation

Chapter 2 Planning for Value Creation: Growth Strategy

- Strategic assessment
- Market targeting
- Investment objectives

Chapter 3 Implementing the Growth Strategy

- Candidate identification
- Qualification
- Engagement
- Assessment
- Pursuit

Investigation

The book's second part includes activities that traditionally are employed in the evaluation phase of the acquisition process. This includes the planning and execution of the review, as well as the communication of its findings and recommendations.

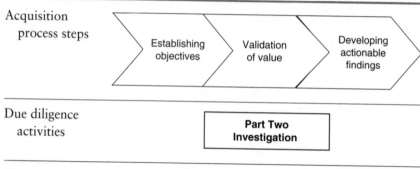

Acquisition process steps

| Establishing objectives | Validation of value | Developing actionable findings |

Due diligence activities

**Part Two
Investigation**

Chapter overviews

Chapter 4 Preparing for Due Diligence

- Environmental factors
- Due diligence team
- Due diligence objectives
- Program development

Chapter 5 Conducting the Due Diligence Review

- Components of the review
- Objectives-driven approach
- Key areas of review
- Cross-functional coordination

Chapter 6 Reporting on Due Diligence: Deliverables and Decisions

- Findings
- Recommendations: withdrawal, renegotiation, decision to proceed
- Outputs and reports

Execution

The third and final part of the book deals with the closing of the transaction and with postacquisition integration. It demonstrates how organizations can best translate due diligence findings into actions, with respect to both transaction structure and integration implementation.

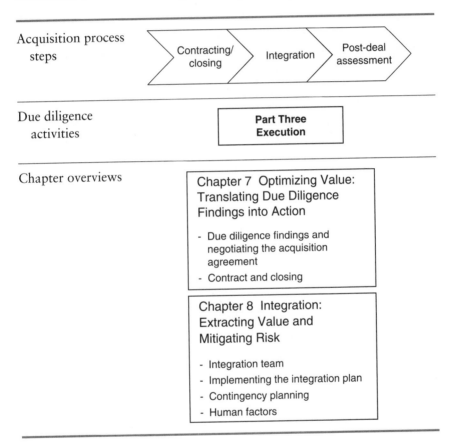

During our collaboration on *Due Diligence*, we dedicated considerable thought to the question of how to share our experience in a way that is informative, useful, and readily accessible by those actually at work on live transactions. We understand how busy professionals are in today's business environment and have a good sense of how much busier they become when working on an acquisition. So we wrote *Due Diligence* with an eye toward optimizing its usability. The chapters, as mentioned, replicate the transaction flow, so that readers can turn to the relevant phase to navigate through its process steps. The discussion within each section is compartmentalized into bulleted segments so readers can rapidly scan the segment headings for points of interest. Alternatively, a recap with cross-references (Key Points) is presented at the end of each chapter. Readers can start there, scan our bottom-line thoughts for that phase of the transaction, and then turn back to the more detailed discussion if desired. In addition, a detailed index is included at the end of the book for readers who need to locate information on the treatment of a specific topic. We also present numerous exhibits throughout the book, which readers may find helpful as templates, checklists, and reminders for the corresponding aspects of their transaction.

About the Authors

William J. Gole is a business consultant, educator, and author of professional books and continuing professional education courses for CPAs and other financial professionals. As Senior Vice President, Planning and Business Development for Thomson Healthcare, a large international publishing and communications company, he had responsibility for strategic planning and mergers and acquisitions activities from 1998 through 2004. Prior to that, Gole was a senior executive at a number of operating companies affiliated with Thomson Reuters, Inc. Gole also served as President of Frost & Sullivan, an international market research firm, in the early 1990s, and as Director of Publications at the AICPA in the mid-1980s. He initially entered the accounting profession in 1976 as a staff auditor with Coopers & Lybrand.

Paul J. Hilger is a business consultant and author with over two decades of experience as a financial executive. Over this period, in addition to his other operational responsibilities, he directed and managed the acquisition and divestiture of dozens of business properties. Hilger served as Chief Financial Officer of several divisions of Thomson Reuters, Inc., including Thomson Healthcare, Institute for Scientific Information, and Warren, Gorham & Lamont, from 1990 to 2007. Prior to Thomson Reuters, Hilger held a number of financial management positions with the McGraw-Hill Companies from 1984 to 1990. He began his career with Arthur Andersen & Co. in 1981.

Mr. Hilger and Mr. Gole have written *Corporate Divestitures: A Mergers and Acquisitions Best Practices Guide*, a book published in April 2008 by John Wiley & Sons, Inc., containing comprehensive coverage of the corporate divestiture process.

Due Diligence

Planning

CHAPTER 1

Introduction

OVERVIEW

Mergers and Acquisitions: A Way of Corporate Life

Consider the following scenario. You take an end-of-weekend look at your e-mail, only to find a message from your division's CEO about a certain company that is in play . . .

> . . . *The company's founders have apparently decided that it's time to sell their business and have retained a broker to advise them on their strategic alternatives. The broker contacted me and outlined the auction process that will be conducted. An offering memorandum will be distributed upon execution of a nondisclosure agreement. Participants will have two weeks to review the offering materials, after which nonbinding offers are expected. A selected group of bidders will be invited into the second round, which will consist of a management presentation and access to a data room, after which definitive offers are expected.*
>
> *We have to move quickly in order to have a chance of acquiring this property. Three activities should be initiated immediately:*
>
> 1. *The legal department should review and negotiate the nondisclosure agreement terms in order to receive the offering materials.*
> 2. *Business development should draft a briefing document for the corporation regarding the company: who they are, the market segment in which they operate and its attractiveness, how the*

acquisition would help us, and how an acquisition by one of our competitors would hurt us. They should work with finance to prepare an initial valuation for sizing. We have to get the corporation up to speed and excited about this market segment and the company fairly quickly because, not surprisingly, the broker has established an accelerated timetable for this deal.

3. *The data room will be open in approximately three weeks. Business development, legal, and finance should assemble a due diligence team, making sure that the necessary internal experts and external advisors are lined up and ready to hit the ground running.*

I hope your weekend was restful—we have a lot of work ahead of us.

If this scenario sounds familiar, it is because mergers and acquisitions (M&A) have become a way of corporate life. During the last five years, over 46,000 transactions were announced in the United States.[1] This statistic, however, does not take into account the many prospective transactions that progress far past an initial evaluation and never come to fruition. If 46,000 transactions were completed and announced, it is probable that corporations spent significant time and resources working on several hundred thousand potential transactions over the same period.

Why have there been so many acquisitions? The answer is relatively straightforward. Corporations compete to provide shareholders with a superior return on investment. Executives of publicly traded corporations, in particular, feel pressure to generate and sustain growth in earnings, the factor upon which corporate valuations are typically based. Earnings growth is derived from three main sources:

- Revenue from existing and newly developed products and services
- Mergers and acquisitions
- Productivity increases and cost reduction initiatives

---

[1] *Mergerstat Review* 2007 (Santa Monica, CA: Factset Mergerstat, LLC, 2007), 8.

While productivity and cost reduction represent important drivers of profits, in the absence of increasing revenues, these types of initiatives cannot produce sustainable, year-on-year earnings growth. As a result, revenue growth tends to dominate the agenda of corporate leaders, with internal (organic development) and external (acquisitions and alliances) growth strategies competing for priority and capital allocation. Further, as corporations grow, mature, and capture an ever-larger market share, organic growth produces diminishing returns and executives find themselves increasingly reliant on external options such as acquisitions to boost revenue growth.

Contrary to the impression fostered by the extensive media coverage of high-profile takeovers of publicly traded companies, the majority of acquisitions occur without much fanfare. Over 95 percent of transactions involve "below the radar" acquisitions of privately owned companies. Further, with an average transaction value of $66 million, many of these deals tend to involve comparatively small businesses, as shown in Exhibit 1.1. Indeed, many corporations view the smaller, more agile businesses in their markets as incubators for new ideas that, if proven successful, can then be swept up into the acquirer's portfolio of products and services.

The good news for acquirers is that there is seemingly no shortage of such acquisition targets because small businesses represent a significant part

EXHIBIT 1.1 Number and Size of Announced M&A Transactions

Year	Total Transactions	Number of Nonpublic	Percent Nonpublic	Average Value of Nonpublic ($ millions)
2002	7,303	6,892	94.4%	$61.4
2003	7,983	7,520	94.2%	$55.8
2004	9,783	9,411	96.2%	$66.8
2005	10,332	9,884	95.7%	$64.6
2006	10,660	10,172	95.4%	$77.6
TOTAL	46,061	43,879	95.3%	$66.1

Source: Mergerstat Review, 2007.

of the U.S. economy and generate a disproportionate share of its growth. More specifically, small firms:

- Employ about half of all private sector employees
- Generate about half of the gross domestic product
- Created 60 to 80 percent of the nation's net new jobs[2]

As a result of the high volume of deals, the acquisition process has become a routine business activity within many corporations, supported by a staff of full-time business development professionals and subject to formal acquisition policies and procedures. The high level of acquisition activity has also required the regular involvement of a broad array of executives and managers from across corporate departments. In large corporations, it is not uncommon to see executives spending almost as much time scouting smaller businesses for potential acquisition as they do tending to their responsibilities for ongoing business operations.

Mixed Results

Despite the well-established role that acquisitions play within their overall growth agenda, corporate acquirers have generally not achieved good results. In fact, the business literature has consistently stated that, on average, mergers and acquisitions have failed to achieve their acquirers' objectives. A sampling of typical findings presents a bleak picture:

- More than three-quarters of corporate combinations fail to attain projected business results... most produce higher-than-expected costs and lower-than-acceptable returns.[3]
- Fully 65 percent of major strategic acquisitions have been failures... resulting in dramatic losses of value for shareholders of the acquiring company.[4]

---

[2]U.S. Small Business Administration, Office of Advocacy, *"The Small Business Economy: A Report to the President"* (Washington, DC: U.S. Government Printing Office, 2009). Available at www.sba.gov/advo/research/.

[3]M. Beth Page, *Done Deal: Your Guide to Merger and Acquisition Integration* (Victoria, BC: Authenticity Press, 2006), 6.

[4]Mark L. Sirower, *The Synergy Trap: How Companies Lose the Acquisition Game* (New York: Free Press, 1997), 17.

- According to a PricewaterhouseCoopers survey, up to 80 percent of merger and acquisition transactions destroyed or failed to create value.[5]
- Thirty years of evidence demonstrates that most acquisitions do not create value for the acquiring company's shareholders . . . recent research shows that acquisitions in the 1990s have just as poor a record as they did in the 1970s.[6]
- Numerous studies demonstrate that, on average, M&As consistently benefit the target's shareholders, but not the acquirer's shareholders.[7]

This is hardly new information; documentation of acquirers' overall record of failure stretches back decades. But a high rate of failure certainly does not suggest that all deals fail. In fact, the literature covering mergers and acquisitions is replete with case studies of individual deals whose results fall everywhere within a broad spectrum bounded by clear failures and unqualified successes. Outcomes of individual transactions across, and even within, organizations vary widely. And in practice, a track record that includes at least a few solidly performing acquisitions may convince organizations that, while difficult and perhaps uncommon to achieve, success is possible.

As a result, this history of mixed results has not caused corporations to turn away from acquisitions as an important part of their growth strategy. In fact, the pace of transactions, despite the risks, continues seemingly unabated. The practical question that corporations face, then, is not whether to continue to pursue acquisitions, but what can be done to increase their odds of success.

Acquisition Risk and Due Diligence

Other aspects of the scenario presented in the previous sections should sound familiar: the prospective buyer's mobilization of a due diligence effort, often in the context of a competitive auction.

---

[5]Alexandra Reed Lajoux and Charles M. Elson, *The Art of M&A Due Diligence* (New York: McGraw-Hill, 2000), xi.

[6]Robert G. Eccles, Kersten L. Lanes, and Thomas C. Wilson, *Harvard Business Review on Mergers and Acquisitions* (Boston: Harvard Business School Press, 2001), 46.

[7]David M. Schweiger, *M&A Integration: A Framework for Executives and Managers* (New York: McGraw-Hill, 2002), 4.

As the business literature makes clear, acquisitions are inherently risky investment decisions. One factor contributing to this risk is acquirers' lack of detailed knowledge about the businesses they pursue. Although a general level of familiarity may exist, crucial data about targeted companies is often beyond the reach of prospective acquirers, buried in books and records, or residing in the experience of the target company's management team. This forces organizations to make their acquisition business cases dependent on *assumptions* about the condition and future prospects of targeted businesses; and faulty assumptions may mean the difference between success and failure. Consequently, corporations are generally unwilling to make an acquisition of any magnitude without the opportunity to first take a closer look—to gain comfort that a target business is what it is represented to be, to validate key assumptions, and to mitigate the risk that an acquisition will bring unwelcome surprises.

This closer look that potential buyers take at targeted businesses is referred to as *due diligence*. Due diligence, as a general concept, is a familiar one in business. The term has its roots in common law, and its usage in the United States dates at least as far back as the U.S. Securities Act of 1933, which required certain parties involved in a security offering to conduct an investigation into the company as a way to defend against accusations of inadequate disclosure to investors. Over time, the term has come into use in a number of other settings, including the investigation of potential mergers and acquisitions. In the context of mergers and acquisitions, due diligence traditionally encompasses those activities:

- Performed by a team of internal experts or external advisors
- Performed during a specified period of time in a transaction when the seller provides access to the target company
- Performed when the team strives to discover as much as possible about the true state and future prospects of the business
- That inform decisions the acquirer must make about the deal
- That, by validating key assumptions, search for previously undisclosed risks, support or alter the valuation, and provide input for the negotiation of the definitive purchase agreements

Driven by this focus on validation and risk mitigation, due diligence teams typically include contingents of legal and accounting professionals, along with selected corporate managers and executives, who scrutinize key aspects of target business, such as:

- *Financial.* Financial statements and tax returns, assets and liabilities, and debt and credit arrangements
- *Legal.* Corporate documents, contracts and agreements, ongoing, pending, and potential litigation, environmental matters, legal and regulatory compliance, and international transactions
- *Business.* Strategy and plans, customers, products, and markets and competition
- *Operations.* Technology, property plant, and equipment, facilities, real estate, and insurance coverage
- *Human resources.* Organization, management, personnel, employee benefits, and labor matters

Due diligence teams also provide a critical intangible benefit to acquirers, acting as a needed voice of skepticism within acquiring organizations, counterbalancing the potentially blinding enthusiasm exuded by deal champions. In making decisions about potential acquisitions, corporations rely on the performance of due diligence to function as a key gating factor, to ensure that both positive and negative factors are evaluated and weighed.

Recognizing the legitimate concerns of potential buyers, sellers customarily provide some level of access to target companies' business and financial information and senior management personnel before definitive offers for acquisition are expected. It should be kept in mind, however, that sellers are focused on their own interests, including:

- Creating a competitive field of multiple potential acquirers while minimizing disruption to the target business
- Ensuring that the sale process is fair—that all potential acquirers have access to the same information
- Protecting competitively sensitive information, especially from the majority of bidders (who will ultimately be unsuccessful)
- Maximizing the value of the sale

Sellers normally bring businesses to market through auction-style sale processes, managed by professional business brokers or investment bankers.

Although auctions usually accommodate acquirers' need to perform due diligence, their fundamental purpose is to optimize the transaction for the seller, putting into play a clash between buyers' concerns and sellers' interests. In fact, sellers often use the competitive leverage provided by auctions to constrain the level of due diligence performed by potential acquirers. They accomplish this by limiting access to a predefined period when target company leadership is showcased through management presentations and detailed information is provided via actual or virtual "data rooms." Sellers limit buyers' access because they see more downside than upside in providing greater access. If a target business is optimally presented within its marketing documents (typically its offering document or prospectus), by definition, due diligence will offer little prospect of further enhancing its image (and value). At best, favorable aspects can be confirmed and, at worst, unfavorable aspects can be unearthed. As a result, sellers normally attempt to push participants to complete their due diligence rapidly and control the amount of information made available, creating an environment of dynamic tension for buyers, and further adding to acquirers' existing risk.

Looking at the intrinsic risk of acquisitions and the difficult environment within which they take place, it is understandable why so many transactions fail. But many acquirers also succeed or fail for reasons that are within their control. We strongly believe that *a soundly planned and well-executed due diligence review* remains the best way to make a major difference in an acquisition's results. Such a due diligence process leaves a potential acquirer much better positioned against other bidders, mitigates acquisition risk, and increases its odds of success. Likewise, an organization that gives insufficient attention to the critical but frequently overlooked details of due diligence does so at its peril. Our goal in writing this book is to present and discuss a comprehensive, step-by-step guide for performing due diligence based on practices and principles that we observed to be most effective in practice.

PREVENTABLE CAUSES OF FAILURE

We begin by examining some of the potential causes of acquisition failure that can be attributed to poor execution by the acquirer. Our intent here is not to provide an exhaustive study of every possible reason acquiring businesses can be unsuccessful, but to focus on a number of preventable causes of failure and then to outline a due diligence approach that we believe will lead to better results. An acquisition team's errors can be grouped into several categories, namely:

- Myopic approach to due diligence
- Reacting to deals
- Compartmentalized behavior
- Inactionable findings
- Exclusive focus on risk mitigation

Myopic Approach to Due Diligence

A critical mistake that acquirers can make is to view due diligence too narrowly; that is, as an exercise compressed into the period when the seller makes its books, records, and people available to prospective buyers. This perspective can have potentially disastrous consequences: The due diligence team may be assembled too late, disbanded too early, and operate in a manner that is disconnected from other acquisition activities. Perhaps worst of all, this narrow window of time might become the only period during the transaction when acquisition team members think about a deal's potential risks.

Risks exist throughout the entire transaction cycle. The root cause of a poor due diligence process may exist early in the development of an organization's growth strategy. Likewise, a postacquisition integration that does not translate due diligence findings into action can completely undermine the benefits of sound preacquisition analysis. Exhibit 1.2 illustrates the risk factors faced throughout the acquisition process. Note that "poor management of due diligence—overlooking something important" is only one of many potential risks that an acquiring organization faces.

Reacting to Deals

To some extent, mergers and acquisitions are inherently reactive because buyers have little control over owners' decisions about whether and when to sell their businesses, but this does not excuse a lack of planning. Organizations that do not give advance consideration to those market areas and the kinds of prospective acquisitions that best serve their interests are poorly positioned to respond to deals when they materialize. We illustrated just such an organization in the scenario in the section titled "Mergers and

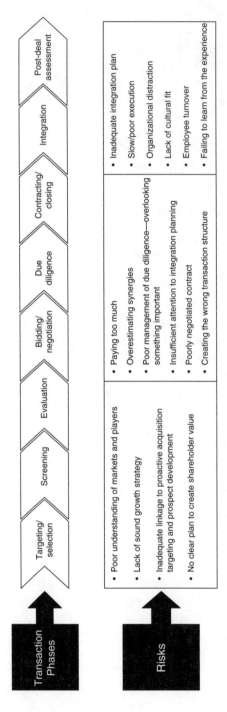

Transaction Phases

Targeting/ selection → Screening → Evaluation → Bidding/ negotiation → Due diligence → Contracting/ closing → Integration → Post-deal assessment

Risks

- Poor understanding of markets and players
- Lack of sound growth strategy
- Inadequate linkage to proactive acquisition targeting and prospect development
- No clear plan to create shareholder value

- Paying too much
- Overestimating synergies
- Poor management of due diligence—overlooking something important
- Insufficient attention to integration planning
- Poorly negotiated contract
- Creating the wrong transaction structure

- Inadequate integration plan
- Slow/poor execution
- Organizational distraction
- Lack of cultural fit
- Employee turnover
- Failing to learn from the experience

EXHIBIT 1.2 Risks Exist throughout the Entire Acquisition Process

Acquisitions: A Way of Corporate Life." One may have wondered why the division needed to introduce corporate management to both the candidate and to the market segment in which it operated. This organization faces an uphill battle in terms of its internal decision making, and the acquisition team may confuse justification of the transaction with analysis of its merits.

The launch of a particular deal should not mark the occasion of the first conversation within the potential acquirer about its growth strategy. If organizations are continually reacting to deals as they are brought to market, they run the risk of being enticed into randomly acquiring businesses unaligned with their organizational goals and objectives.

Compartmentalized Behavior

As mentioned in the section "Acquisition Risk and Due Diligence," due diligence teams can consist of an eclectic group, including specialists such as legal, tax, business development, and accounting professionals, along with corporate managers who provide expertise in areas such as technology, human resources, operations, sales, and marketing. The benefit of involving multiple parties is that a thorough examination of an acquisition target can be conducted within a reasonably short time span, especially if the seller's data is made available for simultaneous electronic access.

There is, however, a related risk of bringing too many perspectives to the due diligence review: It can cause the process to become compartmentalized and allow important items to be overlooked. By definition, specialists tend to look at issues through the filter of their training. For example, if a due diligence team relies on its legal experts to review customer contracts in an asset purchase, it can rest assured that the key terms will be reviewed and abstracted and relevant legal issues, such as assignability provisions, will be studied. But without coordination across the team, the contract review may not address other issues of business significance, such as the target's approach to pricing and its implications for competitive positioning and profitability. Larger, cross-functional, deal-impacting questions may thus fall victim to the minutia of specialist scrutiny.

Inactionable Findings

Perhaps the most relevant question for a due diligence team to answer is whether it has discovered any reason why a potential acquirer should not proceed with a transaction. The objective of finding potential "deal break-ers" is so important that some organizations may believe that if none are found, all that remains of due diligence is for the team to document its find-ings that support the decision to proceed. Although negative assurance (i.e., "no reason not to proceed") is the most critical finding of a due diligence team, it also provides an acquiring organization with no road map for ac-tion other than to go ahead with the transaction. Additionally, limiting the mission of a due diligence team to this one question squanders the potential value of this assemblage of expertise. Due diligence should do more than act as the brakes on a train; it should also help to choose the right track.

Exclusive Focus on Risk Mitigation

Even in situations where an acquisition target is fully supportive of the strategy articulated by the acquirer and the risk mitigation focus of the due diligence team results in the acquisition of a good business, there is still a risk that the investment may be a bad one. This is because an acquisition of a good business is still a failure if it destroys shareholder value—if the price paid for the business exceeds the total value of the deal to the acquirer. So risk mitigation is a necessary aspect of due diligence, but it is not sufficient. There must be two essential objectives for the due diligence team: risk mitigation and value creation.

KEY SUCCESS FACTORS

The identified areas of failure can be translated into a set of operating principles that comprise a due diligence approach that better serves the acquirer's interests. These principles, or key success factors, are illustrated in Exhibit 1.3 and discussed in the sections that follow.

Holistic View of Due Diligence

An acquisition team's chances of identifying and mitigating risks are best if it looks broadly across the entire transaction continuum and methodically addresses the areas where risks can occur.

In our view, the scope of due diligence should be broad—to identify and address the full range of risks and opportunities that exist throughout

- Myopic approach
- Reacting to deals
- Compartmentalized behavior
- Inactionable findings
- Exclusive focus on risk mitigation

- Holistic view
- Growth strategy
- Integrated management
- Purposeful action
- Value orientation

EXHIBIT 1.3   Translating Causes of Failure into Key Success Factors

the transaction cycle. We will use the term *holistic due diligence* throughout the discussion to emphasize this point. Specifically, holistic due diligence should follow a sound growth strategy, inform the decision to acquire and the terms and structure of the transaction, and then guide the actions to be taken before and following the transaction.

Growth Strategy

As mentioned, an organization's decision to pursue an acquisition should be an outgrowth of a sound strategic planning process. Having such a process would provide an acquiring organization with an agreed-upon strategy for a particular market segment and, ideally, a related acquisition target list, facilitating a clear and quick assessment of the strategic merits of a given acquisition candidate. This process also provides the due diligence team with a well-thought-out set of key variables and critical assumptions to be validated during its investigation. We further discuss the linkage between strategic planning and acquisitions in Chapter 2.

Integrated Management

Methodical coordination, communication, and information sharing are essential in the management of due diligence activities. Foundational to effective cross-team management is a top-down assignment of due diligence objectives based on a transaction's particular risks and opportunities, a topic discussed in detail in Chapter 4. We also address methods and techniques for communication and information sharing in Chapter 5.

Purposeful Action

Due diligence teams should be presented with a challenge far greater than playing a key part of the go/no-go decision. Their work should also ask: What actions should the acquirer take leading up to and following the transaction to mitigate the full range of risks it faces and to fully exploit available opportunities to create shareholder value?

This notion carries into the conduct of due diligence itself. Rather than being led by the information requested and received from the targeted business, the conduct of the entire due diligence examination should be objectives-driven. Further, due diligence cannot end with the creation of a static findings report. Those findings must be expressed in terms of actions that must be taken both before and following the deal, including the negotiation and structuring of the transaction and the planning and implementation of postacquisition integration, which we address in Chapters 6, 7, and 8.

Value Orientation

To ensure that a transaction results in both the acquisition of a good business and in a profitable investment for the acquirer, due diligence must focus equally on risk mitigation and value optimization. The due diligence team should approach the process with the mentality of an investor as well as that of an auditor and use value creation as a guiding principle for many of its activities. In the next section, we will further address this notion of due diligence and value creation.

DUE DILIGENCE AND VALUE CREATION

Plan to Create Value

An organization needs more than the intention to generate a return to make an acquisition successful. Two influential authors, David Harding and Sam Rovit, point out that many companies are "terrifyingly unclear" to themselves and investors about why they are making an acquisition, and advocate that every transaction start with a clear statement of how that particular deal would create value for the acquirer.[8] We think this idea is fundamental to a

---

[8]David Harding and Sam Rovit, *Mastering the Merger: Four Critical Decisions That Make or Break the Deal* (Boston: Bain & Company, 2004), 50–51.

successful acquisition, and our guide for the conduct of due diligence builds on the requirement to develop what we refer to as a "plan to create value," in which the prospective acquirer states explicitly *why* it intends to make an acquisition and *how* it proposes to generate a return. This plan serves as a framework for the acquirer's acquisition team, to ensure that actions taken from due diligence through integration are consistent with its purpose. A plan to create value, as we define it, includes the following elements:

- *Strategic purpose.* A compelling reason to pursue the acquisition, including both a sound strategic rationale and an explicit depiction of the increase in value expected from the transaction
- *Value drivers.* An assessment of the magnitude and variability of the sources expected to generate the increased value, framing the key assumptions to be validated in due diligence
- *Key risks.* A comprehensive examination of a deal's inherent downside risks, outlining the most important issues to be mitigated before or after the acquisition

Strategic Purpose   An organization's plan to create value should begin with an explicit statement about how a given acquisition would further an organization's progress toward its strategic goals and objectives. We discuss this concept at length in Chapter 2. For now, suffice it to say, an acquisition needs to have a clearly communicated strategic rationale. This way the organization (both executive management and the deal team) knows why it is embarking on a transaction, and that the essential reasons for the acquirer's interest can be fully vetted in the due diligence team's investigation. For example, if the primary reason a corporation is interested in a particular acquisition is to acquire a certain technological capability, a fundamental goal of the due diligence team should be to validate the key assumptions made about the technology (e.g., to make sure that the target has full and unencumbered ownership rights to the technology, that it has been properly maintained, that the competitive and financial advantages afforded by the technology are sustainable, etc.). Absent a clear strategic rationale, the due diligence team might conclude that the target is a generally good company, but might not investigate certain matters to the level of depth necessary to ensure the acquisition's ability to fully deliver on its expectations.

Another critical element of the plan to create value is a calculation of the increase in value expected from the transaction. The acquirer's business case for the transaction would normally include a financial forecast showing a rate of return that exceeds the corporation's "hurdle" rate, resulting in a positive net present value for the investment. In our view, this forecast needs to be supported by the specific assumptions and actions that will *create* the return on investment, so that these can be validated during due diligence and acted on following the close of the transaction. A tight linkage between the financial drivers of value, key assumptions, required actions, and the implications for due diligence and integration planning is critical to an acquisition's success. For this reason, we now elaborate on each component of value. Exhibit 1.4 presents a visualization of the sources of value created by an acquisition investment.

The exchange between acquirer and seller can be broken down into several components:

- The acquirer delivers the *purchase price*, which consists of the *stand-alone value* of the target business, plus an *acquisition premium*.
- The acquirer receives in return the *combined value*, which is the *stand-alone value* of the target business plus the *synergy value* resulting from the integration of the target with the acquirer.

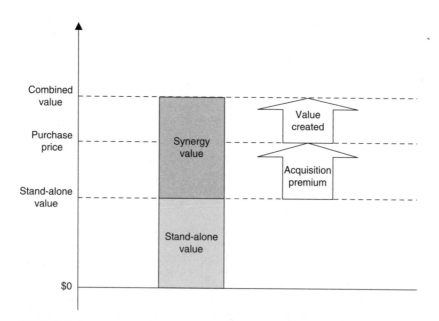

EXHIBIT 1.4   Sources of Value Created by Acquisition Investment

- The deal's success for the acquirer is measured by the *value created*, which is the *combined value* minus the *purchase price*.

A description of each term follows:

- *Stand-alone value.* Represents the potential acquirer's estimated value of an acquisition target as managed by its current ownership. If the target is a privately held business, the acquirer will need to calculate this number as the starting point for determining its bidding strategy. It is also important to calculate a stand-alone value even if the target is publicly traded in order to estimate how much future growth the market has *already* factored by into the target company's share price. The stand-alone value can be determined by calculating the present value of forecasted revenue, income, and cash flows over a 5- to 10-year period, based on factors such as:
  - Historical financial results
  - Current market position
  - Organizational strengths and weaknesses
  - Existing growth strategy
  - Projected ceiling for sustainable market size, growth, and share
  - Assessment of whether the target can attain this potential on its own
  - Assessment of key obstacles to achieving the future growth potential

    The more detailed and explicit the potential acquirer can make its assumptions in support of the forecast, the more effectively it can then validate those assumptions during due diligence. In order to ensure that the calculated stand-alone value is reasonable, it should be compared with the market value of comparable businesses.
- *Acquisition premium.* The acquisition premium represents the amount required to induce ownership to sell. If the target is a publicly traded company, the acquisition premium can be readily computed as the difference between the sale price and the market capitalization of the target preceding the acquirer's offer. If the target is privately held, the acquisition premium is the amount by which the purchase price exceeds what the acquirer thinks the business is worth on its own.
- *Purchase price.* This is whatever value is negotiated between the buyer and seller, though, as stated, it can be thought of as the stand-alone value plus the acquisition premium. It is useful to think of the purchase

price as consisting of these two components because it helps to illustrate some of the contrasting perspectives shared between the parties during price negotiations, and it underscores the direct relationship between the acquisition premium and risk. Acquirers are normally reluctant to offer more than what they view as the stand-alone value for a business (i.e., an unwillingness to pay for value that would only be created by their prospective ownership) because any acquisition premium reduces the value creation opportunity and increases the acquirer's level of risk.

Conversely, sellers expect the purchase price to include an inducement to sell, because at the stand-alone value they are theoretically and, if well-advised, practically content to hold onto their ownership stake.

- *Synergy value.* Synergy is the term commonly used by prospective acquirers as they contemplate the financial benefits of combining with the businesses they target. The synergy value of an acquisition is normally envisioned to be attainable from one of several sources:
    - *Revenue synergy.* Additional revenue growth spurred by activities such as joint product development and marketing, or cross-selling
    - *Cost synergy.* Cost reductions driven by actions such as sharing organizational infrastructure, streamlining redundant operations, or achieving economies of scale.

        The synergy value is a potentiality unique to the combination of two specific organizations, and it is produced only as the result of the postacquisition integration activities planned and implemented by the acquiring organization.
- *Combined value.* Represents the total incremental value received by an acquirer, including both the stand-alone value of the targeted company, plus full realization of the synergy value resulting from the combination of the two organizations. The combined value is best thought of as a maximum potential number.
- *Value created.* Represents the incremental value created for the shareholders of an acquirer as a result of its acquisition investment, calculated as the difference between the combined value received and purchase price paid.

Value Drivers   By making explicit its calculation of the sources of value envisioned from an acquisition investment, a prospective acquirer can clearly see which key assumptions underlie the valuation of a target business. This sets the stage for conducting a comprehensive examination of the possible variability in an acquisition's key assumptions. We use the term *value driver* to describe each key assumption addressed in the analysis to emphasize two points:

1. The analysis should be shareholder value-oriented. The focus of the analysis should center on the assumptions that have the largest bearing on the combined value of the transaction to the acquirer.
2. The analysis should be biased toward action: key assumptions to be validated in due diligence, and actions to be taken before and following the close.

We now reexamine the sources of value in an acquisition by looking at each component as a value driver:

- *Stand-alone performance.* As illustrated in Exhibit 1.5, the stand-alone value of an acquisition should not be perceived as a fixed, or "given," amount. It is dependent on the how the target business performs under

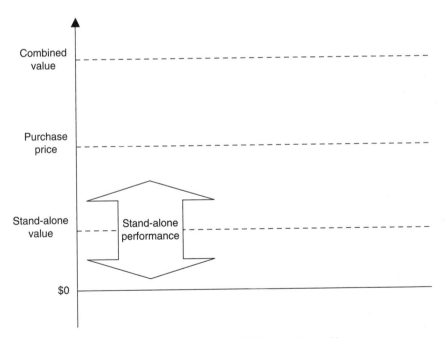

EXHIBIT 1.5 Stand-Alone Performance (and Value) Is Not a Given

the ownership of the acquirer, which has a lot to do with whether the acquirer's key assumptions about the business and its markets turn out to be correct, and how well the business is managed by the acquirer.

- *Acquisition deal structure.* It is useful to consider the purchase price to be a variable amount as well. Acquirers can and should seek to optimize all of the elements of the acquisition deal structure, not only the headline purchase price, but also the contractual terms and conditions, which can shift risk and value back and forth between buyer and seller, and even the tax structure of the transaction, which can also gain or lose value for the acquirer. This idea is illustrated in Exhibit 1.6.
- *Synergy opportunities.* The term *synergy opportunities* emphasizes that the synergy value is an amount that will accrue to the acquirer only if everything goes right with the acquisition and integration—it is a potentiality, far from a given. The acquirer will not realize the synergy value

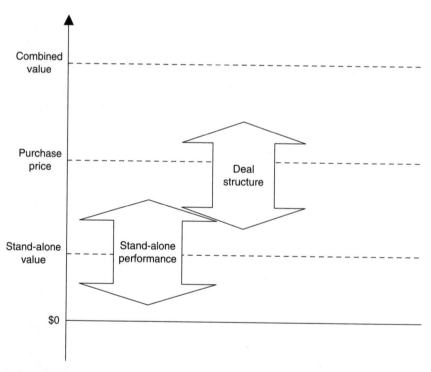

EXHIBIT 1.6 Deal Structure Can Increase or Decrease the Purchase Price

without intensive planning and well-coordinated action; and not all synergies will deliver to the full level of their potential. This area should be a major focus of both the due diligence review and the integration plan.

Exhibit 1.7 highlights the importance of synergy opportunities in value creation.

Key Risks   As discussed in the section "Myopic Approach to Due Diligence," there is a wide range of potential risks to an acquisition, either inherent in the acquired business or borne out of integrating the operations of a target business with those of the acquirer. Any number of these risks can conspire to undermine a lot of hard work and value created from synergy. Yet an acquirer is not a passive witness to the things that may or not happen to its acquired business. While it cannot control all key factors, it can influence many of them by directing its actions in a way that mitigates the downside risks inherent in a given transaction. Critical to this process is

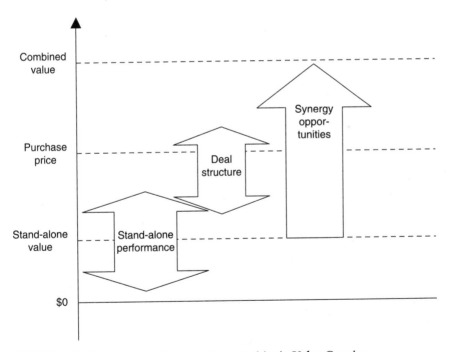

EXHIBIT 1.7   Importance of Synergy Opportunities in Value Creation

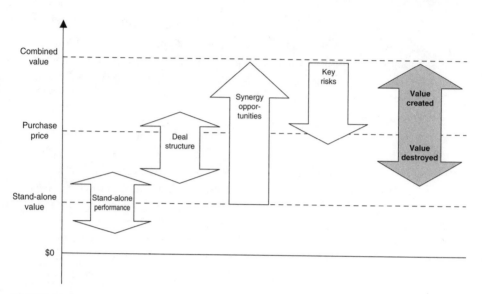

EXHIBIT 1.8 Management of Opportunities and Risks Can Mean the Difference between Value Creation and Value Destruction

assessing the full range of risks, determining which ones are most significant to the value expected from the acquisition, and methodically creating plans to mitigate the risks.

Exhibit 1.8 displays the interplay of all the key value drivers and risks and dramatizes their combined potential to either create or destroy shareholder value.

Purposeful Behavior

By preparing a plan to create value, an organization creates a solid understanding of what it hopes to achieve from a given acquisition, as well as a deep awareness of the factors that could truly make a difference to the transaction's success. This insight then needs to form a guiding framework for purposeful, proactive behavior on the part of the acquisition team to mitigate the identified risks and to optimize the value drivers of the acquisition. Absent a sound plan and a tight linkage to action, the acquiring organization risks seeing its team buffeted by the moment-to-moment events of the transaction, unsure of whether the things that absorb its time are the things that should.

Since the risks and opportunities inherent in an acquisition span the entire transaction cycle, as discussed in "Myopic Approach to Due Diligence," it follows that close direction of the acquisition team should not end with the creation of the due diligence report. As we will discuss further in Chapter 3, the plan to create value should influence action during three critical time periods:

1. *Before acquisition.* Issues requiring specific focus during the conduct of due diligence, plus items requiring resolution before the acquisition closes
2. *At acquisition.* Items that must be resolved within the acquisition transaction structure and underlying legal agreements
3. *Following acquisition.* Items that should be incorporated into the postacquisition integration and contingency plans

Key Points

1. Acquisitions have become a way of corporate life, most commonly involving small, privately held businesses. ("Mergers and Acquisitions: A Way of Corporate Life")
2. Results for acquirers have been mixed. The risk inherent in acquisitions has given rise to formal preacquisition due diligence investigations. ("Mixed Results" and "Acquisition Risk and Due Diligence")
3. Risks and opportunities exist throughout the transaction's lifecycle, necessitating a broader view of due diligence. ("Myopic Approach to Due Diligence")
4. Acquiring a good business does not guarantee an adequate return on investment. We believe that acquisition teams should possess the perspective of both an auditor and an investor in order to achieve two critical objectives: risk mitigation and value creation. ("Exclusive Focus on Risk Mitigation")
5. Holistic due diligence, a cross-transactional perspective, is required to address a transaction's full range of risks and opportunities. ("Key Success Factors")

6. We advocate a plan to create value to serve as the framework for purposeful behavior leading up to, during, and following the close of the acquisition. The plan to create value includes the following elements ("Plan to Create Value"):

- Strategic purpose
- Value drivers
- Key risks

CHAPTER 2

Planning for Value Creation

Growth Strategy

INTRODUCTION

Central Role of Strategic Planning

We believe that it is a central tenet of M&A best practice that investment strategy, and acquisition activities in particular, should be guided and driven by purposeful strategic planning. Strategic planning should be the first step by an organization in identifying investment initiatives that will provide the best opportunity for profitable growth, superior returns, and, ultimately, value creation. Strategic planning also serves as a mechanism to minimize investment risk by clearly documenting long-term objectives and their rationale, and by providing the grounding for downstream decision making, specifically those decisions associated with investment initiatives. In the absence of such grounding, organizations are much more likely to be exposed to behaviors that are opportunistic in nature, undisciplined in their execution, and inconsistent with the organization's strategic goals.

The strategic plan serves as a linchpin between an organization's overarching goals and the tactics it intends to use to achieve them. Most organizations periodically articulate high-level strategic objectives to shareholders and the broader investment community. These objectives are frequently expressed in quantified form, such as "the corporation will achieve average growth in revenue and income of 'X' percent over the next 'Y' years," and are meant to communicate the organization's intent to profitably grow its business and to enhance shareholder value. The strategic plan is an action-oriented elaboration on those objectives. It is intended to provide the detail behind these broadly sketched objectives and it is the link to specific investment activities that support them. At the operating company level within a large, tiered corporate organization, the strategic plan also serves as a communication vehicle that enables the operating company to provide corporate management with an early view of the tactics (internal or external investment) that it plans on using to accomplish its growth and value creation objectives.

It is also important to note that the strategic plan is not a static document. Its development is not intended to provide a linear path to a specific investment. As discussed and illustrated in the sections that follow, once the organization has identified its investment objectives, it must then prioritize them and then consider the mix of tactics it plans to employ to accomplish them. Tactics or investment types identified in the plan—whether to build internally, acquire, or ally with a strategic partner—are not meant to be immutable. Although the organization's best thinking should be put forth in the planning stage, there should also be sufficient flexibility in the plan so that the organization can make the *optimal* choices of investment types, in light of the facts available at the time that choice is made, and alternative approaches should be identified if circumstances dictate that the original choice or choices are not feasible.

Chapter Focus

The focus of the discussion in this chapter is on the strategic planning process employed by most large corporations and the importance of its relationship to investment decisions. The chapter outlines the planning process and how investment decisions flow from that process. It specifically covers the following:

- An overview of the *planning process* and important aspects and characteristics of that process
- A description of the *strategic assessment* aspect of the planning process, including the clarification of the organization's mission and objectives and the consideration of the market and internal factors that drive or influence investment strategy
- A discussion of the types of *investment objectives* that result from that assessment, and their prioritization and selection, as well as the risks and potential rewards associated with each

- A discussion of various aspects of the *investment vehicles* (internal development, acquisition, and strategic alliance) available to execute an organization's investment objectives and an approach to identifying those vehicles that best meet the organization's investment objectives

It is important to note that the scope of this discussion is narrowly focused. It is intended to provide context for understanding the *acquisition investment decision-making process* and the follow-on activities of acquisition due diligence and postacquisition integration. As a result of this narrow focus, it does not cover important but unrelated portfolio issues; namely, divestment and financial restructuring initiatives, such as corporate divestitures, equity carve outs, and stock buy backs.

Additionally, the discussion is biased toward smaller acquisitions of nonpublic businesses (either private companies or divestitures of business units by larger companies) by public companies. That bias is influenced by two factors: First, even though transactions involving two publicly traded companies affect large numbers of stakeholders and frequently get extensive coverage in the financial press, acquisitions of nonpublic entities by corporations have consistently accounted for the overwhelming number of all M&A transactions, as discussed in Chapter 1. Second, acquisitions of privately held businesses have characteristics and transaction dynamics that clearly distinguish them from M&A transactions involving publicly traded companies. The lack of publicly available company information, constraints on buyer due diligence, and the often competitive nature of the selling process (i.e., auctions) conspire to make these types of transactions substantially different from their public counterparts.

THE STRATEGIC PLANNING PROCESS

Most companies, but especially multidivisional corporations with robust investment agendas, routinely update or reinforce their growth strategies annually. These efforts generally take the form of structured strategic planning processes whose output is a formal planning document that outlines the organization's investment strategy for the next several years and identifies specific investment initiatives designed to promote profitable, long-term growth. The approach to the planning process employed varies among organizations and its form is influenced by factors such as the size, structure, maturity, and culture of the enterprise. However, the general outline of the process is fairly standard from organization to organization and shares the same basic characteristics. The planning process leading to an investment decision is illustrated in Exhibit 2.1. It shows that the planning process requires an affirmation or modification of organizational objectives, an assessment of the environment in which the organization operates, a determination of investment objectives, and a decision on how to pursue those objectives.

Managing the Process

The development of a fluid planning process generally evolves over time as an organization matures. Initially, organizations may engage planning consultants to assist them and, as they evolve and grow, create staff functions (business development or strategic planning) with responsibility for driving the planning process and coordinating investment and divestment activities, such as acquisitions, corporate divestitures, and the development of strategic alliances.

The executive management of most large organizations will generally provide their operating units with broad guidelines and assign the planning

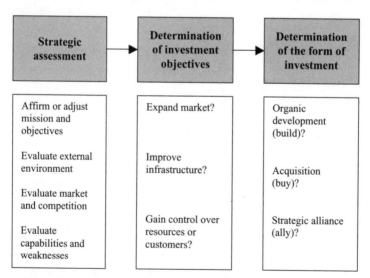

EXHIBIT 2.1 Outline of the Strategic Planning Process

team (senior operating executives of divisions and business units, along with strategic planning and finance staff members) with responsibility for developing the plan and identifying initiatives to enable its execution. In this way, corporate headquarters provides general direction and parameters for investment, while planning professionals assist those closest to the business and the markets served in developing a market-focused plan that will then be reviewed, possibly modified, and approved by corporate management.

Characteristics of an Effective Planning Process

The elements of the planning process are briefly described in the following sections. However, it should be understood that the mere existence of a structured and efficient process does not guarantee effective planning. For it to be effective, it must also be buttressed by characteristics that enhance the process and add credence to its output. Accordingly, the process should adhere to the following guiding principles:

- *It should be adaptive.* As discussed, strategic planning is not a static or linear process. To a great extent, it involves the regular modification of the organization's direction by mapping its resources and capabilities in response to the threats and opportunities presented by the environment—an environment that is often complex, dynamic, and frequently characterized by uncertainty. This dynamism requires an approach to planning that is both ongoing and iterative. The plan should be a living document and the process should have periodic checkpoints where there is intense focus on strategy, and be open to modification in the interim, when strategically disruptive events requiring course correction are encountered.
- *It should be inclusive.* Although the basic outlines of strategic planning are shared by virtually all organizations, the approach or methodology employed will vary among entities. Some may adopt a top-down or command and control approach and others may favor a bottom-up approach. Regardless of approach, it is clear that there must be a mechanism in place to ensure buy-in and ownership at all relevant levels of the organization. Meaningful input from line management is particularly important. If the plan is viewed as "imposed from above," the organization risks the loss of support from those operational managers critical to the plan's successful execution.

- *It should be credible.* The process must be sanctioned by the highest levels of the organization. It cannot be viewed internally as a mere "exercise." Corporate management must behave in a manner that reinforces the importance of the process and its output. It should be made clear that the plan will guide the actions taken by the organization, in particular its allocation and deployment of resources.
- *Its output should be clear and actionable.* The results of the planning effort must unambiguously identify the investment objectives, their rationale, and potential investment initiatives to meet those objectives. These initiatives must be more than simply vague prescriptions for growth. There should be preliminary identification of investment initiatives, along with high-level estimates of investment costs and benefits (measured by growth in revenue, profits, and cash generation) for the plan period and beyond, to provide measurable benchmarks outlining a path to reach the organization's aspirations and goals.

PROCESS OVERVIEW

Although an expansive description of the strategic planning process is beyond the scope of this discussion, an outline of the general characteristics of that process is provided in the following sections. This outline illustrates the general flow and logic of the planning process, as well as linkage of strategic planning to investment choice and execution and the potential impact of those choices on risk and return.

Strategic Assessment

Strategic assessment is at the core of the planning process. It is here that the mission of the organization (its reason for being) and its objectives (aspirational statements of excellence and quantified expressions of value creation objectives) are affirmed or modified. This is generally followed by an evaluation of the macroeconomic environment, looking closely at trends, such as technological advances, demographic change, deregulation, and globalization, and their impact on the organization's business setting.

The planners would then drill down to evaluate trends in the market(s) it serves and related markets, and the effects of these trends on market growth and profitability. Additionally, the behavior or anticipated behavior of the organization's competitors to these environmental and market trends would be considered. Finally, the planners would map the results of this assessment against the strengths and weaknesses of its business portfolio to determine where the organization should focus its investment efforts. This targeting process is described in the following section.

Market Targeting Process

The major factors influencing entry or expansion decisions relate to characteristics such as market fundamentals, the nature of the competitive environment, and the organization's competitive potential. An evaluation of these factors enables the planners to reach a preliminary conclusion about the most attractive way in which to enter or further penetrate the most promising market segments.

When approached methodically, the planners will first identify the markets with the most attractive basic characteristics, namely, size, profitability, and growth potential. They would ask questions such as:

- Is the market or segment large enough, or potentially large enough, to warrant investment?
- Are the profit margins inherent in the market comparable or superior to those of the present business?
- What has been the historical growth profile of the market? If growth has been strong, are rates sustainable?

If this evaluation survives this first filter and suggests an attractive opportunity for profitable growth, the planners then look to the competitive environment and consider the nature of the participants and potential impact of expansion or entry on their behavior. They would probe the following issues:

- Who are the major players and how much of the relevant market segments do they presently serve?
- How crowded are these market segments? Are they attracting other new competitors whose entry is putting pressure on margins?
- Are there emerging competitors who are capturing share of market at a rapid pace?
- How might competitors react to a new entrant? Are they aggressive or complacent?

The answers to these questions shape a view of the competition that enables the planners to perform a comparative assessment. They can then consider the organization's strengths and weaknesses in relation to market threats and opportunities. This, in turn, spawns questions such as:

- How do we measure up to those we consider major existing and potential competitors? Do we have strengths that can be leveraged or weaknesses or gaps that need to be addressed?
- What opportunities for market expansion or entry do conditions suggest? Does the emergence of new competitors signal a market opportunity? Does it suggest a particular form of investment? Does the disposition of major competitors (aggressive or complacent) in an attractive segment suggest a preferred form of investment?
- What level of threat do existing competitors present? Now? In the foreseeable future? Do these threats suggest initiatives to protect our market position?
- What barriers to entry exist? Are they surmountable without extraordinary effort?

The responses to these series of questions present planners with a comparative view of market and competitive conditions and will enable them to come to preliminary conclusions about the nature of the market and the appeal of expansion or entry. It will also suggest whether it makes more sense to compete through internal development initiatives, to ally with a strategic partner, or to buy into the market through acquisition (options discussed in detail in the section "Investment Alternatives") and provide a basis for preliminary targeting of potential strategic partners and acquisition candidates. Next, the planners must prioritize the organizations investment objectives and choose the most appropriate form of investment to realize each of them.

Investment Objectives

In the broadest sense, the strategic goal of the organization is to *optimize shareholder value over time*. In reducing that goal to actionable form, the planners must first evaluate the relative importance of those threats and opportunities revealed by the assessment process and translate them into specific investment objectives. They must then prioritize these objectives based on their potential to yield the maximum shareholder return (i.e., capital appreciation, measured by growth in revenue and profits; and yield, the ability of the enterprise to translate that growth into cash). This step is followed by a selection of those objectives that optimize returns in light of the practical limitations on its managerial and financial resources. As we will discuss in the section "Investment Alternatives," the organization would then determine the form of the investment (i.e., organic development, acquisition, or strategic alliance) most appropriate to attain those objectives. This process is illustrated in Exhibit 2.2.

Generally, there is a wide range of investment options available to most organizations. Predictably, the evaluation and prioritization of these options is specific to each organization and subject to the myriad internal and external variables it must consider. However, certain generalizations can be made about their potential for value creation and the identifiable risks associated with the various types of investment objectives being considered.

Investment objectives fall into three general categories: market expansion, vertical integration, and infrastructure improvement. Each of these broad categories and the specific types of objectives that comprise them are discussed in the following sections in the context of the risks and returns associated with each.

Market Expansion Organizations are continually looking at opportunities to expand their market position to grow their revenue base, increase their market share, and, ultimately, enhance their profitability. In doing so, they typically employ a wide variety of strategic tools to evaluate market expansion opportunities, including matrices that identify product/market growth and profitability potential and competitive models that analyze industry

EXHIBIT 2.2 Identifying Investment Objectives

structure, dynamics, and attractiveness. Such models suggest the desirability of a limited number of potential initiatives, namely:

- *Developing or acquiring new products or services for current markets.* This is one of the most common types of investment objectives. It focuses on filling apparent gaps in the organization's business portfolio and enabling it to extract more revenue and profit from its core market. Arguably, the more related the investment initiative is to the core market of the organization, the less risk is associated with that objective. This is a function of the organization's collective knowledge and understanding of the market as well as its expertise, in areas such as production, marketing, and distribution, in servicing that market. However, it is also true that, as a general rule, the more mature the market, the more likely that the upside potential of this type of initiative will be limited.

- *Extending distribution by reaching new markets with existing products or services.* This frequently takes the form of geographic or international expansion. Successful implementation can create substantial value especially if the products or services do not need to be significantly modified. The major risk associated with this type of initiative is a misreading of the new market. In the case of international expansion, this can result from a superficial understanding of needs, tastes, and preferences of "foreign" customers. An organization may also encounter regulatory barriers that could inhibit market penetration.

- *Extending brand recognition of products or services to increase pricing power.* Brand leveraging can be accomplished in a number of ways. A business with strong brands may leverage an existing brand by bringing some of its existing products/services under that brand "umbrella" or by developing or acquiring a new portfolio of products or services with the intent of leveraging the brand. Conversely, a business may acquire a strong brand with the intent of leveraging that brand by relabeling its existing products/services. Because strong brands provide substantial market advantages (loyalty and pricing power), leveraging them successfully can generate great value. However, attempts to extend the benefits of a well-earned brand identity are difficult to execute and have significant downside risk, specifically the dilution of brand power. If the products or services that are brought under the brand umbrella are not consistent with the values and identity of the brand, the extension can work in reverse, undermining the branding power of the entire portfolio of the organization's products.

- *Developing or acquiring new products or services for new markets.* This is a market entry objective that is generally most effective when an organization wishes to enter an adjacent market. However, significant risk attaches to this objective. It should also be clear that increased risk does not necessarily translate into greater upside potential. Rather, the farther an organization steps outside its comfort zone (i.e., its indigenous market), the greater the risk and the more uncertain the reward. This reality certainly does not preclude consideration of new-market investment initiatives. However, it does place an added burden on the organization to thoroughly consider the heightened risk associated with such initiatives.

Vertical Integration   Vertical integration initiatives are executed to gain control over an organization's sources of supply by expanding operations toward suppliers' markets (backward integration) or to gain control over operations in an organization's customer markets (forward integration). Vertical integration clearly is a form of market expansion, but it is a very specific type of market expansion activity—enough so to warrant its own separate and distinct discussion. This is because the organization will expand within its value chain (i.e., the continuum that might include raw material extraction, intermediate production, final production, wholesale distribution, and retail distribution) requiring knowledge, skills, and expertise that are distinctly different from those in its core business.

Both forms of vertical integration provide certain *potential* benefits. These include the certainty of economic relationships (whether the supply of goods or the availability of distribution channels), control, and certain overall value chain efficiencies, such as better control over inventory management. In addition, forward integration can provide a valuable window into the behavior of an organization's customers. However, vertical integration presents certain disadvantages or risks that can be substantial in their impact. By in-sourcing functions that can be contracted for with independent firms, the organization trades certain variable costs for fixed costs, increasing basic business risk. It can also cause loss of any advantage associated with competitive pricing, if the relevant functions were outsourced. In addition, the organization puts itself at risk of loss of market focus and flexibility of action. This type of objective is generally high risk and anticipated returns should be commensurate with that risk.

Infrastructure Improvement   Organizations also regularly evaluate opportunities to lower production and processing costs and thereby increase margins as part of the planning process. These evaluations typically focus on expanding capacity to benefit from better economies of scale or through process improvement to increase efficiency. Capacity expansion is a double-edged sword in that it has the potential to reduce unit cost, but also increases fixed cost and also introduces the risk of idle capacity. Process improvement, whether through more efficient procedures or technology adoption, is generally an ongoing effort by most organizations and more often than not yields continuous incremental improvement.

The appropriateness and prioritization of these various investment objectives are peculiar to each organization. The ultimate choice of executable objectives (i.e., those within the context of the organization's resource base) should be subject to risk-reward analysis. Once the recommended objectives have been identified (what is to be done) the organization must determine the appropriate vehicle for its execution (how it is to be done), the topic of the next section.

Investment Alternatives

Once investment objectives have been established and prioritized, the organization should then make a preliminary assessment of the type of investment vehicles that best meet the objectives it wishes to pursue. The options available are (1) to develop the relevant capability internally (*build*); (2) to obtain that capability through acquisition (*buy*); or (3) to establish a strategic alliance with another independent entity to jointly develop that capability (*ally*).

The assessment of investment alternatives is a dynamic process because of the many variables that have to be taken into consideration. Each investment type has its own inherent advantages and disadvantages. In addition, the choice or choices are influenced by factors particular to each specific investment, such as the competitive environment, the availability of potential acquisition candidates or strategic partners, and the compatibility of those candidates and partners. Finally, the organization will not want to approach the investment decision without an alternative course of action (i.e., a "Plan B"), in the event that the initial plan does not materialize for some reason. Because of these factors, the assessment process should be seen as a filtering effort that preliminarily identifies what are believed to be optimal choices, but leaves the organization with the flexibility to modify its approach in light of new information. The following sections discuss the elements of the assessment process, leading to a preliminary plan that represents the best thinking of the planners to optimize value before actual implementation (i.e., execution of specific investments) occurs.

Characteristics of Investment Types   Whether an organization chooses to build, buy, or ally will be influenced by some of the innate characteristics of each investment vehicle. Those characteristics are suggestive, not determinative, since each decision will depend on the specifics surrounding any individual investment choice. However, those involved in the planning process should be mindful of the strengths and weaknesses of each form of investment. The potential generic advantages and disadvantages are illustrated in Exhibit 2.3.

In addition to the consideration of these innate characteristics, planners will have to assess the practical realities associated with each individual investment. This aspect of the assessment process requires the planners to evaluate each initiative in light of market and competitive forces, the specific characteristics of each individual investment, and factors that can be expected to affect their execution. Whether explicitly or implicitly, planners must then assess the advantages and disadvantages of each and determine the feasibility and the desirability of each investment alternative (i.e., build, buy, or ally) before arriving at the optimal choice. The discussion that follows is intended to frame the issues that would be considered for each of these types of investments.

Internal Development   Internal development, when properly implemented, offers certain clear advantages. For example, an organic (i.e., internal) growth initiative can be thoroughly researched and planned. Research can provide a high level of assurance that the initiative is market focused and based on analysis, devoid of preconceived notions and biases. This increases the likelihood that it will be tightly linked to the organization's strategic objectives. Internal development also provides control over the execution process and development costs. This approach affords the organization the

EXHIBIT 2.3 Build, Buy, or Ally?

	Internal Development (build)	Acquisition (buy)	Strategic Alliance (ally)
Potential advantages	Control over execution Focused development Control over cost	Speed of execution Cross-company synergies Complementary expertise Removal of a competitor Low market entry risk	Low entry cost Cross-company synergies Complementary expertise Low market entry risk Ability to learn
Potential disadvantages	Lengthy execution period Inbred perspective Uncertain market acceptance Increased competition	High integration risk High entry cost Unwanted assets and unwelcome liabilities	Shared benefits Complex management Disagreements regarding control Questionable sustainability

ability to clearly lay out the components of the initiative, to establish bench-marks for development, and to monitor progress and costs on a continuous basis. The ability to create a new, more market-focused offering can provide a significant competitive advantage in cases where existing providers have been slow to respond to changes in customer preferences and expectations.

These advantages must be measured against certain innate disadvantages associated with internal development. Organic development can often require significant lead time for research and development, allowing the window of opportunity to narrow or even close before the new offering can get to market. And there is the risk of plans giving way to a myopic view of the market. This is a particular risk when the initiative involves entry into new market segments where competitor and customer behaviors are unfamiliar to a new entrant. In any event, even the best researched initiatives live under the cloud of uncertainty until the time of launch.

In addition, the planning team must answer the threshold question, whether the organization has the *ability* to develop the relevant capability internally. The answer more often than not will be "yes," but there will be those situations where the initiative requires access to special assets, such as intellectual property, proprietary processes, or unique capabilities that do not exist within the organization. Clearly, in such situations planners would have to look outside the organization to obtain that capability.

If the planners believe that the organization has the ability to develop the capacity internally, they must then weigh the pros and cons of doing so. This requires an in-depth understanding of the market being targeted for the initiative. The planning team may have a clear picture of what the market wants and the confidence that it can deliver it. This is likely to be the case when the initiative addresses the needs and preferences of a market familiar to the organization, that is, one in which it has strong presence and intimate knowledge. A typical example of such an initiative is one that extends a company's existing product line. In such cases, the organization has superior market intelligence and the ability to leverage product identification, development capabilities, and distribution channels.

As initiatives move farther away from that "comfort zone," the dis-advantages associated with internal development increase. When entering entirely new markets, the risk profile of organic development is significantly elevated. In addition to unfamiliarity, the planners should consider the impact of increasing productive capacity in the market being entered. The organization will effectively be adding a new competitor and additional supply to that market. If the initiative is large in size and scope, this can have a material impact on the ability of the organization to penetrate the market, as well as on its flexibility in pricing and its ability to generate acceptable margins. This is particularly the case if the new entrant can expect aggressive competitive behavior on the part of market incumbents. However, these risks may be mitigated if the market is mature and the competitors are complacent and slow to react. This may enable the organization to experience rapid penetration, especially if the new offering reflects some significant competitive advantages. Most or all of these factors will be considered as the planners navigate through this assessment process.

Acquisition   Acquisition, as an investment vehicle, has many innately attractive features. It can enable an organization to establish a strong position in a new market very quickly. It also provides the basis for drawing on complementary expertise and differing market perspectives of the acquired and acquiring companies on the market, potentially generating synergistic benefits. Acquisitions also have some positive impacts on the constitution of the market. Unlike organic development, they do not increase market capacity. Rather, from the acquirers' perspective, they eliminate a competitor, removing one aspect of market risk—the risk associated with market entry and product acceptance. Although value creation remains a challenge to the acquirer, market acceptance of an incumbent provider's offerings is virtually assured.

The offsetting disadvantages of acquisition as an investment vehicle relate to the risks inherent in this type of investment. Acquisitions are risky primarily because details of the target business are beyond the reach of acquirers, who are forced to rely on *assumptions* about the state of the business and its prospects for the future. Layered on top of these assumptions are the inevitable need for the acquirer to pay a purchase price premium and the challenges of postacquisition integration. These factors conspire to significantly raise the risk profile of acquisition transactions. For these very reasons, a well-planned and well-executed due diligence (as described in detail in Chapters 4 through 6) is a critical component of the acquirer's effort to mitigate these risks.

Insofar as premiums are concerned, it is a virtual certainty that the acquiring company will pay a price in excess of the acquired company's stand-alone value. As previously discussed in Chapter 1, in the section titled "Strategic Purpose," the extent to which a premium can be justified is a function of the acquirer's ability to generate synergistic benefits in excess of that premium. Given the historical track record of acquirers, it is clear that extraction of synergistic value is a substantial challenge. That challenge can be exacerbated if the company being acquired is saddled with nonstrategic assets and liabilities that inhibit the acquirer's ability to create value. In addition, acquisitions are almost invariably accompanied by a range of postacquisition integration demands, including the harmonization of product offerings, infrastructures, and cultures. Accordingly, poorly planned, untimely, or poorly executed integration are primary inhibitors of value creation.

Beyond these conceptual considerations, the planners must consider the practical issue of feasibility. With respect to acquisition, this will mean determining whether there are, in fact, attractive candidates that may be available to buy. If there are such candidates, the organization will have to determine whether they have characteristics sufficient to warrant consideration. Candidate attractiveness will typically be a function of some combination of size, market position, and profitability. Frequently, organizations will want candidates that are major players in the market segment in which they wish to expand. That may mean that the corporation will be strongly inclined to consider one of the two or three top competitors in any given segment for acquisition. Of course, there may be exceptions, such as when the candidate is an emerging player in a market niche that is developing quickly or undergoing substantial dislocation due to underlying forces such as technological, demographic, or regulatory change.

In addition, the planning team will want to consider potential synergies between the organization and candidate businesses. Obvious synergistic benefits, particularly those that can be mined more effectively by the organization, will be strong factors in determining attractiveness. Conversely, additional baggage in the form of unwanted assets and liabilities will influence the planner's evaluation and, at a minimum, may make an acquisition feasible only under certain circumstances (e.g., the availability of a specific segment or division or the necessity of structuring the acquisition as an asset purchase).

In this initial culling process, the planners will also want to look at potential downside risks associated with individual candidates. They would specifically focus on the relative ease or difficulty of transaction execution. This might include a troublesome ownership structure, the reputation of principals, or cultural differences between the organization and the candidate. Owners who are at odds with each other, principals with reputations as mavericks, and the existence of a culture that is clearly incompatible with that of the acquirer are red flags and are factors that may influence the choice of an acquisition candidate (one over another) or may tip the scale in the direction of other investment alternatives.

Strategic Alliances   There are many types of tactical, intercompany arrangements that fall short of what are generally considered "strategic" alliances. These might include licensing agreements and comarketing or distribution arrangements. Frequently, these tactical arrangements provide a basis for building trust and confidence with a potential strategic partner or a possible acquisition candidate. However, for purposes of this discussion, a "strategic alliance" implies something more than these types of arrangements. It suggests a major commitment between partners to extract substantial value from a market or market segment. Additionally, it assumes the comingling of assets, talent, and capabilities and the sharing of the benefits derived. These alliances can take a number of forms, the most common of which are joint ventures (JVs) and minority investments. Such arrangements can be valuable investment vehicles. The primary benefits of strategic alliances are that market entry costs are generally low and synergistic benefits generally high. These arrangements also provide the organization with the ability to learn about the market in real time, a benefit that is particularly valuable when attempting to enter unfamiliar or foreign markets. In addition, they provide a courtship opportunity during which the principals are able to learn more about the other party. This is particularly important if the relationship leads to an acquisition because it can increase the odds of a successful transaction by possibly lowering acquisition cost, establishing a solid market position, and facilitating integration.

As with the other investment vehicles discussed, there are several generic disadvantages associated with strategic alliances. With shared risks come shared rewards. By definition, alliances require a division of profits and this can cause an organization to suboptimize its investment opportunity. In addition, alliances can be difficult to manage. The issue of control is generally a major consideration between the partners. This can be a disruptive issue since the interests of the partners are rarely if ever entirely coincidental, especially over time when there are changes in personnel, the market being served, and the individual entities' underlying strategies. This issue feeds into the longer-term issue of sustainability. Strategic alliances are almost invariably not an "end game." By their very nature, they are bridges to the future. For them to provide value to the participants, that future has to be defined in fairly specific terms, not an easy task in a dynamic environment.

Beyond these generic issues, there is the threshold question of whether or not there are viable candidates for alliances. The answer to the question will generally boil down to attractiveness as defined by compatible and complementary competencies. Such features are essential for synergistic collaboration, a strategic alliance's reason for being. However, availability and compatible competencies are just necessary but not sufficient characteristics for a successful alliance. These characteristics can be offset by lack of compatibility on other levels, such as the personalities of a candidate's principals or its cultural disposition. Aggressively competitive organizations generally reflect the personality of their leadership and, although that quality may be the hallmark of the company's success, it is generally not a good basis for cooperative behavior. As a result, planners may want to factor these characteristics into their assessment. Additionally, and as previously noted, alliances are a bridge to the future. They are rarely sustained indefinitely, so the partners should agree on where the relationship will lead. With that in mind, planners should have a preliminary view of what a desirable end game would be for the organization and assess the potential of getting there.

Backup Planning

Once the planners have evaluated the target markets and alternative investment initiatives and have identified what they believe are the most promising markets and the optimal choice for each initiative, they will craft an overall plan around these conclusions. That plan should support the organization's strategic objectives and reflect the best thinking of the planners. It should also incorporate a flexible approach to their proposed investment portfolio. It should be understood that, at this stage of the investment process, the planners are equipped with incomplete knowledge. The plan will be based on *assumptions* about availability and willingness of candidates to partner with or be acquired by the organization. It also *assumes* that the organization can negotiate transactions on a basis acceptable to it. These assumptions require a level of flexibility in the plan that provides the organization with other potential ways forward to implement its strategy, if those assumptions are found to be in error.

The path to arriving at the preferred form of each investment would have included a detailed assessment of the other options available to the organization. The costs, benefits, and other influencing factors for each investment option should be rigorously analyzed to determine whether acquisition, strategic alliance, or internal development yield the best opportunity for value creation; or if acquisition appears to be the appropriate path for a given investment, whether buying company A is preferable to the acquisition of company B. This comparative analysis is not only important to the decision-making process, it also provides the organization with critical information if course correction is needed as more information becomes available. For example, if the value creation assumptions associated with an acquisition are found to be faulty as a result of the due diligence review, the organization will want to revisit alternative approaches that had been considered during the planning process. Absent such thoroughly considered fallback positions, the organization is left with simple "go, no-go" courses of action if value creation expectations are not met at the diligence stage. This situation also leaves the organization with little in the way of leverage in dealing with the seller. Left with that type of binary choice, the organization would have to go back to the drawing board if it chose not to proceed or, potentially worse yet, to talk itself into suboptimizing its investment—and possibly destroying, rather than creating, value in the process—by overpaying for the acquisition.

Plan Outputs

Exhibits 2.4, 2.5, and 2.6 illustrate several components of a strategic plan and provide insight into the logic and content of certain plan deliverables. From the perspective of logic, these exhibits collectively demonstrate the thought process involved in proceeding from market opportunity to high-priority investment initiative, to comparative analysis of investment alternatives, to the preferred form of initiative execution. The resulting content outlines the form of the initiative, its method and timing of execution, and, in the case of acquisitions and strategic alliances, the high-potential targets for investment.

More specifically, Exhibit 2.4 identifies plan initiatives and their preferred form—internal development, acquisition, or strategic alliance—within the context of the markets chosen for investment. That is, those markets offering the organization the greatest opportunity for value creation.

EXHIBIT 2.4 Target Market and Investment Options

Target Market	Initiative	Preferred Form of Execution	Fall-Back Option
Core	Extend existing product line in core market	Internal development	Acquisition of small, rapidly growing competitor
	Enhanced distribution capability in core market	Strategic partnership	Acquisition of proposed partner
	Retrofitting of production process for core products	Internal development	N/A (i.e., no attractive option to self-development)
Adjacent	Establish strong market position in adjacent market	Acquisition of market leader	Acquisition of number 2 player
	Acquire technology to support entry	Acquisition	Internal development
Related market niche	Roll up niche players in emerging market	Acquisition of largest player and build critical mass with additional acquisitions	Acquire number 2 or number 3 player in the market and build critical mass
International	Establish strong market position in European Union	Acquisition of market leader	Acquisition of number 2 player in market

EXHIBIT 2.5 Investment Plan

Target Market	Investment Initiative	Plan Period YR1	YR2	YR3	Description
	Market Expansion				
Core	Product line extension	Build			Introduce three new products to fill out existing line over first two years of plan period
Adjacent	Adjacent market entry		Buy		Acquire a major competitor in the X market in year 2 of plan period
International	International expansion	Buy			Acquire European market leader or number 2 competitor in Y market in year 1 of plan period
Related niche	Roll-up of niche competitors		Buy		Acquire market leader in emerging niche and roll up smaller competitors during plan period
	Vertical Integration				
Core	Distribution channels	Partner/Buy			Acquire or partner with intent to acquire with major distributor of company core products
	Infrastructure Improvement				
Core	Production process		Build		Incrementally retrofit production process over plan period
Adjacent	Product technology	Buy			Acquire firm with proprietary technology to support adjacent new market entry

EXHIBIT 2.6 Acquisition/Partner Target List

Target Market Segment	Target Company	Market Position	Acquire or Partner
Primary/core	AlphaCo	The target company is the major distributor of company products and is the established leader in this sector.	Partner
Related niche	EmergeCo 1	The target company is the leading competitor in this emerging market niche. Market intelligence indicates that it is three times the size of its closest competitor and is experiencing revenue growth in excess of 20 percent for the last three years. It will provide the foundation for the organization's plans to roll up other competitors in this rapidly growing market.	Acquire
	EmergeCo 2	The target company is believed to be the second largest competitor in this niche and has a strong market position in the western half of the United States.	Acquire
	EmergeCo 3	The target company is one of the smallest competitors in the niche, but has developed proprietary software that is believed will provide competitive advantage this segment.	Acquire
	EmergeCo 4	The target company is one of the first entrants into this niche and has developed good brand recognition and a small loyal following. It is believed to have grown steadily, although slower than the market average, but its position presents an opportunity for pricing leverage.	Acquire

(Continued)

EXHIBIT 2.6 Acquisition/Partner Target List (*Continued*)

Target Market Segment	Target Company	Market Position	Acquire or Partner
Adjacent/Related	NewCo 1	The target company is the largest competitor in this adjacent market and provides a strong entry position.	Acquire
	NewCo 2	The target company holds the number 2 position in this segment and has demonstrated strong growth in recent years after a series of successful product introductions.	Acquire
	TechCo	The target company is the competitor with the strongest technology orientation in the market. Its technology, layered onto one of the two top players in the market, would result in a powerful position.	Acquire
European market	EuroCo 1	The target company is the leading competitor in the European version of the company's primary or core market. Its acquisition would create substantial synergies in the form of branding and cross-selling.	Acquire
	EuroCo 2	The target company is the second largest competitor in the European market. It possesses superior production capabilities and is believed to be the lowest-cost provider in the EU market.	Acquire

It also identifies fallback positions that have been thoroughly analyzed and considered.

Exhibit 2.5 outlines the investment plan, based on the preceding analysis. It elaborates on the initiatives, describing them and their preferred form of execution in more detail. It also documents time frames and identifies specific candidates for partnership and acquisition.

Exhibit 2.6 captures and expands upon the information about specific candidates and provides the basis for the organization's target list. This list will generally be the starting point for the screening process the organization will employ in pursuing companies for partnership or acquisition.

CONCLUSION

While the strategic plan is explicit, it is not etched in stone. It should provide a balance between a firm commitment to growth initiatives and flexibility on the tactics that will be employed. At this planning stage, the team will have put forward its best thinking on tactics, with the realization that those tactics may change as they approach implementation and more information (such as the expectations of acquisition candidates relative to price and other terms of sale) becomes available.

The results of this process will have positioned the organization to focus on its investment priorities. It will have identified the markets with the greatest potential and the vehicles best suited to extract value from them. From an acquisition perspective, it has homed in on specific candidates that constitute the primary targets for those tasked with implementation. The follow-on activities associated with the screening and qualification of those candidates is discussed in Chapter 3.

Key Points

1. A central tenet of M&A best practice is that investment strategy in general, and acquisition activities in particular, should be guided and driven by purposeful strategic planning. Strategic planning should be the first step by an organization in identifying investment initiatives that will provide the best opportunity for profitable growth, superior returns, and, ultimately, value creation. ("Central Role of Strategic Planning")

2. The mere existence of a structured and efficient process does not guarantee effective planning. For it to be effective, it must also be buttressed by characteristics that enhance the process and add credence to its output. ("Characteristics of an Effective Planning Process")

3. The major factors influencing entry or expansion decisions relate to characteristics such as market fundamentals, the nature of the competitive environment, and the organization's competitive potential. An evaluation of these factors enables the planners to reach a preliminary conclusion about the most attractive way in which to enter or further penetrate the most promising market segments. ("Market Targeting Process")

4. The strategic goal of the organization is to *optimize shareholder value over time*. In reducing that goal to actionable form, the planners must first evaluate the relative importance of those threats and opportunities revealed by the assessment process, and translate them into specific investment objectives. ("Investment Objectives")

5. That plan should support the organization's strategic objectives and reflect the best thinking of the planners. It should also incorporate a flexible approach to their proposed investment portfolio. ("Backup Planning")

CHAPTER 3

Implementing the Growth Strategy

FROM IDENTIFICATION TO PURSUIT

Choosing an Acquisition Strategy

As described in the previous chapter, corporate strategic planners select desirable market segments and then evaluate alternative growth tactics: whether to build, ally, or acquire. Each of these tactics presents different implementation issues that affect an organization's relative enthusiasm for one or another as it sets out to act on its strategic plan. To summarize:

- *Build.* Internal development is a tactic largely within control of the organization, but it has two main risks: execution (completing the project to specification on time and within budget) and customer acceptance. Customer acceptance, in particular, can be a formidable hurdle, depending on competitive circumstances.
- *Ally.* A strategic alliance may reduce some of the execution or customer acceptance risk inherent in building because the two partners usually start out with deployable assets, such as established capabilities or market presence. The initial focus is on one-on-one discussions between two organizations, where they attempt to determine whether there is a convergence of strategic interest. The alliance then becomes managed like a "build" project if additional development or integration is required. The alliance relationship itself can be complicated and require ongoing management attention.
- *Acquire.* An acquisition may be seen as an even better way to mitigate execution and acceptance risk, especially when an established business

is the targeted asset. However, a prospective deal may not be a "pure play." With coveted assets may come unwanted ones, which can distract the management of the acquiring company. In addition, acquisitions are generally complex transactions and present their own execution issues and risks.

Although this book focuses on cases where an acquisition is the chosen approach, it should be noted that the "optimal" approach for an organization is not a fixed, unchanging position. As discussed in Chapter 2, the strategic plan process determines the preferred growth strategy based on sometimes limited knowledge and assumptions formed at a point in time. We deliberately incorporated a mentality of open-mindedness in strategic plan outputs such as Exhibit 2.6 with its acquisition/partner target list. Because an organization learns more as it looks more deeply at specific opportunities, which may alter its assumptions about their relative merits, we advocate sustaining active consideration of alternative approaches (alternative acquisitions, strategic alliances, or internal development) *even after an organization has chosen to pursue a particular acquisition.*

Once the first step is taken toward acquisition, a deal can take on a life of its own, making the evaluation of alternatives much easier said than done. But we believe it is worth the effort. Significant issues may be discovered during the investigation of an acquisition target, or might emerge during the deal negotiations, altering the relative desirability of a transaction. Absent viable alternatives, the potential acquirer can only make a binary decision to acquire a particular company (at what cost?) or do nothing at all in a segment. Having realistic alternatives, conversely, would allow an organization to know when an acquisition would make the most sense and under what circumstances the next best alternative becomes superior.

Winnowing Process

The progression from identifying targets to pursuing acquisitions should follow a methodical, ongoing winnowing process consisting of the following steps, which are illustrated in Exhibit 3.1:

1. Identifying potential acquisition targets
2. Qualifying them
3. Engaging with them

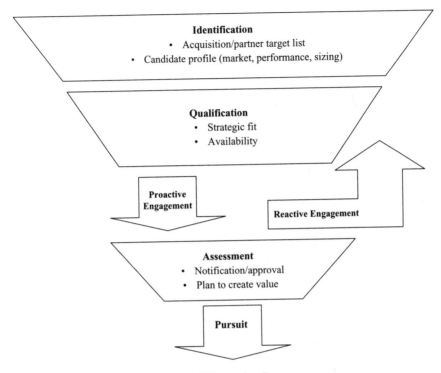

EXHIBIT 3.1 Acquisition Prospect Winnowing Process

4. Further assessing them
5. Deciding to pursue a transaction

- *Identification.* Coming out of its strategic plan, a corporation is armed with three key documents that set the stage for implementation: a list of targeted markets (Exhibit 2.4), an investment plan (Exhibit 2.5), and an acquisition/partner target list (Exhibit 2.6). These documents form the logical starting point for an organization's search for acquisition targets, and they should not be allowed to become static and out of date. The acquisition/partner target list, in particular, should be continuously updated and revised, fed by ongoing research, input from advisors, and feedback from management's industry networking. A candidate profile should be prepared for each company, serving as a repository of knowledge about the business, addressing three main aspects: markets

(Who are its customers?), performance (What does the company do and how has it fared?), and sizing (How valuable is the company and how expensive might an acquisition be?). These themes are elaborated on in the section "Identification."

- *Qualification.* Because the acquisition/partner target list may include multiple players within each targeted segment, it is not realistic for an organization to set out in pursuit of every company on the list. A high-level qualification process can quickly reduce the list to a manageable number for active targeting. This initial screening of candidates should consist of two groups of questions to be answered by the prospective acquirer.

  The first area of focus centers on strategic fit. How closely do the capabilities of a potential target fit with the corporation's strategic aims? Is the target big enough and attractive enough to make a strategic difference to the acquirer, yet small enough to be afforded, integrated, and managed? The second set of questions should address availability. Is the transaction likely enough to make the cost and uncertainty of pursuit worthwhile? This should go beyond the question of whether a business is for sale; rather, the focus should be on whether a deal is feasible. What is the ownership structure? Is the company privately held or publicly traded? How approachable is its ownership and management? Is it a stand-alone entity or an integrated component of a larger organization?

  The answers to these two sets of questions informs the yes or no judgment of whether or not a company should be actively engaged and are further discussed in the "Qualification" section.

- *Engagement.* Given the level of uncertainty that exists at this early stage of the process about the viability and nature of a potential deal, we advocate gradual, proactive engagement of targeted organizations, preferably before they have decided to initiate a sale. Proactive engagement, as we define it, is a combination of courting and information gathering conducted by management. This approach can significantly reduce some of the inherent risk of acquiring, while keeping alternatives open to consideration. Its dual focus allows an organization to vet a target while mutually determining *with the target company* the best way to pursue a given market opportunity. It enables discussions to evolve naturally and the level of trust to increase between the two management teams as they consider various forms of collaboration, ranging from partnership to acquisition. Alternatively, if a target is queried immediately about its interest in being acquired, discussions can quickly degenerate into price negotiations, with the prospective acquirer no better informed about whether or not a particular deal would serve its interests than when it initiated contact.

We recognize that proactive engagement is a best-case scenario. Many transactions will also come to potential acquirers at a time and method of the seller's choosing. When a prospective deal is presented to an organization, a process we refer to as reactive engagement, there is a risk that an organization can be drawn into pursuing a transaction before fully evaluating the opportunity's strategic merits. In these cases, when potential acquirers are reacting to an opportunity instead of cultivating it, we believe they must first take a quick step back and give careful strategic thought to a prospective deal before entering the frenetic, consuming process of a competitive sale. Having a well-developed growth strategy in place, along with a systematic process for evaluating opportunities, will position an organization to be thoughtful yet responsive, enabling it to make an informed judgment in a rapid but not hurried manner. This process is discussed in detail in the "Engagement" section of this chapter.

■ *Assessment.* Before formally deciding to pursue a particular acquisition, the acquiring organization normally goes through an internal assessment process. The form of this process can vary based on the level of empowerment of the transaction sponsor (i.e., the executive responsible for the business unit championing the acquisition) within the organization, but it usually consists of a written proposal either notifying senior management of the intention to initiate nonbinding acquisition discussions with a particular target and its advisors, or asking for corporate permission to do so. In either case, the proposal should address how the prospective deal fits with the organization's growth strategy and should present a quantified case for how the transaction will create value.

This is a step that should not be rushed through, nor thought of as an unavoidable bureaucratic hurdle. It provides assurance that analysis will not veer from clear-eyed assessment to justification, "supported" by unrealistic assumptions about an acquisition's benefits (to justify a competitive price). The assessment of the acquiring organization should not be limited to a notification/approval document either. It should also include a supporting plan to create value (a document and approach discussed in detail in the "Assessment" section). Suffice it to note here that the plan to create value bridges aspiration and action. It sets the stage for effective diligence and informed decisions, and establishes a clear plan for purposeful behavior.

- *Pursuit.* The next step in the winnowing process is the active pursuit of the acquisition transaction. Acquisitions follow a well-defined process and generate dynamic tension between players and their advisors as they pursue their particular interests. This explains in part why deals tend to take on a life of their own, consuming the time and attention of the acquirer and making the notion of maintaining alternatives difficult. We outline the typical acquisition process and the players involved in "Pursuit" and more fully frame due diligence in the context of the realities and pressures of an active, competitive sale process in Chapter 5.

In the remaining sections of this chapter, we discuss each of these steps in more detail.

IDENTIFICATION

Marketplace for Acquisitions

Active acquirers are no doubt aware that a well-established, relatively efficient M&A marketplace (i.e., where businesses are bought and sold) exists, the result of a trend spanning decades and driven by two factors, namely, globalization and relatively cheap capital. This has implications for those involved in the acquisition process. The accelerated pace of globalization has been a significant stimulant to the acquisition market. Advances in technology, decreased regulation, and the lowering of cross-border barriers in the form of beneficial trade agreements have increased competition worldwide. To a greater extent than ever, this has caused organizations to focus more intensely on aggressive market expansion and on rapidly attaining greater economies of scale and substantially enhancing efficiencies. Relatively cheap capital, in turn, has provided fuel for this expansion, with leverage helping to make the economics of growth through acquisition more attractive to corporations.

These trends have created favorable conditions for M&A transactions. They have attracted an increasing number of players into the process, both prospective acquirers and professional intermediaries. As a result, the market has matured and become very sophisticated, generating a wealth of information (such as values of comparable transactions) and a predictable process for buying and selling. However, the increased number of potential acquirers and availability of pricing data have also had the expected result of making the market more efficient. Even while the cost of capital has been at historically low levels in recent years, its benefits have been mitigated by more buoyant valuations, reducing acquirers' potential to generate outsized returns from acquisition investments.

Yet, the maturity of the market can also be an asset to potential acquirers. Professional intermediaries, in particular brokers and investment bankers, provide a good source of industry knowledge and have extensive contacts, which can help identify potential acquisition targets and connect prospective buyers and sellers. Experienced acquirers understand both the pros and cons of dealing with intermediaries, using them as a source of industry consensus about markets and participants and frequently tapping them to identify prospects and facilitate contact. They are also mindful that intermediaries' self-interest can lead to a less than objective stance on some issues. Therefore, seasoned acquirers seek to combine intelligence and assistance gained from these players with information gleaned from other more objective sources, as further discussed in the next section.

Identifying Prospects

There are three main outputs from the strategic planning process that establish the starting point for identifying potential acquisitions: a list of targeted markets (Exhibit 2.4), an investment plan (Exhibit 2.5), and an acquisition/partner target list (Exhibit 2.6). The first step in implementing the strategy is to make the acquisition/partner target list a continually updated and enhanced data set by:

- Establishing sources for identification of prospects
- Implementing an information-gathering process
- Distilling information on market, performance, and sizing into a standardized acquisition candidate profile for each firm
- Feeding and updating the acquisition/partner target list with information sources

There are a variety of ways in which organizations prospect for candidates for acquisition or partnership. The effort is essentially one of intelligence gathering, which consists of two basic tactics: research and networking. To be effective, research and networking should not be seen in the context of a single transaction; rather, they should be established as ongoing operational processes integral to an organization's acquisition efforts.

To this end, larger organizations often dedicate entire departments to researching markets and businesses (e.g., business intelligence) and others to networking and strategic planning (e.g., business development). Smaller organizations with fewer resources often cannot afford the luxury of dedicating resources to these types of activities. But if an organization is serious about developing an active acquisition program, it must somehow create a mechanism for filling the prospect "pipeline." Even smaller organizations, therefore, should seek to operationalize research and networking activities, by formally assigning responsibility to existing departments or functions.

- *Research.* Research draws on a range of information sources, some housed internally and others available from external repositories. Internal records and analysis are generally extremely valuable intelligence sources. For example, most companies maintain files of some sort to track the behavior and intentions of competitors. These internal records can be foundational to the screening process and if they are maintained and updated routinely and integrated with the acquisition prospect list.

  These internal sources can easily be supplemented by readily available secondary business, industry, and specific company information from a wide array of resources. There is a universe of relevant, easily accessible databases that can enhance a company's research efforts. Although data for publicly traded companies are more easily accessed, there is also a rich reservoir of information available on private companies. These include:

  - *Dun & Bradstreet* (D&B) maintains one of the largest business information databases in the world, with risk and market information on more than 100 million businesses in almost 200 countries.
  - *Ward's Business Directory of U.S. Public and Private Companies* lists over 100,000 companies, the vast majority of which are privately held.
  - *Lexis-Nexis* delivers profiles of more than 43 million companies worldwide and in-depth information on key industries.
  - *Hoovers,* a D&B company, provides access to information on 43,000 public, nonpublic, and international companies, as well as 600 industries in the United States, Canada, United Kingdom, Europe, and Asia/Pacific.

- *Factiva*, a Dow Jones company, provides access to 600 newswires and 2,500 newspapers, as well as information on 32,000 nonpublic and public companies.

There is also much that can be gleaned from industry publications and reports, and company analysts' reports. Industry publications, such as trade journals and newsletters, provide ongoing, current views of developments in the industry and at individual companies within that industry. In addition, most industries are closely followed by equity analysts, market research firms, and industry experts or consultants. These industry monitors produce research reports, industry overviews, market trends, and company profiles. Even if a targeted company is privately held, it is quite possible that an equity analyst covers the market served by its publicly traded competitors, which could provide useful data on market size, trends, and competitive positioning.

Finally, there is a large volume of freely available information that can be accessed through Internet search engines. The challenge here is in sorting out the quality and credibility of sites pointed to by a search engine. Sources should be carefully vetted and information viewed with a level of healthy skepticism. For example, individual company Web sites can be very useful, providing company profiles and current, detailed product or service information, but they should be viewed as essentially promotional in nature. Company filings or governmental databases, conversely, can at least be expected to meet certain reporting standards, although compliance rather than full disclosure is often the root objective of those preparing the underlying information. News items are helpful sources of company information, but sometimes can represent no more than uncritically prepared summarizations of company-prepared press releases. Listserves (i.e., electronic mailing lists or e-lists) can sometimes contain interesting, unfiltered commentary about an organization, but the objectivity and even truthfulness of the content should be considered highly suspect and, if used at all, should be first subjected to validation through other, more trusted sources.

- *Networking*. Organizations should not restrict themselves to an "arms-length," or data-centric, search. Even with the ease of access to data enabled by technology, there are few substitutes for human interaction when it comes to prospecting for acquisition candidates. Two groups are most useful in this regard: internal management and professional intermediaries.

Company management may be an organization's best source for identifying candidates, particularly those that operate within markets already served by that organization. In this context we are using the term "company management" broadly. Intelligence may be garnered from sales executives obtaining customer feedback (e.g., which competitors are making inroads, winning sales pitches, or are mentioned frequently by customers as a quality provider), or from managers attending industry and trade events. These efforts may also be complemented by dedicated business development executives, whose primary function is to spend time at various industry forums to identify promising acquisition opportunities.

As mentioned in the preceding section, intermediaries such as financial advisors (e.g., brokers and investment bankers) are a good source of candidate identification. Establishing relationships with advisors and indicating areas of potential interest to these firms is normally a core responsibility of the business development function. Intermediaries, given their connections and contacts, can be extremely helpful in actually making contact with prospects, as we further address in the section "Engagement."

Using some combination of the techniques and practices described above, development of a systematic mechanism for candidate identification and evaluation should be an organizational objective. Having accomplished that objective, the next critical part of the process should be to organize, distill, and house this information in a way that facilitates rapid retrieval and ease of comparison, discussed next.

- *Acquisition candidate profile.* The first question that tends to be asked by executive management about an acquisition prospect is "What do we know about this company?" It is a simple question, but one that suggests that an organization should not simply amass raw data about targeted companies obtained from the various sources. Instead it should be collected in a focused and methodical manner and is distilled into a standardized summary format that provides an informative overview of each organization.

The sequence of questions asked below provides a focus and an organizing principle for information-gathering efforts, as well as the outline for the primary output—a form we refer to as the acquisition candidate profile. Questions about a target company fall into the following three broad categories:

1. *Market.* Which market segment does the company serve, who are its typical customers, and where does it stand relative to its competitors?

2. *Performance.* What does the company do and how has it fared? Who runs it and what is their strategy? What steps have they taken in implementing it? What has their performance looked like?

3. *Sizing.* How big/expensive might an acquisition be? What is their ownership structure?

The acquisition candidate profile should be a high-level, quick-reference document of just a few pages, addressing basic questions, such as those noted above, and backed up by more detailed information. It should also be periodically updated (perhaps monthly or quarterly for top prospects, and less frequently for companies chosen for longer-term monitoring), via a regular check of the company Web site and other sources for key financial metrics, company announcements, product and organizational changes, and acquisition and alliance activity. Exhibit 3.2 contains an illustrative outline of an acquisition candidate profile.

EXHIBIT 3.2   Outline of Acquisition Candidate Profile

Company	Name, ticker symbol (if public), location(s), and ownership form
Market	Market served Market share Customer base
Performance	Business overview/history Products and services: revenue composition Management and strategy Company news summary: key events Financial trends: growth, profitability
Sizing	Market valuation (if publicly traded) or comparable multiples
Sources	Source(s) of information (e.g., company Web site, news releases, industry reports, proprietary market research, input from financial advisors, discussions with company management) Date updated

QUALIFICATION

In contrast to the identification process, which entails casting a net as wide as possible to identify the largest potential pool of relevant acquisition targets, the qualification process is the first step in the effort to narrow the field to a manageable number for active engagement. It is only a first step because information available at the early stages of the process is not always sufficient to fully vet potential acquisition candidates, and further investigation is normally required to reach a definitive view on whether or not to pursue an acquisition (actually, that decision should remain open until the purchase agreement is signed). However, the list of candidates can be trimmed and prioritized based on broad criteria. The goal should be a yes or no determination about whether to begin efforts to engage a target company in strategic discussions. The two key factors for qualification are *strategic fit* and *availability*, which are discussed next.

Strategic Fit

The first area of focus in qualifying a potential acquisition target is strategic fit. Assessing strategic fit involves comparing a prospect's assets and perceived strengths with the corporation's stated strategic objectives, specifically examining the market segments served by a target and its capabilities within those market segments. It is understood that detailed information at this early stage is likely to be limited, and judgments about market position and capabilities, while perhaps supported by some data, will be somewhat qualitative and subjective. Because of this, organizations may shy away from attempting to make such preliminary judgments without access to detailed information, creating something of a chicken-and-egg paradox, and potentially wasting effort "kicking the tires" of too wide an array of acquisition prospects. We believe it is critical to make even a subjective judgment at the qualification stage so that a hypothesis can be formed about why a target is strategically attractive to the acquirer, and *which specific attributes it needs to bring to the acquirer in order to make a strategic difference.* This sets in place the essential strategic rationale for an acquisition and creates a sharp focus for further information gathering, without which the evaluation of a prospective deal could remain essentially a mathematical exercise.

Exhibit 3.3 illustrates an example of how a qualitative assessment of strategic fit might be structured. The corporation, in its strategic plan, has

EXHIBIT 3.3 Qualitative Assessment of Strategic Fit

Offering Strength 0–4	Market Segment [X]				
	Product/ Service A	Product/ Service B	Product/ Service C	Product/ Service D	Product/ Service E
Acquirer	3	2	2	1	0
Acquirer + Target	3	2	3	3	4
Competitor 1	2	0	3	2	2
Competitor 2	1	1	1	0	1

determined that market segment X, based on its size and growth characteristics, should be targeted for expansion. It has a reasonably strong competitive position in three product/service areas, A, B, and C, but is relatively weak in two others, D and E. It believes that in order to be successful and capture the largest share of this segment, it must have a comprehensive product/service portfolio, inclusive of A through E. Acquiring the target would fill out these gaps in its product/service portfolio, making it the only such organization in the segment with a full range of capabilities. Note that the assessment is comparative to the competition, and that Competitor 1, since it also appears to have some strength in product/service areas D and E, might be a possible alternative acquisition or alliance partner.

This type of analysis lends itself to preliminary judgments about both due diligence and the potential deal structure. It suggests that, in the due diligence review, the team should place particular focus on product/service areas D and E, since they are the main reason for the acquisition. Absent this focus, the due diligence team may treat all product/service areas alike and give insufficient attention to the question of whether D and E have the capacity to fulfill the promise underlying the deal's strategic rationale.

In terms of deal structure, a candidate will often possess some assets or capabilities that are an excellent strategic fit, but others that are not. Assume the target company also has product/service lines F, G, and H—not shown in Exhibit 3.3—in which the acquirer has no strategic interest. In such a case, the acquirer will have to determine whether the desired assets or capabilities alone can be acquired or, if not, whether an acquisition of the entire company would still make strategic and financial sense. At a minimum, the acquirer should establish for itself the due diligence goal of identifying all extraneous operations of the target, and placing discrete values on the desired business segments and the impact of the acquisition of the undesired segments.

Finally, the acquirer should determine whether the target is the right size. Would a deal be within the acquirer's financial capacity and comfort zone? Is it big enough to make a strategic difference to the acquirer, yet small enough and to afford, integrate, and manage?

Availability

The second area of focus should be the target company's availability. This includes an analysis of the ownership structure of the target, plus a qualitative assessment of its posture toward acquisition. Is it a publicly traded or privately held business? Does the target represent an entire corporation or is it a division that could be separated and divested? If it is a division of a larger corporation, does it seem central or peripheral to the stated strategic aims of its ownership? What is its history? Has it ever been approached for a deal involving the targeted business? Does the corporation have an active portfolio (as both an acquirer and a divester)? If the target is well known to the potential acquirer, many of these questions may be easily answered. If it is not, the acquirer will have to rely on publicly available information and, perhaps, the input of an intermediary.

While it may not be obvious if a particular business is "for sale" (because at some price most everyone could be), in the case of a public company, it is important to seek to determine in advance whether an acquisition overture would be received as friendly or hostile. This factor may not preclude a desirable acquisition, but it must be considered as part of the decision to proceed. A hostile deal would obviously be far more difficult, expensive, and risky, raising the bar considerably for creation of shareholder value.

U.S. Antitrust Considerations

It is worth noting here that for transactions above a certain size, acquirers should approach the evaluation of markets, competition, and the impact of potential acquisitions with a high level of care and discipline from the very beginning of the information-gathering process. The Hart-Scott-Rodino Antitrust Improvements Act of 1976 (HSR) established a premerger program requiring those engaged in certain mergers and acquisitions to notify the Federal Trade Commission (FTC) and the Department of Justice (DOJ) of an impending transaction. The parties to such a transaction must submit a notification and report form with detailed information about their businesses (along with their analyses related to the deal) and wait a specified period of time, usually 30 days, before consummating the transaction. The government has the right to request additional information via a "second request," which can considerably extend the time, cost, and risk of the process. (The Appendix contains a comprehensive overview of the HSR program.) Following are a few points about HSR requirements and their implications for acquirers.

- HSR affects a significant number of transactions. An HSR filing is generally required for transactions with an aggregate value above $65.2 million, adjusted annually.
- For transactions anywhere near this threshold, guidance should be given to the acquisition team at the outset of the process to ensure there is a consistent understanding of the requirements of HSR, and that analytical documents in particular are assembled and reviewed during the course of the transaction so that time is not lost rushing through this critical process once the deal is signed. At the point in the process where a transaction is actively pursued, expert antitrust legal counsel should be engaged as advisors to the acquisition team.
- In preparing all forms of documents and communications related to the transaction, the team needs to be precise and consistent in characterizing markets, and in explaining the rationale for the deal. Any such documents should accurately characterize the market position of the acquirer and the target based on an objective, consistent set of market measures. Documents should be written clearly and factually, avoiding hyperbolic (and often inaccurate) references such as "market dominance," thoughtfully characterizing how a prospective combination would affect market competitiveness.

ENGAGEMENT

Once the acquisition/partner target list has been reduced to a manageable number of qualified prospects, a methodical program for establishing and developing relationships with these organizations should be initiated.

Because of the level of uncertainty that exists at this early stage about the viability and nature of any potential deal under consideration, we advocate gradual, proactive engagement of targeted organizations, preferably before they have decided to initiate a sale process.

Proactive engagement is a best-case scenario for the buyer, one that allows the acquirer to simultaneously explore and evaluate strategic alternatives, thereby reducing risk. We recognize that many, if not most, transactions do not develop this way. They usually come unsolicited to potential acquirers. When a potential deal is presented to an organization, a process we call reactive engagement, there is a risk of being drawn into a transaction before fully evaluating the opportunity's strategic merits. In these cases, when potential acquirers are reacting to an opportunity instead of cultivating it, we believe they must first take a step back; careful strategic thought must be given to a prospective deal before entering the frenetic, consuming process of a competitive sale.

We discuss each type of situation in the following sections.

Proactive Engagement

Proactive engagement, as we define it, is a combination of courting and analysis, a process that can significantly reduce some of the inherent risk of acquisition while keeping alternative collaborative options open to both buyer and seller. This type of approach, with its dual focus, allows an organization to vet a target while mutually determining the best way to pursue a given market opportunity. Discussions could evolve naturally, a level of trust developing between the two management teams as they consider various forms of collaboration ranging from partnership to acquisition. Alternatively, if a target is queried immediately about its interest in being acquired, discussions can quickly degenerate into price negotiations, with the prospective acquirer no better informed than when it started about whether or not a particular deal would serve its interests.

The advantages of methodical, gradual, proactive engagement are several:

- *Longer initial evaluation period.* As discussed in the section "Qualifying Acquisition Candidates," much of a corporation's strategic rationale for an acquisition at this point may still be hypothesis. Therefore, a critical goal of approaching a prospect in a gradual fashion should be to gather information that supports or refutes the strategic merits of an acquisition, so that a transaction can be pursued with greater confidence and less risk. Acquisition targets can often be curious enough about the upside of a potential deal to agree to a preliminary information exchange. The corporation should try to learn as much as it can about the target, using this information to inform its evaluation of a potential acquisition, preferably against strategic alternatives (i.e., building and allying).

- *Critical period for relationship-building.* Too often, mergers and acquisitions can be thought of in purely financial terms: price-earnings multiples, net present value, and so on. It is important to keep in mind that the sale of the business can be turbulent for the management and employees of the target, and that the human aspects of an acquisition can have a significant impact on the value of the transaction. No acquirer, to cite just one example, would want to face a large turnover of employees immediately following the close of the transaction. We discuss this further in later chapters when we address integration planning.

    The main point is that the acquirer's first efforts should be to establish one-on-one relationships with the key leaders of acquisition targets. This facilitates an open dialogue on key issues as the discussions between the organizations as they progress from exploration to execution. Initially, the focus of relationship building should be on establishing trust, determining if there is a shared strategic vision, and obtaining information. In addition to shaping and informing the acquirer's own strategic views, this process allows the acquirer to evaluate the quality of the target's management, determine whether the management philosophies and company cultures mesh, and to highlight areas for further investigation in the due diligence review.

- *A window for exclusive discussions.* In the section "Marketplace for Acquisitions," we discussed how an organized marketplace for mergers and acquisitions exists, an environment in which a structured, competitive sale process is normally exploited to benefit sellers. For this reason, it makes sense for acquirers to try to preempt competitive auctions whenever possible. In preemptive situations, buyers get an opportunity to establish relationships and discuss the strategic and organizational merits of doing a deal with the seller. Once intermediaries are involved, discussions are channeled through a narrow framework of competitive bidding, driving up prices, lowering the value creation opportunity, constraining information gathering, and increasing acquirers' risk. Potential acquirers should anticipate even preemptive deals to become competitive at some point—when a seller seriously considers a sale, they usually will be strongly urged by their advisor to evaluate the full range of "strategic alternatives" to optimize their value. As a result, opportunities to consummate preemptive deals are dwindling. Still, they are worth pursuing even if only to establish relationships and jump-start the information-gathering process.

Role of Management versus Intermediaries Accountability for development of relationships with each targeted organization should be assigned to an individual executive. Ideally, the executive should be knowledgeable about the targeted market segment and involved in the development of the corporation's growth strategy for that segment. Often, executives in business development or strategic planning manage the outreach to prospective acquisition candidates, especially in initial exploratory conversations, but it is important to involve operating executives early and at key stages in the development of the organizational relationship. That involvement is important for several reasons. It enables those close to the market and acquirer's internal operations to provide early input into the decision-making process. It accelerates the executives' understanding of issues critical to the effective execution of due diligence if an acquisition is pursued. And, it establishes internal support for the transaction if it is consummated.

Intermediaries such as business brokers, investment bankers, and industry consultants can also be helpful in engaging with targeted organizations. The best of them have their fingers on the pulse of the industry in which they operate, and very often they have business relationships with a wide range of organizations within their area of expertise. But there is a cost of employing such intermediaries if conversations result in an acquisition, so they should be retained only if no better avenue of approach is available to the potential acquirer. And, importantly, using intermediaries does not supplant the need for management accountability for relationship development; management needs to direct the intermediaries.

Confidentiality of Information: Nondisclosure Agreement (NDA) Because the initiation of contact with a targeted organization is often accompanied by an initial exchange of confidential information, there is a need to establish legal protection against the damage that can be created by disclosure or misuse of this information. This legal protection normally takes the form of an NDA.

The NDA is the first legally binding agreement executed between the targeted organization and the potential acquirer. It requires the potential acquirer not to disclose any information about the business that is deemed to be confidential, or about the existence or contents of any deal discussions. The NDA may also prevent the potential acquirer from hiring or soliciting employees of the targeted organization (known as a "no poach" provision). These restrictions may endure for several years. Most terms of an NDA (such as the definition of, and the limitations on, what is deemed confidential information, the restrictions on the parties, and the procedures if discussions terminate) are fairly noncontroversial. Where the difficulty usually comes is in the no-poach provision.

The no-poach provision is normally the first item that the potential buyer and seller have to negotiate. From the seller's perspective, the no-poach provision should be written as broadly as possible—for example, covering any employee, whether involved in the sale or not, for as long as possible. From the potential acquirer's perspective, the fact that it has entered into potential acquisition discussions should not impair its hiring practices. This is particularly the case if it is an active acquirer with numerous NDAs in circulation. It will prefer as narrow a no-poach provision as possible—for example, covering only employees it meets or becomes aware of during the diligence, and for a short period of time. Also, the potential acquirer may want to provide for an exception, or carve out, in case employees come to its attention as a result of normal, broad-based solicitations, such as job advertisements in industry publications or on company Web sites. Negotiations of no-poach provisions can become a significant impediment for some potential acquirers, especially for large organizations who may find no-poach agreements cumbersome to internally administer. As a result, active acquirers are well-advised to establish and communicate clear guidelines on no-poach terms and be prepared to adhere to them.

Reactive Engagement

Although we believe that proactive relationship development is the optimal path to strategic conversations between a potential acquirer and a targeted organization, we acknowledge that in many transactions originate with a call from the seller's financial adviser with the message that the business is for sale, a situation we refer to as reactive engagement. In practice, acquisitive organizations engage regularly in both proactive and reactive deals.

We described the risk of reacting to deals in Chapter 1. Reactive engagement can easily result in the acquisition team getting swept up in the momentum of the deal and being tempted to *justify*, rather than *assess*, the strategic merits of the potential transaction. In organizations looking toward acquisitions to boost growth, there can be significant internal pressure to pursue deals. That pressure can originate with a seller's financial advisor who will have artfully packaged the property and created positive industry "buzz" about the market opportunities the offered company provides. That buzz, in turn, can generate leading inquiries from corporate headquarters (which may have been lobbied by the advisor) and concerns at the operating level about the competitive impact if the property is not pursued ("if we don't buy it a competitor will"). Under these circumstances, those screening the opportunity must exhibit a high level of discipline and a willingness to advocate against pursuit when there is a disconnect between the established strategy and the "opportunity."

Our concern about the consequences of an organization's opportunistic, nonstrategic reaction to incoming solicitations is why an entire chapter (Chapter 2) is devoted to the strategic planning process and its relationship to the acquisition process. As noted, a successful acquisition program must be rooted in an organization's investment strategy, regardless of how opportunities originate. That means that all opportunities should be driven by the organization's strategic plan and should be subjected to the same high level of disciplined analysis and evaluation. An organization with a well-developed growth strategy and a systematic process for evaluating opportunities will be better positioned to be thoughtful yet responsive, making an informed judgment in a rapid but not hasty manner. Before deciding to pursue an incoming opportunity, the prospective acquirer should first ask itself the following questions to establish a link between the potential transaction and the corporation's growth strategy:

- Is the market segment served by the offered property targeted by the corporation for expansion based on its size and growth characteristics? If not, why should a deal be pursued?
- Is the offered property listed on the corporation's acquisition/partner target list? If not, why was it missed if it serves a targeted market segment?

- Does the offered property compete with an organization that is listed on the corporation's acquisition/partner target list? If so, where does it stand competitively and would it be an equivalent or superior alternative to acquiring the listed organization? If not, why should the deal be pursued?

ASSESSMENT

When engagement with a targeted company progresses to the point where pursuit of an acquisition appears desirable, the acquiring organization normally conducts a formal assessment process. We present an overall acquisition transaction framework in more detail in the section "Pursuit," but for purposes of this discussion we are referring to the internal steps the deal sponsor, the executive championing the transaction, must take to receive corporate authorization or concurrence to initiate nonbinding acquisition discussions with the target and its advisors.

In this section, we first discuss the corporate notification/approval document. Then, we address the plan to create value, which we view as the lynchpin that *links intentions to actions*. It connects the strategic and financial assumptions comprising the business case for the acquisition to their validation in the due diligence review and to decisions made and actions required before and after the close of the transaction.

Notification/Approval Document

Most acquiring organizations have an internal process whereby the sponsoring executive notifies the corporation of the intent, or receives corporate approval, to initiate formal acquisition discussions with a target (in an auction this would be to make a nonbinding bid and to conduct preliminary due diligence). While formats vary, this process normally involves drafting a notification/approval document (sometimes referred to as a *position paper* or *early alert*), which typically covers the following topics (see Exhibit 3.4 for an illustrative outline):

- *Purpose.* The document should clearly indicate whether the transaction sponsor is informing the corporation about a prospective transaction, or requesting its approval to submit an offer within a defined range.
- *Strategic rationale.* The rationale should connect the acquisition opportunity to the corporation's growth strategy. If there is a documented

EXHIBIT 3.4　Illustrative Outline of Notification/Approval Document

Purpose	Notification of intent (or request for approval) to initiate nonbinding acquisition discussions
Strategic rationale	Linkage to growth strategy Desirability of market 　• Size, growth Desirability of target company 　• Market share, customer base, products and services, management, organization, strategy Desirability of acquisition 　• Relative merits versus building or allying Shareholder value created by proposed transaction
Financial impact	Financial metrics 　• Supporting the investment (market measures such as comparison to comparable transactions) 　• Supporting return on investment (discounted cash flow analysis, internal rate of return, net present value, usually accompanied by a preliminary financial forecast model) Value drivers 　• Key assumptions about transaction structure, core business growth, revenue synergy, cost synergy
Transaction considerations	Sale process, timeline, next steps Preliminary bidding strategy Preliminary risk assessment and key issues of focus for the due diligence review

growth strategy, this section would link to the targeted market segment, to the acquisition/partner target list, and to the assessment of strategic alternatives (buy, build, or ally), placing the particular target on an already established strategic road map and quantifying the value creation opportunity. The absence of a well-developed growth strategy places much more pressure on this section of the document (and its authors). It would need to define and sell the corporation on a growth strategy and then build interest in the target—an uphill battle for the acquisition team at exactly the moment it is seeking to pivot into a transaction mode.

- *Financial impact.* The purpose of this section is to detail the value creation opportunity, addressing two basic questions: How much is the target worth, and how much might it cost? Because this document must be created prior to negotiations and due diligence, there is generally uncertainty about both value and price. Typically at this stage, the acquiring company prepares a number of "upside" and "downside" financial scenarios based on optimistic or conservative assumptions, resulting in a range of potential valuations, within which the acquisition would make financial sense. While the sophistication of financial models varies from one organization to another, most approach valuation in a similar way: calculating the present value of after-tax cash flows of the targeted business based on assumptions about future growth and profitability, and comparing the price of the potential acquisition with revenue or earnings multiples attained in comparable transactions. The most important aspect of the financial analysis at this stage is not its level of technical sophistication, it is the depth of thinking about the sensitivity of the valuation to specific business assumptions, and the documentation and communication of those assumptions.

- *Transaction considerations.* This section briefs those with approval authority within the corporation on the nature and status of the sale process, such as whether it is a preemptive sale or a competitive auction and the time period over which it will be conducted. It also provides preliminary thoughts on bidding, especially if value and price have been expressed in ranges, with a recommended bidding floor and ceiling. Finally, the acquisition sponsor should specify the key things that are *not* known about the target, important factors and risks, which need to be validated during the due diligence review in order for the team to recommend moving forward with a definitive agreement.

Even if the transaction sponsor is authorized to initiate acquisition discussions without prior approval, we believe it is highly desirable for the acquirer to document and communicate the strategic purpose and the value creation expected from the envisioned transaction. That communication should be both upward, to corporate management to set expectations, and downward, to the acquisition team to guide its actions. It is important that the acquisition team does not look at this step as a bureaucratic hurdle. Time spent developing the notification/approval document presents an opportunity for the prospective acquirer to think about what a successful transaction should look like, in terms of both its strategic and financial benefits. Only by pushing itself, to make assumptions about what conditions are necessary to result in a successful deal, will the acquisition team know how to direct its due diligence review and guide its negotiations and its postacquisition activities.

The drafting of the notification/approval document also sets the stage for the development of a more thorough and actionable analysis, the team's plan to create value.

Plan to Create Value

The plan to create value addresses many of the issues discussed in the notification/approval document, but it differs from that document in its elaboration of the detailed thinking behind the proposed transaction. It lists and quantifies the assumptions, risks, and opportunities at a granular level, and by so doing, establishes clear priorities for the due diligence review team.

We introduced the concept of the plan to create value in Chapter 1, defining it as a document in which the prospective acquirer states explicitly *why* it intends to make an acquisition and *how* it proposes to generate a return. It serves as a guide to ensure that actions taken from due diligence through integration are value-driven. In this section, we address the plan to create value from a tactical perspective. It is best to think of the plan to create value as a bridge between planning and action; it connects the assumptions that underlie the acquisition's business case to the actions of the deal team.

Specifically, the plan to create value should itemize the key factors that underlie the deal's strategic and financial rationale, quantify each factor's impact on the valuation, and identify the actions required to address the deal's major unknowns and mitigate the key risks. It asks:

- What is assumed about the business and the value created by the proposed acquisition?
- Can each assumption be quantified in terms of its contribution to the projected value of the deal?
- Which of these assumptions need to be validated and what actions need to be taken to extract this value?

Exhibit 3.5 illustrates how a plan to create value might be structured. All of the deal's key elements can be listed within one of three categories:

1. *Strategic purpose.* In this section, assumptions are articulated about the relative merits of acquisition versus the alternatives, about the quality

EXHIBIT 3.5 Plan to Create Value

	Key Assumptions	Required Action
Strategic purpose	Desirability of acquisition	Relative merits of acquisition vs. building or allying	Validation, assessment
	Characteristics of acquired business	Markets served, strength of offerings, organizational capabilities, management, etc.	Validation, assessment
	Impact of combination	Areas of expected benefit: e.g., market share, combined offerings, newly developed offerings, relative competitive strength	Validation, assessment, integration planning
Value drivers	Calculation of shareholder value created by:		
	• Transaction structure $X million	Optimal deal structure (purchase of assets vs. stock, tax benefits)	Validation, negotiation
	• Core business growth $X million	Future growth and profitability of the acquired business	Validation, assessment, integration planning
	• Revenue synergy $X million	Initiatives to increase revenue growth: e.g., cross-selling existing products/services, development of new products/services	Validation, assessment, integration planning
	• Cost synergy $X million	Initiatives to increase profitability: e.g., shared infrastructure, elimination of redundancy, economies of scale	Validation, assessment, integration planning
Key risks	Preliminary risk assessment and key issues of focus for the transaction	Specific risks that could impair the value of the transaction: e.g., integration, management strength, key personnel retention	Validation, assessment, integration planning, negotiation

of the business being considered, and about the benefits from the transaction expected to accrue to the acquirer.

2. *Value drivers.* This section puts a dollar figure next to each of the key assumptions in the acquisition's business case (i.e., it allocates the deal's present value to the factors that generate that value). This includes the transaction structure, the expected performance of the acquired business on a stand-alone basis, and the expected increases to revenue and profit growth generated by synergy between the acquirer and the target. Asking the acquisition team to produce this level of detail can be revealing. If a preliminary valuation has been prepared, financial forecast assumptions have been made, either explicitly or implicitly. The more explicit the thinking, the more the due diligence team has to work with and the better it can then focus its efforts. It is entirely possible that the valuation model at this early stage may simply assume that revenue growth rates, profit margins, or cash flows will increase by some percentage after acquisition, based on rules of thumb or past experience. The point here is for the due diligence team to *understand the deal's financial targets, and to begin the process of identifying the key areas and actions necessary to achieve those targets.*

3. *Key risks.* This section lists the key risks and unknowns that have been identified by the prospective acquirer. While it may not be possible to quantify the risks (for example, a risk such as differing business cultures impairing the integration effort might be very difficult to put a number on), they should be identified and prioritized in some manner so that the team's limited resources can be applied to the most important issues.

With a plan to create value in place, the prospective acquirer has the ability to guide and direct the acquisition team's behavior to focus on the issues that matter most to the value of the deal, spanning from due diligence to the transaction's close and subsequent integration, as shown in Exhibit 3.6. We will demonstrate the usefulness of having such a framework in more detail in the subsequent chapters.

PURSUIT

Although no two acquisitions play out in exactly the same way, most follow a similar general pattern. We outline that pattern in this section, first focusing on the differing perspective of the players involved, and then looking at the

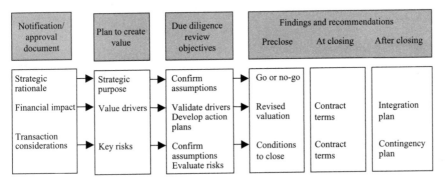

EXHIBIT 3.6   Plan to Create Value Bridges Planning and Subsequent Action

initial major step the acquirer takes toward an acquisition, the formation of its core acquisition team.

Transaction Framework: Sellers' and Acquirers' Different Perspectives

Most acquisitions follow a transaction flow consisting of three phases, as illustrated in Exhibit 3.7. In the first phase, each party conducts its own assessment of the strategic merits of engaging in a transaction and, after deciding to proceed, shifts to the preparation stage of the process. The timing of the buyer's and seller's actions differs depending on which party makes the decision first and initiates engagement with the other. If the buyer is proactive, it has conducted candidate screening and selection and approaches the seller before the seller has begun its preparation. If the buyer is reacting to a seller's offer, the seller has likely already engaged advisors, developed offering materials, and may have completed a financial audit, before contacting prospective buyers. During this first phase, the amount of interaction between the parties is by definition limited.

The second phase of the transaction is its most intense. For purposes of this illustration, the assumption is that the seller is conducting a competitive auction, which is common, if not the norm, for many transactions. The inter-action between the parties is defined according to a sale process outlined by the seller's financial advisor, typically following these steps (this aspect of the process is described in greater detail in Chapter 5, in the "Auctions" section):

- Distribution of an offering document, or confidential information memorandum, following execution of a nondisclosure agreement

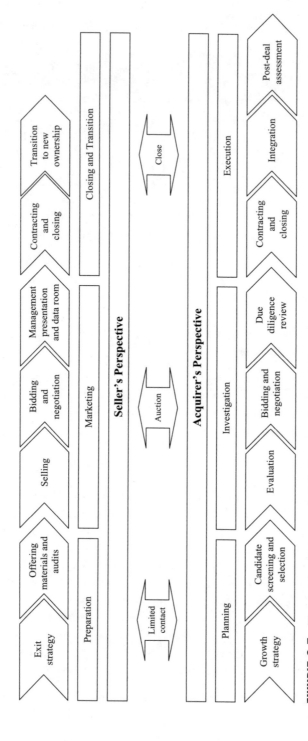

EXHIBIT 3.7 Transaction Framework: Seller's versus Acquirer's Perspective

- Solicitation of preliminary nonbinding offers
- Selection of a limited number of prospective acquirers to enter a second round, based on the initial bids
- Prospective acquirers conduct "preliminary due diligence," which normally consists of a management presentation and access to a "data room" containing detailed information about the business
- Solicitation of definitive acquisition offers, which normally include mark-ups to a draft acquisition agreement circulated by the seller
- Conduct of final, or "confirmatory," due diligence

In Chapters 4 and 5, we will discuss the added degree of difficulty the prospective acquirer faces when it must conduct its due diligence review within the constraints of a competitive auction. Suffice it to say here that there is an inescapable conflict between the interests and goals of the parties at this stage, which creates dynamic tension and makes the due diligence review a major logistical challenge for the buyer. The seller is, after all, conducting a sale, and while it wants to address buyers' questions and information requests, its primary posture is marketing the business. The buyer, in contrast, is attempting to address a long list of questions, uncertainties, risks, and unknowns within a short period of time, and is looking for access and answers, not salesmanship.

In the third phase, a definitive acquisition agreement is negotiated and executed, and the ownership of the target business is transitioned from the seller to the buyer. At this point, the seller's work ends and the buyer's begins, as it integrates and takes over management of the acquired business.

Taking Action: Assembling the Core Acquisition Team

The final step of the planning stage, for the buyer, is to establish the core acquisition transaction team. The core acquisition team is normally a small number of individuals tasked with:

- Interfacing with the seller and its representatives
- Engaging and managing external resources and advisors
- Calling upon and managing additional internal resources from within the acquirer, when and as needed

The key roles on the core acquisition team are as follows:

1. *Transaction sponsor (deal champion).* This is normally the executive responsible for the business unit pursuing the acquisition. While this individual does not usually lead day-to-day activities of the transaction, he or she must be kept apprised of the transaction's status and key issues as they arise. The transaction sponsor should be centrally involved in the acquirer's decisions about whether or not to pursue the transaction, and if so, at what price. If the value of the transaction exceeds this individual's authority, it is the transaction sponsor's responsibility to secure any required corporate approvals, with the core acquisition team's support.

2. *Acquisition project lead/deal negotiator.* The acquisition project lead has day-to-day responsibility for the management of the acquisition. This role is typically filled by an executive from the business development or strategic planning function, but it could be filled with any executive with substantial mergers and acquisitions experience. The project lead also is the primary interface with the seller and its advisors, and so will also normally serve as the voice of the acquirer in negotiations of the various elements of the deal. Typically, the project lead will be supported by the senior financial executive on the team and the lead member of the team's legal contingent. While other specialists will be drawn into the process at various points, these two professionals will play a continuous support role throughout the transaction.

3. *External resources.* Acquisitions normally require the support of various external experts. The specific resources utilized will depend on the size and complexity of the transaction, and on the acquirer's capabilities and capacity. For a large transaction, the acquirer may seek the involvement of an investment bank to assist in valuation or financing. The acquirer's legal counsel may also enlist outside attorneys to assist with the transaction, particularly if advice on specialized topics, such as antitrust regulation, or international transactions, if the transaction involves a multinational company. An independent accounting firm may also be retained to perform certain activities in the financial due diligence.

4. *Internal resources.* The core acquisition team is expanded at specific times to include a collection of individuals from a variety of functions

across the organization (most commonly, human resources, tax, technology, product management, sales, marketing, and operations). One such expansion is the creation of the due diligence review team, which we discuss in Chapter 4, and another is the integration team, addressed in Chapter 8.

Key Points

1. The progression from identifying targets to pursuing acquisitions should follow a methodical, ongoing winnowing process consisting of:
   - Identifying potential targets
   - Qualifying them
   - Engaging
   - Assessing
   - Pursuing a transaction
     ("Winnowing Process")

2. The acquisition/partner target list should be continually updated and enhanced by:
   - Establishing information sources for identification of prospects
   - Distilling information on market, performance, and sizing into a standardized acquisition candidate profile for each firm
     ("Identifying Prospects")

3. It is not realistic for an organization to set out in pursuit of every company on its target list. A high-level qualification process can quickly reduce the number of targets based on strategic fit and availability. ("Qualifying Acquisition Candidates")

4. Proactive engagement is a best-case scenario for the buyer, one that allows the acquirer to simultaneously explore and evaluate strategic alternatives, reducing risk. ("Engagement")

5. Assessment involves receiving corporate authorization or concurrence to initiate acquisition discussions with the target, and should also include a plan to create value, connecting the strategic and financial

assumptions comprising the business case to their validation in the due diligence review, and to required actions before and after the close of the transaction. ("Assessment")

6. There is an inescapable conflict between the interests and goals of the seller and buyer in a competitive auction, which creates dynamic tension and makes the due diligence review a major challenge for the buyer. ("Transaction Framework: Sellers' and Acquirers' Different Perspectives")

Investigation

CHAPTER 4

Preparing for Due Diligence

INTRODUCTION

Once a live sale process is underway, the transaction enters its most intense phase. This is when the dynamic tension between seller and buyer, described in Chapter 3, peaks. The seller is motivated to showcase the business while controlling access to information and personnel. In contrast, the buyer is prepared to launch its due diligence review with a mind-set that is decidedly evaluative and investigatory.

To this point, the buyer's acquisition team has probably received only summary information about the target company and is anxious to validate a host of assumptions it has made about the transaction. However, it is likely to be faced with constraints on personnel and information access as it seeks to do so. Under these conditions, the due diligence team must place a premium on the efficient and effective use of its finite resources.

We believe that the acquirer is best served in this environment if it conducts its due diligence review in a top-down, objectives-driven manner, where the objectives are informed by its plan to create value and its findings guide its negotiating posture and its postacquisition action plans. This approach is meant to unify and coordinate the efforts of the due diligence team members around those objectives that will have the greatest impact on the value of the transaction.

In this and the following two chapters, we present a step-by-step approach to the conduct of due diligence where, *throughout the process,* the acquirer sets its priorities based on the dual over-arching goals of risk mitigation and value creation. In Chapters 7 and 8, we turn to additional benefits derived from an integrated approach, the due diligence review's importance in shaping the definitive transaction terms and structure (discussed in Chapter 7) and the postacquisition integration (the focus of Chapter 8).

Due Diligence Reviews

The due diligence review, seen as an integrated component of the broader acquisition process, has the following characteristics and objectives:

1. It is performed *by a team* of internal experts and/or external advisors. Once it is clear that a due diligence review will occur, the initial acquisition team is expanded to include a cross-functional group of functional experts in areas such as technology and operations and subject matter experts in areas such as accounting, taxation, and business operations. The requisite skills and expertise of these members of the diligence team are discussed in detail in the section "Creation of the Due Diligence Team."

2. Much of the review occurs *during a specified period* of time in the transaction when the seller agrees to provide access to the target company. This access consists of the exposure of detailed business and financial information, as well as contact with key members of the seller's management team. The degree of access may vary based on the nature of the selling process; that is, whether the transaction takes the form of an auction sale or a negotiated sale. Issues and processes affecting access are discussed in the section "External Constraints of the Sale Process."

3. The review by the team endeavors to *discover* as much as possible about *the true state and future prospects of the business*. To this point in the process, the acquisition team has typically had limited exposure to target company information (e.g., an *offering document*) and company management (i.e., major principals such as an owner/manager or CEO, if at all). Because of the additional constraints on access that are likely to be imposed by the seller, the acquirer should use its plan to create value to set clear priorities for the due diligence team, so that its limited resources are directed at the factors having the greatest impact on the deal's value.

4. The team's findings inform decisions the acquirer must make about the deal by *validating key assumptions and identifying previously undisclosed risks*. To date, the acquirer's analysis and projections will largely have been based on assumptions about upside potential (i.e.,

cross-company synergies) and downside risks. The review enables the team to confirm or modify those assumptions relative to that potential and those risks, as well as identify any previously unforeseen exposures and opportunities.

5. The findings resulting from the review *support or alter* the acquirer's preliminary *valuation and provide input for negotiation* of the terms of the definitive purchase agreement. A well-planned and executed review results in the documentation of actionable findings (discussed in Chapters 5 and 6) that can be used by the acquisition team to negotiate and structure a transaction that minimizes risk and fully exploits value creation opportunities.

6. The review also enables the acquirer to begin to *prepare a plan for postacquisition integration.* A key aspect of the due diligence review is to outline an integration plan that enables the acquirer to operationalize measures that minimize integration risks and optimize opportunities to extract the benefits presumed in its acquisition business case.

The due diligence review, by definition, is ambitious in scope. It endeavors to cover all material aspects of the candidate's operation, consisting of intense document review and analysis, extensive discussion with management, and often an evaluation of physical plant and operations. Given the time constraints under which a due diligence review is generally conducted (typically, less than 10 days for acquisitions involving nonpublic companies), it is critically important that the process is properly targeted, effectively organized, and efficiently conducted. Accordingly, this chapter discusses planning issues, measures, and procedures affecting the efficiency and effectiveness of that process.

Chapter Focus

As noted in Chapter 1 (Mergers and Acquisitions: A Way of Corporate Life), the most common type of acquisition transactions is that involving smaller, privately held businesses by midsize and large companies. This discussion, therefore, focuses on the process involving these types of transactions, although most of the concepts and procedures described are applicable to all types of acquisitions, regardless of the size of the acquiring company or the one to be acquired. The discussion outlines a disciplined, structured, and well-documented process that will result in the optimization of an acquirer's time and personnel and in the development of actionable findings.

The remainder of this chapter is divided into the following sections:

- Environmental factors that influence planning and executing a review
- Creation of the due diligence review team
- Development of the due diligence review program
- Planning the due diligence review

ENVIRONMENTAL FACTORS

There are several factors that significantly influence the planning and conduct of the due diligence review. They include (1) external forces shaping the environment in which the transaction takes place; (2) internal limitations that an acquirer typically encounters in preparing for and executing the review; and (3) the nature of the target company. These environmental factors are discussed in the sections that immediately follow.

External Constraints of the Sale Process

Under ideal circumstances an acquirer may have the luxury of extended review time, abundant resources, and extensive access to prepare for and conduct due diligence. In these uncommon situations, candidate companies and their principals are courted directly, without intermediaries, over an extended period of time, the acquirer has the competitive benefit of a preemptive bid, and the seller is willing to tolerate the disruption and distraction associated with a buyer's extensive review. As discussed in Chapter 3, the marketplace for companies has matured to the point where such situations have become a rarity.

In contrast, in the overwhelming majority of acquisition transactions, buyers are provided a narrow window of opportunity, in a competitive environment, to prepare for and perform due diligence. Acquirers typically become aware of a company's availability only weeks before they must mobilize a due diligence team. In addition, sellers are routinely represented by knowledgeable and skillful financial advisors who manage competitive sales processes (generally auctions) regularly. These competitive offerings are often designed to maximize sales proceeds, as well as other benefits (such as transaction structure and limitations on post transaction recourse) for the seller. Even in those cases where transactions are conducted on a noncompetitive basis (i.e., a preemptive bid as opposed to an auction), they are usually managed by advisors who are extremely knowledgeable about the industry and are very skilled at extracting a price premium and restricted diligence conditions in exchange for preemption.

The constraints on the due diligence review that result from the prevailing competitive environment in which they are usually conducted take the form of limited access to company information and management, as well as constricted time frames in which to review and analyze intelligence for decision-making purposes. For example, in a typical auction sale, potential buyers are provided with access to data on a gradual, incremental basis. Information is disclosed in a measured fashion, first to stimulate buyer broad interest (generally in the form of a "teaser"), then to more fully describe the opportunity to those expressing interest (in the form of an offering document or prospectus), and then to a small subset of qualified potential buyers in the form of access to the "data room" (described in this section) for preliminary due diligence purposes. Only the final bidder or bidders receive access to the most sensitive, proprietary information in the review's final, "confirmatory" stage, detailed information that may have been redacted, or perhaps not provided in any form, in preliminary due diligence. Finally, the winning bidder will receive representations and warranties as to its validity in the form of the final agreement and associated schedules. Exhibit 4.1 illustrates this phased disclosure process.

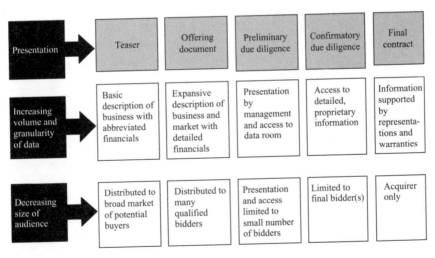

Presentation	Teaser	Offering document	Preliminary due diligence	Confirmatory due diligence	Final contract
Increasing volume and granularity of data	Basic description of business with abbreviated financials	Expansive description of business and market with detailed financials	Presentation by management and access to data room	Access to detailed, proprietary information	Information supported by representations and warranties
Decreasing size of audience	Distributed to broad market of potential buyers	Distributed to many qualified bidders	Presentation and access limited to small number of bidders	Limited to final bidder(s)	Acquirer only

EXHIBIT 4.1 Phased Disclosure Process

Similarly, access to company management is controlled to the advantage of the seller. Management presentations to buyers are developed, rehearsed, and delivered with an emphasis on salesmanship. They are delivered in a controlled environment over a constrained period (several hours) and generally in advance of buyer access to detailed proprietary company information in a *data room*. The diligence review in total (management presentation and data room access) is typically limited to a period of one or two weeks. This entire process is designed not only to stimulate a sense of competitiveness but also to limit the buyers' ability to probe and identify transaction risks and vulnerabilities of the target company.

Internal Limitations of the Acquirer

It is also important to note that acquisition transactions do not occur in a vacuum. The acquiring company will almost certainly be involved in other strategic initiatives, such as other acquisitions, divestitures, corporate restructuring, internal development efforts, and strategic alliances. As a result, any given acquisition effort will be vying with these initiatives for attention and resources. The competition for resources can diminish the ability of the organization to involve those managers and experts with optimal knowledge and skills, forcing the acquirer to place more reliance on external resources.

Nature of the Target Company

The nature of the target company itself can have a significant impact on planning for the due diligence review. If, for example, the target company is an early-stage, fast-growing organization with an entrepreneurial culture, the due diligence team should expect to encounter a sparsely populated data room, with business policies and practices either informally documented or not documented at all. The team, consequently, may not be able to accomplish certain of its objectives through document review alone; it may need to place a greater reliance on face-to-face meetings with company management to fully understand and gain comfort with the target business.

At the other extreme, if the target company is a large, mature, well-established business, the number of contracts and other documents housed in the data room may be overwhelming. In this case, the acquirer should consider retaining legal and financial advisors with the capacity to rapidly scale up the number of professionals participating in the document review.

Impact of Environmental Factors on the Review

The factors described in the preceding paragraphs underline the need for a well-planned and targeted review. External and internal constraints generally preclude the ability of the acquirer to take a broad "kitchen sink" approach to the review. Limitations on time and access to information and target company management put a premium on an approach that focuses on issues of greatest importance. Consequently, planning for the review should include establishing transaction-wide objectives with the intent of assigning specific goals and objectives to each of the due diligence team members. We discuss this use of a "top-down," directive approach further in the "Key Aspects of the Due Diligence Program" section of this chapter.

CREATION OF THE DUE DILIGENCE TEAM

Introduction

Even the largest organizations will generally not have a standing due diligence team. From a practical standpoint, the volume of acquisition activity over time is too uneven to justify dedicated staff in all areas where expertise is needed. In addition, needs change from one assignment to the next, further complicating any attempt to build a staff of dedicated professionals.

As discussed in Chapter 2, however, larger and more acquisitive companies may have a core team consisting of M&A or business development professionals; peopled by staff (versus line) personnel with specific expertise in areas such as strategic planning and financial modeling; and supported by finance professionals within the acquiring organization; and by corporate staff with expertise in areas such as acquisition law, taxation, and insurance. In these cases, business development and finance personnel, as transaction leaders, generally drive the acquisition process, but they rely heavily on managers from various parts of their overall organization to supplement their efforts once it becomes clear that the acquisition is likely to materialize. Accordingly, line managers from the departments responsible for technology, human resources, sales and marketing, and operations are typically enlisted as part of an acquisition team to supplement the finance and business development staff.

In smaller organizations, a selected business manager and finance professional would generally be assigned as team leaders by the acquiring company's CEO, with responsibility for shepherding the acquisition process. Once a decision is made to proceed with due diligence, these leaders would organize a team consisting of a mix of internal and external professionals and coordinate their involvement in the diligence review. Typically, smaller organizations will rely more heavily on external consultants and professionals to flesh out the due diligence team. This may include legal, tax, human resource, and acquisition advisors, as well as an independent accounting firm. This approach enables the organization to limit the distraction of internal managers and to fill gaps in transaction expertise. However, the organization must realize that it cannot entirely outsource the transaction. Involvement by internal managers is critical to ensuring a sense of ownership in the transaction, as well as responsibility for the successful postacquisition integration.

Composition of the Due Diligence Team

As it becomes clear that the acquisition is likely to be pursued, the individuals assigned to the due diligence team would be formally apprised of the prospective transaction and informed of the specific role that they will play in the due diligence review process. The team would generally be constituted along the lines indicated in the following list. For each functional area, if there is more than one reviewer involved, there would be a lead member for that function who will have responsibility for coordinating the review of that area and for reporting on the results.

- *Finance and accounting.* The financial aspect of the review is clearly of great importance and, accordingly, is an area where substantial resources should be brought to bear. The number of financial professionals on the due diligence team from the acquiring company is largely dependent on the size and complexity of the company being reviewed and the volume of documents to be reviewed. It is also dependent upon whether or not outside accounting firm assistance is enlisted. The lead member of the financial team will frequently manage or comanage the diligence process with a business development colleague and will coordinate the inputs and involvement of other financial professionals, such as tax, accounting, and acquisition specialists on the team. Additionally, that individual would be the liaison to the finance and accounting managers at the candidate company, as well as its accounting firm.

- *Independent accountants.* The decision to utilize an independent accounting firm may stem from a number of considerations. It may simply be a matter of a desire for increased manpower and enhanced expertise. Notably, most full-service firms have transaction services groups that can perform any or all aspects of the financial due diligence for clients. This is a major consideration for smaller organizations and those with financial staffs that have limited M&A experience or gaps in their expertise (in an area such as taxation or acquisition modeling). Or it may result from a desire to have a third party to review and validate the target company's key financial information for the comfort this may provide to the executive management of the acquiring organization. In addition, if the financial statements of the prospective candidate have not been audited, it may be necessary to engage an independent firm.

- *Business development.* As noted, the existence of a business development function is dependent upon the size and appetite for acquisitions of the acquiring company. In those instances where the function exists, the acquisition process in general, and the due diligence review in particular, will significantly benefit from the participation of business development staff seasoned in the organization's strategic planning process and acquisition justification efforts and experienced in managing due diligence reviews. The senior member of the business development staff would frequently be a comanager of the diligence process, and he or she would provide valuable guidance in shaping the due diligence objectives, in developing the due diligence program, and in efficiently and effectively conducting the review.

- *Legal.* Whether inside or outside counsel or both are used, those staffing of the legal arm of the team would have been involved early in the process, at least as early as the drafting of the governing confidentiality agreement and the letter of intent (LOI), if applicable. Their continued participation in the process is critically important from a number of perspectives. They will provide the necessary expertise to review legal documents and assess legal issues of all sorts during due diligence. In addition, because they will also be intimately involved in negotiating and drafting the purchase agreement (see Chapter 7), their participation will provide the knowledge base to effectively address legal aspects of business issues that typically emerge during final negotiations.

- *Human resources.* HR staff involvement should take into consideration the need to cover the range of issues associated with personnel management, compensation plans, change of control issues, and benefits management, and should be staffed accordingly. In addition, human resource staff will frequently play a central role in harmonizing practices and procedures and in spearheading cultural integration, if the company is acquired. Smaller and less frequent acquirers will benefit from the use of HR advisers experienced in dealing with acquisition and cultural integration issues.

- *Information technology.* The technology function generally has a number of issues to address. The IT professionals will have to gain a clear understanding of the purely operational aspects of the candidate's technology (i.e., systems, hardware, software, and connectivity) and the implications for operational integration. They will also have to evaluate product or product support technology (particularly in technology-intensive businesses such as software development, communications, financial services, and entertainment) and its compatibility with that of the acquiring company. Depending upon the nature of the business being reviewed, this area can require a substantial commitment of internal and external resources.

- *Sales and marketing.* The sales and marketing aspect of the due diligence review would include an assessment of the quality of the candidate's products and services, customer perceptions of those products and services, and the company in general, as well as the state of its customer relationships. There should be particular emphasis by the sales and marketing reviewers on the confirmation of assumed cross-company revenue synergies and the ability of the combined entity to generate growth consistent with the projections in the acquirer's assumptions.

- *Product management.* Whether the function goes under the title of product management, product development, research and development (R&D), or something else, the reference here is to that department within the organization responsible for the development and management of products or services. The detailed review of this area is critical because this element of the review team is charged with determining whether there is sufficient life in existing products, and a healthy enough pipeline of new products, to support the growth assumptions embedded in the valuation model.

- *Production/operations.* The operational review would generally concentrate on production/manufacturing processes, facilities, fixed assets, and real property leases, with a strong bias toward identifying or confirming the existence of cross-company efficiencies. The individuals handling the operational review are also the most likely candidates to manage the non-IT operational or cost-savings aspect of postacquisition integration. As a result, much of the attention of these reviewers will be focused on projected expense synergies and preliminary plans for integration implementation.

A Caveat

As noted in the previous section, "Internal Limitations of the Acquirer," there may be limitations on the availability of internal resources for a due diligence review due to competing organizational initiatives, such as other acquisitions or divestitures. However, it is incumbent on the acquiring organization to dedicate or engage the best available combination of internal and external resources to the diligence review and to ensure that team assembled is capable of executing at a high level. If the organization is unable or unwilling to field a knowledgeable and experienced team, it should consider passing on the opportunity, since this would suggest that the investment is not a high enough priority to warrant the transaction risk that routinely accompanies an acquisition.

Other Considerations

In addition to the previous observations, it is important to note that there are other areas of review that may either be taking place off-line or that should be considered, due to special circumstance. An example of the former is the work of the acquiring company's tax professionals or advisors. They would have been involved in early stages of the process to determine the tax and financial ramifications in structuring the acquisition. They would also be involved in the post–due diligence stage to ensure optimal tax treatment going forward.

An example of special circumstances that might require additional outside assistance is one in which proprietary product information of the target company must be reviewed by an independent third party to ensure against potential litigation, in the event the transaction is *not* consummated. For example, this can be the case when a software company is being reviewed and the quality and documentation of source code are important due diligence issues that cannot be handled by the acquiring company, in the event that the acquisition effort is terminated.

Initial Preparation Measures

At the time team member involvement is formalized, members should be provided with the following documents to enable them to prepare their portion of the due diligence program and to prepare for the execution of the due diligence review:

- The plan to create value or the organization's functional equivalent that outlines the assumptions about the transaction's ability to enhance the enterprise's value
- The approval document presented to corporate management to justify the transaction and the accompanying valuation model, including detail of projected growth, profitability, and synergies
- Information, such as the offering document or other preliminary data, that may have been provided by the seller or its representative
- Company and product information, such as promotional materials, that may be available
- A copy of the Information Request presented to the seller
- The acquirer's standardized preacquisition checklist such as the one found in Appendix 4A

The team members should then be assembled and thoroughly briefed by the team leaders on the contents of the documents noted in the previous list and on the key issues associated with the acquisition. Due diligence team leaders should focus the attention of the team on the risks and opportunities assessment to ensure that the members' validation efforts are on those areas of greatest exposure and opportunity. That focus should drive the identification of the due diligence objectives and shape the form of the due diligence program (discussed in detail in the following section). Because it is not unusual for this to be the first diligence experience for some members of the team, the team leaders should provide first-timers with sufficient opportunity to ask questions and obtain clarification about the process and their roles in it.

In addition, at this point in the process, the team members would be briefed on the confidential nature of the prospective transaction and the restrictions outlined in the governing confidentiality agreement (and the LOI, if applicable). The need to safeguard internal communications regarding the transaction, particularly those that contain valuation information (e.g., its plan to create value and its valuation model) should also be emphasized. This would also be the point at which potential regulatory requirements, such as Hart-Scott-Rodino Act (HSR) compliance, are outlined (see the "Closing" section of Chapter 7 for a discussion of HSR and the Appendix for a comprehensive overview). To stress the importance of these issues, that briefing should be conducted by the lead member of the legal staff.

DEVELOPMENT OF THE DUE DILIGENCE PROGRAM

The due diligence program is the "playbook" used in conducting the review. It consists of a functional breakdown of procedures to be performed and questions answered in the course of the review. The program provides a structured approach to obtaining and documenting a detailed understanding of the candidate's operation and validating key assumptions of the acquirer embedded in its plan to create value and in the supporting valuation model. The process employed in doing so consists of document review, presentations by and interviews of the candidate company's management team, and an assessment of its facilities and operations.

Program Development Process

The starting point for the development of a program is the documentation provided team members and listed in the section "Initial Preparation Measures." If thoughtfully assembled and reflective of diligence team input, the *information request* will be organized along functional lines and it will identify key documents to be provided that will suggest questions and procedures relevant to the area being reviewed. A comprehensive due diligence checklist will also be helpful in identifying issues that may otherwise escape the attention of the reviewer. However, slavish adherence to a checklist approach is not what is being suggested. These documents provide a guide and a framework for the due diligence program, but its development and particularly its objectives must be strongly influenced by the acquirer's plan to create value. The limitations on time and access (discussed in the "Environmental Factors" section of this chapter) make it imperative that reviewers focus on the areas with the greatest upside and downside potential.

After being provided clear direction in this regard, the various team members should be assigned the development of the section of the program for their respective functional areas. They should be directed to create a proactive, procedural document that will induce them to review the appropriate materials, ask the right questions, and focus on the issues of greatest importance. The resulting document should clearly articulate the objectives of the review for that functional area. It should also cause the reviewers to draw specific conclusions about the results of the review (i.e., their findings and recommendations), particularly observations that suggest that assumptions embedded in the plan to create value are flawed, as well as to identify any items that should be addressed prior to or after the close of the prospective transaction. The drivers of due diligence and its outputs are illustrated in Exhibit 4.2.

Key Aspects of the Due Diligence Program

Although all programs are situation and company specific, there are key aspects of the program that should always be included, regardless of the nature or size of the company being reviewed. It is important to remember that the overarching objectives of due diligence are the mitigation of acquisition risk and validation of enhanced shareholder value of the acquisition to the acquiring company. Accordingly, the items below, to varying degrees, are reflective of those goals.

Review objectives. The program should contain clearly stated objectives, for both overall review and for each individual functional area. The explicit inclusion of objectives serves as an important point of focus for the

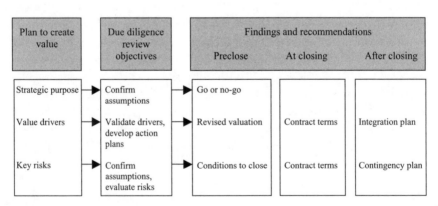

EXHIBIT 4.2   Due Diligence Continuum

reviewer. Objectives for individual functional areas should focus on two areas: any evidence that supports or alters the organization's value drivers; and establishing, confirming, and documenting the reviewers' understanding of processes, policies, and procedures for that area. The overall objectives of the review should be to confirm the team's understanding of the business and to validate or modify the major assumptions made in the plan to create value. Examples of these types of objectives would address:

- *Stand-alone growth.* The examination of the target company's expected stand-alone growth questions whether the forecasted growth rates are supportable, and specifically, whether they are attainable under the ownership of the acquirer. The due diligence review presents the acquirer with the opportunity to determine whether there are any previously unforeseen impediments to growth. This assessment is situation specific, but areas of risk may relate to such things as the ability to retain key personnel, the robustness of the company's product/service pipeline, the strength of the target's reputation with customers, continued contractual relationships with major customers, and ownership of key assets, particularly intellectual assets.

- *Profitability.* The assessment of projected profitability centers on the adequacy of assumed foundational or run-rate expenses and the assumed pricing power of the target. With regard to expenses, the issue is whether future growth can be supported by the existing infrastructure without extraordinary investment or whether there is sufficient infrastructure investment assumed in the underlying financial model. Insofar as pricing power is concerned, the major concern is whether the target company's offerings can sustain the product/service pricing levels assumed by the acquirer.

- *Synergies.* Assumed synergies can be broken down into two broad categories: revenue synergies and expense synergies. Revenue synergies embody the concept that the combined entity can generate greater revenue and profits than the sum of its parts. That assumption is based on the belief that combining certain assets and capabilities will result in new, profitable revenue streams. Those combinations are specific to the transaction being contemplated but take the form of such things as leveraging product development or distribution capabilities, brands recognition, or R&D capabilities. The ability to benefit from expense synergies is based on the assumption that costs can be removed from the combined entity through the elimination of redundant functions or through process improvement. These will generally take the form of headcount reduction for duplicative functions, the elimination of facilities, plants, and equipment, and the improvement in product development, production, and distribution processes.

- *Integration.* Assumptions about growth, profitability, and synergies not only have to be validated, there must also be a plan for implementation and integration. A conceptually accurate view of the benefits that will be derived from a transaction are of little value if it is not accompanied by a postacquisition plan to extract them. It is during the diligence review phase of the transaction that such a plan should begin to crystallize. The review should focus on the attainability of the benefits within the time frames assumed in the model. The questions the team should ask, as assumptions on growth, profitability, and synergies are validated, are:
  - Do we have the capabilities necessary, such as IT skills or HR resources, to implement integration?
  - Are the time frames assumed in the plan realistic?
  - Are there obvious impediments to integration, such as conflicting corporate cultures, that must be addressed?

- *Breadth of coverage.* All major functional areas within the organization being reviewed should be assigned and covered. Although the emphasis in due diligence is on areas of greatest potential exposure, the breadth of coverage should be sufficient to identify any significant risks that may not have been previously known. To the extent that such risks are identified, team leaders should be immediately informed. Such discoveries should result in an expansion in the scope and the depth of the review.
- *Focus of coverage.* The inherent limitations of the due diligence review make it necessary to be selective about the areas that receive in-depth attention. Therefore, the initial focus of the review should be on areas of greatest risk and opportunity that will have surfaced in the course of preliminary evaluation, analysis, and discussions. As noted, the scope of the review should be expanded if additional issues emerge during the course of the review.
- *Conclusions about work performed.* Reviewers should be made to express a general conclusion about the area of their responsibility and its

impact. Accordingly, it is recommended that, at the end of each individual portion of the program, there is a conclusion section requiring the reviewer to explicitly indicate (i.e., express an opinion and sign off) whether there were any issues that came to light that might impact the organization's assumptions about the value of the target company (see Exhibit 4.3 for an illustration of the section of the program requiring a conclusion). This mechanism establishes clear responsibility on the part of the reviewer and introduces a compelling element of individual accountability that, in turn, inspires a high level of professionalism.

- *Development of actionable findings.* In the course of due diligence, numerous important issues arise that will require resolution. They may need to be addressed either before the transaction is consummated; they may have a bearing on the terms of the purchase agreement; or they may require action after the close of the transaction. These issues encompass a broad range of possibilities, but would include such things as determining the impact and options associated with the nontransferability of a license agreement, to contractual mitigation of potential sales returns, to issues associated with postacquisition integration or the need for posttransaction transition services. The program should accommodate the need to efficiently capture and aggregate this type of information. Further, it should cause the reviewer to provide specific guidance on the steps to be taken to address and resolve the issues identified.

Objectives, Procedures and Findings, and Recommendations Illustrated

In Chapter 1, we presented an example where the primary reason for an organization to acquire a business is to obtain ownership of its technological capability. One objective of due diligence under these circumstances would be to validate the candidate company's unencumbered, exclusive ownership rights to that technology and that those rights will be retained for a length of time consistent with the acquirer's assumptions. Under such circumstances the legal aspect of the due diligence program would be aimed at validating that assumption (in addition to other important aspects of the business). Exhibit 4.3 shows review objectives, relevant procedures, and the capture of the resulting findings and recommendations.

EXHIBIT 4.3 Legal Section of Illustrative Due Diligence Program

---

(Note: *This sample program is presented to illustrate the linkage between due diligence review objectives, procedures performed, and findings and recommendations. It is not intended to cover all typical components of a legal due diligence review.*)

Objectives:

A. To obtain and document an understanding of contractual, environmental, litigation, and intellectual property rights issues
B. To validate the company's unencumbered ownership of (named) technology and to determine if and when such rights terminate

Procedures:

1. Obtain and review all copies of facility leases and addenda thereto
2. Determine existence of any environmental permits or environmental issues or violations
3. Review all material contracts and agreements. Document major terms relative to the following:
   a. Agent agreements
   b. Distributor agreements
   c. Customer agreements
   d. Supplier agreements
   e. Licenses
   f. Royalty arrangements
   g. Other agreements
4. Obtain documentation of any outstanding or threatened litigation
5. Review all documentation relative to intangible assets, indicating status of the following:
   a. Copyrights
   b. Patents
   c. Trademarks
   d. Servicemarks
6. Determine states in which the business should be qualified

Findings and Recommendations:

Conclusion (Express conclusions relative to overall objectives, and specific objectives associated with this section of the program, such as a go/no-go recommendation or a recommendation to revise the initial valuation)

EXHIBIT 4.3　*(Continued)*

Preacquisition follow-up (Note any issues or items that must be addressed prior to closing)

Contract Issues (Note any issues that should be specifically addressed in the purchase agreement)

Postacquisition follow-up (Note any items or issues that must be addressed after the close, such as transition services or integration issues)

In this illustration the legal review is concerned with risk (i.e., the verification or nonverification of ownership). It should be noted that other reviewers should also be looking at this key asset from other perspectives. Those tasked with the sales and marketing review should be evaluating the asset to determine whether underlying value creation assumptions are supportable. Those reviewing IT and operations aspects of the target company should be assessing the intellectual property from technical and operational perspectives. In addition, all of these team members should be communicating with one another to ensure that there is a comprehensive understanding of all the risks and opportunities associated with this asset. Cross-functional communication is discussed in detail in Chapter 5.

A Due Diligence Mind-Set

Based on the foregoing, it should be clear that a due diligence review is not simply a mechanical or procedural process of data collection and review. It requires a certain mind-set that combines the risk-assessment mentality of an auditor with the value-creation mentality of an investor. It is important for team leaders to impress the importance of this combined mentality on the members of the team, especially those who are first-time due diligence participants.

A diligence review is, by no means, as comprehensive as an audit. Constraints on time and resources limit the depth of the evaluations conducted. However, a due diligence review is analogous in some respects to an audit; and the types of procedures that should be reflected in the program are not unlike what one would find in an audit program. Also, an aspect of the review that is, arguably, as important as the program itself is the healthy skepticism one would employ when conducting an audit. Because of these similarities, inclusion of financial team members who have audit experience can be beneficial. They can also be of great assistance to other team members in creating and modifying the due diligence program and in coaching those team members who have not previously been involved in a due diligence review.

In addition, reviewers should adopt an investor mentality and not fall into the trap of mechanically recording and evaluating information without subjecting it to a higher level of analysis. The reviewers should be encouraged to step back from the detail of the review on a periodic basis and consider the entire body of what they have seen and its implications. The questions that the reviewers should periodically ask themselves are:

1. Is this a sound investment?
2. Does what I am seeing support the assumptions reflected in the plan to create value?

Whereas the audit mentality referenced above may cause the reviewer to arrive at the conclusion that they see a "good business," this investment mentality should cause the reviewer to determine whether that business is a "good investment."

PLANNING DUE DILIGENCE

Once the individual components of the program have been developed, a meeting should be convened, under the direction of the lead members of the team, to thoroughly discuss the due diligence plan. This meeting should be used to accomplish the objectives described in this section.

Finalize the Program

Before beginning the review, the due diligence program must be finalized. The individuals with primary responsibility for each functional area to be reviewed should submit their final version of their portion of the program to the individuals leading the due diligence review. Team leaders should evaluate its contents and provide input as needed. They should ensure that the objectives established for the individual functional areas will challenge assumptions made in the plan to create value and induce the reviewer to provide actionable findings that can be utilized in the postreview phase of the transaction.

Mechanisms for Team Coordination

It is critically important that team leaders avoid adopting a silo mentality in doing their review. As with many complex processes, due diligence is more than the sum of its parts. An effective process requires periodic interaction among team members during which they should exchange information and impressions. It also requires a holistic, cross-functional mentality that causes them to take ownership in the entire endeavor and not just their piece of it. Team members should be sensitized to the need to share findings and views on issues and a process to do so should be established at this time. At a minimum, the reviewers as a team should plan to meet daily. In addition, as issues of importance surface, team leaders should be apprised so that they can determine when and how such information should be shared among the appropriate members of the team (see Chapter 5).

Resolve Issues of Overlap

There is generally an overlap of interest in certain documents (e.g., contracts, licenses, leases) among various functional areas. For example, this commonly occurs between the legal reviewers and reviewers of other areas, such as human resources, sales, and real estate. The individual doing the legal review will look at many of the same documents as the individuals performing reviews of these other areas, but from a different perspective. In cases where a virtual data room is provided, this problem is obviated by the ability of multiple reviewers to access the same information simultaneously. If a more traditional physical data room, supplied with hard copy documents, is provided, it is advisable to request multiple copies of these documents. If this is problematic, coordinate these efforts so that inefficiencies are minimized and proper coverage is assured. In any event, those whose reviews overlap should communicate and cross-check their findings and conclusions.

Maintain an Aggressive Posture

Sellers and their representatives (i.e., business brokers and investment bankers) will exercise control over access to the management team of the entity being sold. This will usually take the form of limiting the buyer access largely to a formal presentation by the management team. The due diligence team should push the envelope when making requests of the seller for access. It should not automatically acquiesce to the terms and conditions of the selling team and assume that there is no room for negotiation on issues affecting access to personnel (and information) and the ability to extend timelines. The selling team will try to project a degree of competition, which may in fact not exist. Frequently, an acquirer will have more leverage than they think, and the only way to determine if this is the case is to challenge the restrictions established by the seller.

Communicate Logistical Information

This generally takes the form of a memo indicating the location and timetable for review, as well as the responsibilities of the individual team members. This appears to be a relatively mundane matter, but it is a prudent measure that obviates the risk of misunderstandings when coordinating the efforts of a sizable group.

Communicate Responsibility and Timing of Report Submissions

The review will result in a due diligence report composed of the individual fieldwork and findings and recommendations of team members. The individual responsible for the review of each of the functional areas should understand what is to be submitted and when it is due. In addition, it should be clear to all members of the team which team leader or leaders will have responsibility for compiling, synthesizing, and summarizing the team's findings. The deadline for individual submissions should be aggressive, but reasonable. The longer the time between the time the fieldwork is done and reports are finalized, the greater the potential for information to be lost and memory to fade.

Key Points

1. We believe that the acquirer is best served if it conducts its due diligence review in a top-down, objectives-driven manner, a review in which objectives are informed and guided by the plan to create value. ("Overview")

2. In the overwhelming majority of acquisition transactions, buyers are provided a narrow window of opportunity, in a competitive environment, to prepare for and perform due diligence. This entire process is

designed not only to stimulate a sense of competitiveness but also to limit the buyers' ability to probe and identify transaction risks and vulnerabilities of the target company. ("External Constraints of the Sale Process")

3. If the organization is unable or unwilling to field a knowledgeable and experienced team, it should consider passing on the opportunity, since this would suggest that the investment is not a high enough priority to warrant the transaction risk that routinely accompanies an acquisition. ("Other Considerations")

4. In the course of due diligence, numerous important issues arise that will require resolution. The due diligence program should accommodate the need to efficiently capture and aggregate this type of information. Further, it should cause the reviewer to provide specific guidance on the steps to be taken to address and resolve the issues identified. ("Key Aspects of the Due Diligence Program")

5. A due diligence review is not simply a mechanical or procedural process of data collection and review. It requires a certain mind-set that combines the risk-assessment mentality of an auditor with the value-creation mentality of an investor. ("Due Diligence Mind-Set")

APPENDIX 4A: DUE DILIGENCE CHECKLIST

Note: This checklist provides extensive coverage of the areas to be evaluated by a due diligence review team. It is designed to assist members of the team in their evaluation efforts. However, it is not a substitute for a due diligence program that focuses on the risks and opportunities peculiar to a specific transaction. Accordingly, it should be used as an aid to ensure that the team considers all aspects that are relevant to a given transaction.

I. Review Company Background and Organization and Proposed Transaction

A. CORPORATE RECORDS (Note that matters involving identification of shareholders and characteristics of the company's capitalization may not be relevant in asset transactions.)
  1. Review articles of incorporation and bylaws.

2. List of subsidiaries; certificates of incorporation and bylaws of subsidiaries.

3. Minutes of meetings of directors and committees of directors, and minutes of stockholder's meetings.

4. List of shareholders cross-checked against stock certificate book.

5. List of the classes of stock and other equity and convertible debt securities that indicate shares authorized and outstanding, voting and preemptive rights, dividend preferences and amounts in arrears, conversion features, and so on.

6. For all classes of stock, obtain a roster of major shareholders: number of shares of each class held both direct and beneficially; the shareholders' status—minors, trustees, and so on; and note any shareholder agreements with respect to the stock.

7. List of jurisdictions in which the company and each subsidiary are qualified to do business.

8. Any agreements that may limit the ability of the company to compete in a line of business or with a person or in a geographic area.

B. HISTORY AND STRATEGY

1. Obtain an understanding of management's vision, mission, and strategy for the business and its divisions, if applicable. This would include:
   - The company's competitive advantage and any barriers to competition the company enjoys
   - Its current three-to-five-year business plan, including assumptions regarding product mix, price increase, and cost reductions
   - Overall financial strategies, objectives, and major growth initiatives
   - Corporate development activities (e.g., specific acquisitions targeted)

2. Ascertain significant external events and developments (e.g., political, economic, technological) that have recently had, or could have in the future, a major impact on the business. Identify possible constraints on growth.

3. Identify any agreements that may limit the ability of the company to compete in a line of business or in a geographic area.

4. Outline the history of the company, including major transactions. Describe the terms of major transactions and their accounting treatment.

5. Obtain a summary of the principal product development, distribution, and research and development facilities of the company.
6. Obtain plan projections and budgets applicable to current year and any year subsequent.
7. Obtain management's description of the overall financial strategies, criteria, and goals for the company.
8. Obtain details of any loans, liabilities, or commitments (other than trade payables) the buyer would be expected to assume.

C. **REVIEW PROPOSED TRANSACTION**
1. Determine whether there are any provisions in the proposed agreement that would negate the intended tax structure of the transaction. Review the other tax considerations involved in the transaction.
2. Obtain or prepare pro forma financial statements and acquisition models demonstrating the effect of the proposed transaction. In reviewing pro forma data, consider the adequacy of future cash flows.
3. Inquire of legal counsel as to the effect of antitrust regulations on the proposed transaction. Specifically, consider the Sherman Act, the Clayton Act, and Hart-Scott-Rodino Antitrust Improvements Act of 1976 (HSR Act). If a pretransaction filing is necessary under HSR Act, obtain and read a copy of the filing document.

D. **MANAGEMENT**
1. Officers, directors, and key employees:
   - Obtain a listing of officers, directors, and key employees, including name, age, position description, background, length of service, and business affiliations.
   - Review existing employment contracts and outline major provisions.
   - List indebtedness of directors, officers, or employees to or from the company.
   - List of compensation paid to directors, officers, and key employees during the past three years. Include salary, bonus, profit sharing, stock options (note present stock ownership), insurance, and any other forms of compensation or fringe-type benefits (including nonmonetary perquisites) both current and deferred.
2. Depth, structure, and philosophy of management:
   - Comment on the abilities and depth of management.
   - Consider whether there are any indispensable or key managers.

- Compare the organization chart with the actual operating structure. Consider whether the real power is maintained by one or a few officers.
- Determine the function and importance of the board of directors and its major committees.
- Determine if management philosophy is oriented toward specific functions, such as production, marketing, manufacturing, or finance. Considering the industry, competition, and the current economic environment, does this emphasis appear proper?
- If outside advisors are used on an ongoing basis, consider whether this indicates any weaknesses within the company's management structure.
- Inquire into the company's conflict of interest and ethics policy and its policies with regard to "improper payments." Obtain or review a copy of any recent investigative reports.

E. **RELATED PARTY TRANSACTIONS**
   1. Schedule significant related party transactions. The schedule should indicate the relationship and business purpose of such transactions.
   2. Note any family relationships among officers, directors, and key employees. Also note any relationships of officers, directors, and employees with business organizations with which the company has significant dealings.

II. Financial

A. **CURRENT YEAR AND HISTORICAL RESULTS**
   1. Review audited financial statements for the last three years, including report of independent accountants. Financial statements to include income statement, balance sheet, and cash flow.
   2. Review results for the prior three years compared to budgets, with management comments. Reconcile to audited financials if management results are on a different basis.
   3. Determine impact of acquisitions and disposals on revenues and operation profit during the past three years.
   4. Determine impact of changes in currency rates on revenues and operating profit reported for the last three years.
   5. Obtain details of any special write-offs, write-backs, and/or nonrecurring items affecting results for prior years or expected this year.

6. Obtain the last six monthly management reports. For the most recent month, compare the current year's performance to budget, and include management's discussion of results/outlook for the rest of the year.

B. REVENUE

1. Review details of each product or service providing over 5 percent of revenues and/or operating profit in each of the prior three years.
2. Schedule price increases in each of the last three years and the respective impact on revenues and unit sales.

C. OPERATING EXPENSES

1. Determine new product development expense and contribution to sales and operating income for new products launched in this year and each of the last three years.
2. Analyze cost of sales, and sales, general and administrative costs.
3. If the target is a unit of a larger organization, analyze any central infrastructure, shared services, or other corporate overhead costs.

D. BALANCE SHEET ACCOUNTS

1. Obtain a summary of banking relationships and schedule of monthly bank balances during the year. Determine the company's policy regarding the investment of idle balances.
2. Schedule marketable securities; separate into current and noncurrent categories, and list original cost, date purchased, interest rate, maturity date, current basis of recording, and current market value.
3. Analyze accounts receivable, include an aging, details of bad debt provision, and historical write-offs.
4. Analyze inventory and inventory reserves.
5. Analyze changes in working capital, and provide a narrative explanation of the factors affecting these accounts.
6. Obtain a summary of property, plant, and equipment and accumulated depreciation broken down into category totals (e.g., land, buildings, equipment, etc.) for the current and past three years. Show beginning balances, additions (or provisions), retirements, and ending balances. Explain any unusual/one-time capital expenditures made in the current or any of the prior three years.
7. Analyze any other material asset accounts. Obtain details and support for any asset reserves.
8. Analyze goodwill and intangibles. Review support for valuations and examine details of any adjustments.

9. Obtain details supporting any in-process research and development.
10. Provide a detailed trail balance of all material items in trade accounts payable and accrued expenses.
11. Analyze unearned revenue, and provide details of revenue recognition of policies by major product or service.
12. Analyze all other material liability accounts.
13. Obtain a schedule of all short-term and long-term debt and examine the underlying agreements.
14. Obtain details supporting any contingent assets or liabilities (e.g., litigation, environmental issues, or possible product recalls).

E. **OTHER ACCOUNTING MATTERS**
1. Obtain a statement of accounting policies; address revenue recognition by product line.
2. Review auditors' internal control memorandums for the past three years in addition to any other internal control documents developed by the company.
3. Determine details of acquisitions made. Cost, allocation of cost to assets, write-off policy on assets/liabilities, any special provisions made against acquisition cost, performance compared to acquisition expectations.
4. Determine capitalization policies and, outside of fixed asset expenditures, what costs are capitalized and the write-off policy.
5. Perform analysis of revenues and operating profit by country.
6. Detail unremitted earnings and cash flows by country.
7. Determine foreign source income included in financial results.
8. Detail description of accounting, commercial, and management systems.

III. Technology

1. Obtain complete description of computer facilities, hardware, and software.
2. Obtain descriptions/flowcharts of all systems transaction
   - Sales support and customer information
   - Order entry and fulfillment
   - Product development and delivery
   - Work flow and other infrastructure
   - Communications
3. Obtain disaster recovery plan.

4. Obtain strategic plans for major technology upgrades and enhancements, including costs and timing thereof.
5. Determine plans for future search engine/user interface enhancements.
6. Obtain details of capital expenditures (for the past three years) for technology and amounts included in projections.

IV. Products

A. GENERAL

1. Obtain a list of all products and services offered by the company.
2. Describe arrangements and costs associated with raw material/component acquisition. Determine stability of supply.
3. Describe production process from receipt of material through delivery to customers.
4. Describe the value added to products.
5. Describe major product enhancements and new products in development.

B. PRODUCT DEVELOPMENT

1. Describe the production process, including:
   - Technology employed
   - Current development projects and their status
   - Development projects planned over the next three years
   - Analyze by product ongoing expenses, including amortization of accumulated development costs

C. RESEARCH AND DEVELOPMENT

1. Describe the target's research and development effort. Include the extent to which facilities are committed to this endeavor and the number of employees.
2. Inquire whether the target's success is dependent on the development of new and unique products.
3. Obtain a list of significant copyrights/patents (and their expiration dates) developed as part of the research and development effort. Does the company utilize significant patents owned by competitors?
4. Evaluate the importance of research and development within the industry and its importance to the company.
5. Obtain list of major projects currently being worked on, indicating the stage of completion, the expenditures made, and the expenditures needed to complete.

V. Marketing and Sales

1. Obtain details on sales activities: direct mail, sales force, telemarketing, and so on, and the contribution from each source. Provide an analysis of the cost of each marketing activity over the last three years.
2. Obtain details of sales representative agreements/arrangements; describe sales incentive compensation plans.
3. Obtain details on major warehousing, distribution, marketing, production, and advertising arrangements.
4. Obtain competitive analysis of the company's products, accuracy, timeliness, and service compared to those of competitors; statistical analysis to support market share claims.
5. Obtain copies of any recent market research and customer satisfaction studies.
6. Obtain customer information reports by product to validate new orders, payment rates, renewal rates, product migration patterns, and the like.
7. Obtain details on trade names, trademarks, copyrights, service marks, patents, licenses, and royalty agreements and similar documents.

VI. Legal

A. GENERAL

1. List of all litigation, claims or assessments, and judicial, administrative, or regulatory proceedings pending or threatened, including date filed, relief sought, forum in which brought, and status of the matter. Also, list any potential exposure.
2. Obtain all government or regulatory reports/correspondence concerning noncompliance with any laws or regulations (including IRS, Department of Justice (DOJ), Federal Trade Commission (FTC), Occupational Safety and Health Administration (OSHA), Environmental Protection Agency (EPA), Equal Employment Opportunity Commission (EEOC), National Labor Relations Board (NLRB), etc.).
3. Obtain agreements that limit the ability of the company to compete in any line of business or with any person in any geographic area.
4. Obtain details of actual or attempted infringement of trademarks, trade names, patent, or copyrights.
5. Obtain contracts or options relating to the acquisition of any business.

6. Obtain documents relating to unrecorded liabilities, including unfunded vested pension liabilities, unfunded retiree medical and other benefits, multiemployer pension plan liability, product liability, environmental matters, and other contingent liabilities.

B. REGULATORY MATTERS

1. Obtain details of all material licenses, permits, orders, approvals, filings, reports, correspondence, and so on from or with federal regulatory agencies and foreign, state, or local agencies performing similar functions, including:
   - Environmental Protection Agency
   - Equal Employment Opportunity Commission
   - Internal Revenue Service
   - Other (e.g., Department of Justice, Federal Trade Commission, Occupational Safety and Health Administration, Department of Labor, Department of Commerce, National Labor Relations Board, etc.)
   - Agencies governing export/import matters
2. If applicable, provide copies of these public filings:
   - Annual reports on Form 10-K and annual shareholder reports filed during the last five years
   - Quarterly reports on Form 10-Q and shareholder reports, and any reports on Form 8K filed during the last three years
   - Proxy statements for the last five years
   - Any recent prospectus or offering memoranda or circulars

C. MATERIAL AGREEMENTS

1. Obtain standard forms of customer agreements; description of major deviations therefrom.
2. Obtain agreements with distributors and sales representatives.
3. Obtain material agreements with vendors and customers other than purchase or sales orders entered into in the ordinary course of business.
4. Obtain contracts, franchises, licenses, concessions, leases, and commitments that involve an obligation on the part of the company to make payments in excess of $10,000 in any one year, and other material agreements.
5. Obtain loan or other financing agreements, including bank loans, lines of credit, letters of credit, mortgages, indentures, and a list of any property pledged as collateral.

6. Obtain joint venture agreements and partnership agreements.
7. Determine if there are guarantees by the company or its stockholders of any obligation of others.
8. Obtain contracts with any governmental entity.
9. Obtain contracts with providers of data, and discussion of possible constraints on future data availability.

D. FACILITIES

1. Review all deeds, title reports, surveys, title insurance policies, title reports, and legal opinions with respect to title, zoning, and related matters on all real property owned by the company.
2. Review all leases and subleases of real property to which the company is a party.
3. Review copies of any option agreements, earnest money agreements, or other agreements to which the company is a party and that involve the purchase or sale of real property.
4. Review all agreements for use, easements, restrictions, rights of way, construction, architectural services, and any other agreements or documents relating in any way to the ownership or leasing of real property by the company.
5. Review all environmental reports and studies.
6. Review details of computer facilities (use, age, replacement program, backup facilities).

E. TAXES

1. Obtain a description of audits and other tax disputes in progress.
2. Obtain a description of any tax elections in effect.
3. Obtain tax rulings and tax closing agreements with any taxing authority (foreign or domestic) applicable to the assets of the company.
4. Obtain liens for taxes on any assets of the company.
5. Determine if any assets are treated as owned by any other person under the "safe harbor lease" provisions of Section 168(f)(8) of the Internal Revenue Code.
6. Determine the nature and amount of assets by state for possible application of the state, local bulk sale rules, and notification requirements.
7. Review federal, state, local, foreign, and other tax returns for all open years.
8. Review details of any tax-sharing agreements.

9. Obtain a summary of property taxes for the past three years, by individual location.

10. Review last five years' sales tax filings, if applicable.

VII. Insurance

1. Review general liability/umbrella, publisher's liability/errors and omissions, workers' compensation, crime and property/business interruption, and other insurance policies (other than employee benefit policies).

2. Review a schedule of insurance costs over the past three years by type of coverage, including brokerage commissions.

3. Review a schedule of major casualty losses over the past three years, whether covered by insurance or not. List areas where the company is self-insured.

VIII. Human Resources

A. GENERAL

1. Obtain copies of employee handbooks and HR policy manuals and summary benefit plan documents.

2. Obtain complete documentation and understanding of employee benefit plans available to company employees (including pension plan) and costs (total, percent of payroll, and per employee) thereof. Include billing schedules, premium amounts for employee and employer, and levels of coverage for each plan.

3. Obtain complete schematics, organization charts for the company. The charts should include full-time equivalents (FTEs) for all areas, names, and titles for anyone with supervisory authority, and total headcount (FTEs) for employees who report to them. Note where part-time employees or "temps" are used on an ongoing basis.

B. MANAGEMENT

1. Identify all key management employees (include all director-level positions and above), including their position in the organization, their profile, and the likelihood that they will remain with the organization postacquisition.

2. Obtain copies of all senior management's most recent performance reviews.

3. Obtain details of the company management compensation and incentive plans. Include copy of actual plan(s).

4. Obtain information describing any individual (nonsales) incentive or bonus plans in effect during most recent three calendar years, names of participants, percent of salary for which they were eligible, percent actually paid compared to percent eligible.

5. Obtain copies of all employment contracts.

6. Obtain details of special compensation arrangements, including any special arrangements regarding the sale of the company, stock options, grants, golden (or tin) parachute, and "poison pill" benefits.

7. Obtain information concerning any cars, memberships, or other perquisites currently assigned to any current or prospective personnel or director (if over and above what is included in employee handbook or otherwise available to general employee population without specific authorization), including names of such personnel and details regarding arrangements.

8. Obtain copies of all severance benefits plans covering management or employees.

9. Obtain copy of relocation policy.

10. Obtain copy of confidentiality/conflict of interest agreement.

11. Obtain copy of travel and entertainment (T&E) policy and procedures.

C. SIGNIFICANT AGREEMENTS: NONMANAGEMENT

1. Identify all independent contractors performing key or routine work for the company; identify amounts spent over the last three years, estimates of amounts to be spent during the plan period, and FTEs assigned over the respective periods requested.

2. Set forth details of union or collective bargaining agreements in force now or during the last five years. Provide copies of any such agreements.

D. EMPLOYEES

1. Obtain employee list by location, including name (last name, first name, middle initial), date of birth, date of hire, title and job description, department, annual salary, years and months with the company, total compensation (base salary plus all other forms of compensation reported on the employee's form W-2) identified separately for each of the last three years and estimated for the current year. The list should be provided in two formats: one sort by last

name, another sort by estimated current year compensation in descending order. Highlight those employees hired during the previous 12 months.

2. Obtain information describing any team or group incentive plans in effect during most recent three calendar years, including data regarding payout.

3. Determine terms of sales force compensation plans, including discussion of significant changes from the prior year or changes anticipated in projections.

4. Obtain description of performance review system and copies of related reports.

E. DEMOGRAPHICS

1. Obtain data regarding numbers of employees by age broken into these groupings: 15–19, 20–24, 25–29, 30–34, 35–39, 40–44, 45–49, 50–54, 55–59, 60–64, 65+.

2. Obtain a list of hires currently in progress.

3. Obtain job application and "new hire" material provided to new employees.

4. Obtain copy of leave of absence policy as well as history for two years and current status.

F. ISSUES MANAGEMENT

1. Obtain document process for handling employee complaints, concerns, grievances, investigations, and so on.

2. Obtain details of pending employee litigation, including charges of wrongful discharge.

3. Obtain copy of current Affirmative Action program, three most recent Equal Employment Opportunity (EEO)-1 reports, names and titles of personnel responsible for administering-related programs, information regarding any settled or pending suits in this area.

4. Obtain information regarding reductions in force (RIF) for the past three years, or any planned RIF, including numbers, titles of employees terminated, method of selecting employees, claims settled or pending, copies of documents or notices used in the process, savings resulting from the reductions. Include pre-/postorganization charts, noting changes.

5. Obtain copies of any termination agreements entered subsequent during the last three years.

6. For severance plans obtain a summary of payments made in last 24 months.

G. SAFETY MATTERS

1. Obtain copy of OSHA log for the last three years.
2. Obtain copy of injury illness prevention program and any other health/safety programs/forms.
3. Obtain schedule of workers' compensation claims experience over the last two years.

H. DEVELOPMENT

1. Obtain copy of any internal training programs provided to employees over the last three years.
2. Obtain copy of any employee communications, such as newsletters, letters from the president, and the like.
3. Obtain copy of results from any recent employee surveys, including documentation of follow-up to the surveys. Include information on the process used to design, administer, score, and give feedback on surveys.
4. Determine process (e.g., suggestion program) in place to encourage and recognize employees who have ideas that would improve processes and work environment.

I. EMPLOYMENT COSTS

1. Obtain headcount statistics by department for past three years and management projections for the next five years.
2. Obtain reconciliation of growth in total company compensation during the last three years to headcount changes and average compensation (merit increases).
3. Obtain information outlining salary compensation planning for the past three years, including overall percent of target merit increase, grades (including which jobs are in each grade), and salary ranges for each grade, merit increase matrix (if used), percent spread from minimum to maximum, and percent spread between midpoints of ranges.
4. Obtain data indicating overall percent of employees in each salary quartile, including number of employees currently at the maximum of or under the minimum of their respective salary range.
5. Obtain total benefits costs (health and welfare plans as well as employer benefits taxes, e.g., FICA) as a percentage of total pay.

J. BENEFIT PLANS

1. Obtain plan documents, summary plan descriptions (and trust agreements for funded plans) for each of these retirement plans:
   - Pension plan(s)
   - Profit-sharing and other qualified defined contribution plan(s)
   - 401(k) savings plans
   - Nonqualified supplemental executive retirement plan(s)
   - Health care, life insurance, and other welfare benefit plans covering current and/or future retirees
2. Obtain plan documents and summary plan descriptions for each of these welfare benefit programs:
   - Comprehensive medical plan
   - Other medical plan(s)
   - Dental plan(s)
   - Life insurance: basic life, supplemental life, dependent life, business travel accident, accident death and disability
   - Disability: short term and long term
   - Time off: sick pay/vacation/holidays
   - Severance
3. Obtain trust agreements for any Voluntary Employee Beneficiary Association (501(c)(9)) or other trusts.
4. Obtain plan documents and summary plan descriptions for each of these stock-based programs:
   - Stock purchase plan
   - Stock option plan
   - Employee stock ownership plan
5. For each of these plans:
   - Comprehensive medical plan
   - Other medical plans
   - Dental plan (if any)
   - Life insurance: indemnity, optional indemnity, business travel accident
   - Disability: short term and long term

The following information should be obtained:

- Form 5500
- Audit reports for last two years

- Details of actual cost of programs for last two years
- Details of expected cost of programs for current year
- Copy of all insurance policies covering employees
- Copy of latest (and prior) insurance renewals, if insured
- Details of claims experience (for last three years, if possible)
- Details of any rate guarantees, liability limits, and stop-loss provisions currently applicable
- Current status of reserves of each plan
- Information on current financing vehicle(s), including any trusts (and the amount of any trust assets)
- Current premium rate information
- Current Consolidated Omnibus Budget Reconciliation Act COBRA rate information (medical and dental plans only)

6. Obtain health plan census (number of employees enrolled in indemnity plan, health maintenance organizations).
7. Obtain census or health plan coverage status (number of employees in each of these categories): Individual; Employee + l; and Family Coverage.

CHAPTER 5

Conducting the Due Diligence Review

INTRODUCTION

Chapter 4 described the planning and preparation steps leading up to the due diligence review. In this chapter, we set the stage for the actual execution of the plan. First, we discuss the range of possible transaction types a review team may encounter and describe the components of a typical due diligence review. This is followed by a discussion of an objectives-driven, top-down approach to the due diligence review, one that focuses the effort on the major risks and assumed opportunities articulated in the acquiring company's plan to create value.

OVERVIEW OF TRANSACTION TYPES

The dynamics of the sale process are influenced by the type of transaction the seller chooses to employ. That choice is affected by various factors. More often than not, the seller is motivated by the desire to maximize after-tax proceeds and to minimize any posttransaction risk. However, there are situations in which the decision on how to offer the business for sale is influenced by other factors. These may include a desire on the part of the seller to close the transaction quickly and confidentially so as to minimize disruption. This can be the case when a business is small or fragile and a protracted and publicized process may impair its value. The seller may be motivated by the desire to find the best "home" for the business's long-standing and loyal employees or by the desire to find a buyer that the owner believes will protect and extend the company's legacy. These factors frequently influence the owner's approach to selling the business—that is, whether it will be sold via an auction or some sort of preemptive bid. That choice can have a significant impact on the buyer's approach to the transaction and, ultimately, on the environment in which the due diligence review is conducted. The rest of this section describes the range of possible transaction types and how they impact that process.

Auctions

If the seller's objective is to get the highest possible price with the least exposure to after-sale risk (in the form of buyer's recourse), it will generally opt for an auction sale—assuming that the business can withstand the rigors of an extended, public transaction. The auction sale process is illustrated in Exhibit 5.1 and described in the following points.

- *Engaging a financial advisor.* Although most sellers would not attempt to sell their business without the assistance of a financial advisor of some kind, auction-based sales require the involvement of either a business broker or investment banker with expertise in this type of transaction. Auctions are tightly structured transactions and require day-to-day management by professionals that have mastered this process. Most broker and banker organizations have such expertise. The firm engaged by the seller can also be expected to be familiar with the market for the business being sold and have relationships with specific companies in that market, facilitating the auction process. Potential buyers should understand that these firms are highly motivated to maximize the sale price, since they are compensated on a commission basis.

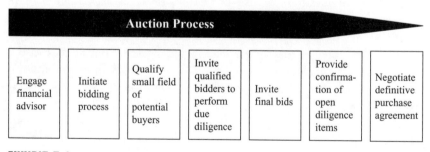

EXHIBIT 5.1   Auction Process

- *Initiation of a bidding process.* Based on its market knowledge, the financial advisor counsels the seller on the scope of the auction, that is, whether to limit it to a narrow field of bidders, or allow a broader, public auction involving a large number of potential bidders. There are a number of preliminary steps (such as the specific identification of potential bidders and the execution of confidentiality agreements with those who wish to participate) that lead up to the distribution of an offering document or prospectus and a preliminary process letter (see Appendix 5A of this chapter for an illustration) outlining the typical transaction process to potential bidders.
- *Qualifying and selecting potential buyers.* The financial advisor and seller will then qualify those who expressed an interest, based on such things as their bid, their reputation for being willing and able to close a deal, and their creditworthiness. Although there is no ideal number of qualified bidders, the field will generally consist of several, perhaps a half dozen interested parties.
- *Inviting the selected potential buyers to perform preliminary due diligence.* This would consist of a management presentation (see the "Management Presentation" section for a discussion of the management presentation process and dynamics); the opportunity to gain access to a data room, populated with a broad array of company information, to perform document review (discussed in the "Document Review" section); and, possibly, a tour of the seller's facilities.
- *Inviting final bids.* The seller in conjunction with its advisor would choose a finalist or finalists. To maintain negotiating leverage and to mitigate the risk of "being left at the altar," the seller will often select more than one finalist. These finalists will be required to submit their best and final offer, along with a marked-up copy of the seller's draft of the purchase agreement for the transaction.
- *Inviting the finalist(s) to perform confirmatory diligence.* The final bidder(s) will obtain confirmation and clarification of any open issues through further document review and discussions with management.
- *Negotiation of the purchase agreement with the winning bidder.* The buyer and seller will negotiate the final aspects of the agreement, comply with any regulatory requirements, and close the deal.

Auctions: The Buyer's Perspective   From the buyer's perspective, involvement in auction sales has both strategic and tactical implications. Strategically, the transaction by definition is the result of *reactive* engagement; that is, one that is initiated by the seller and not by the buyer. The section titled "Reactive Engagement" in Chapter 3 discusses the dynamics and risks associated with reactive transactions, but suffice it to say here that a reactive response to a business's availability should involve a very high standard of analysis and evaluation. Before a buyer engages in an auction sale (no less due diligence), the prospective transaction should be justified on the basis of its ability to support the acquirer's strategic plan and its potential to create shareholder value—not simply its availability. Also, as we have noted, successful acquirers develop and continually update a list of potential acquisition targets. If the available company has not passed through this filter, the organization should approach this "opportunity" with healthy skepticism and be on guard against the tendency to tailor strategic justification to that opportunity.

If the potential acquisition survives the above-mentioned strategic filter, the buyer should recognize the tactical limitations involved in an auction sale. On the tactical level, the dynamics of the auction process can be reduced to a difference in seller and buyer orientation. The seller and its advisors see the auction as a marketing process, whereas the buyer views it as an investigative endeavor (see "Transaction Framework: Sellers' and Buyers' Different Perspectives" in Chapter 3 for a discussion of this difference in perspective). Because the selling group controls the process, the result is a competitive environment (or, at least, the illusion of one) that maximizes the leverage of the seller and minimizes the leverage of the buyer. More specifically, the seller's financial adviser will put itself between buyer and seller and maintain tight control over the process. It will limit the level of detail of company information and the time to review it, and limit access to those who manage the business being sold as well as the duration of that access. These limitations have an obvious constraining impact on the due diligence review process and require the buyer to be well prepared and intensely focused on the issues of greatest strategic importance, specifically its assumptions about the acquisition's ability to create shareholder value.

Preemptive Bids

Preemptive bids can materialize in a number of ways. When it becomes known that a business will be put up for sale, but before an auction process is initiated, an interested potential acquirer may be willing to pay a material purchase price premium to ensure that it will preempt other interested parties. Alternatively, a potential buyer may have been courting the owner of the business for an extensive period of time and, for a variety of reasons, may have gained the inside track on the prospective transaction. These two scenarios are discussed in the following sections.

Purchase Premium Preemption   When an owner decides that it wishes to put its business up for sale, it may be approached by an aggressive acquirer willing to pay a premium for the first right to negotiate a deal. From the seller's standpoint, there may be advantages to entertaining such a proposition. These would include:

- A high probability of getting an attractive price
- The minimization of disruption and the potential business impairment that can come with an auction sale
- The ability to close a sale quickly

The downside of accepting a preemptive bid is the possibility of not optimizing sale price and other terms of the transaction and the risk that the sale does not materialize. Occasionally, sellers believe the risk of not maximizing the value of the property is sufficiently offset by the benefits noted above. In addition, they can take measures to mitigate the risk of a failed transaction by such steps as negotiating a reverse breakup fee (an agreed-to penalty paid by the preemptive bidder to the seller) and by being prepared to pull the trigger on an auction if the transaction gets derailed. In any event, sellers will and do entertain aggressive preemptive bids for their businesses under certain circumstances.

In these circumstances, sellers are typically advised by bankers or brokers who play an active role in managing the selling process. The advisor will endeavor to maintain as much sales leverage as possible. In much the same way as in an auction, the advisor will attempt to limit access to information and to management until it is satisfied that the deal can be closed for the price and on the terms preliminarily agreed to at inception.

Price Preemption: The Buyer's Perspective   The strategic implications of a bid to preempt an auction are no different than those associated with engaging in an auction. The buyer must be able to demonstrate that the acquisition is supportive of its strategic objectives and should articulate a value creation plan that justifies the price it is willing to pay. From a tactical perspective, the degree of leverage on the sell side of the transaction will almost certainly be substantially diminished. As a result, the buyer will generally be in a strong position to push back and make greater demands for access to management and company information. In such situations, the potential for the diligence team to take a somewhat broader and deeper approach to its review can be materially enhanced.

Relationship-Based Preemption As noted in "Proactive Engagement" in Chapter 3, some acquirers go to great lengths to develop relationships with owners of businesses they deem strategically attractive, but not immediately available for sale. Establishing and maintaining these types of relationships can provide acquirers with a preferred position once the owners do decide to sell. It can bolster the seller's confidence in how its business and employees will be treated and that the buyer would provide a good home for the business. Such qualities as cultural compatibility and shared standards for integrity, quality, and customer service are far less tangible than price but can influence a seller when it assesses the field of possible acquirers. Although relationship-building in and of itself will rarely carry the day, it may enable the potential acquirer to preempt the market for a more modest purchase price premium, especially since the courting process suggests that the likelihood of closing a transaction is high.

Relationship-Based Preemption: The Buyer's Perspective Preemption based on a courting process is, by its very nature, a proactive (versus reactive) method of acquisition pursuit. If supported by strategic analysis and evaluation, preemption is the most desirable form of pursuit—although, arguably, the rarest. This type of transaction is very likely to result in a significantly different due diligence review. Purchase price will typically have been negotiated in advance, obviating the need for the leveraging techniques employed by sellers in auction-type transactions. Accordingly, the seller's advisor, if it has one, is likely to be more of a facilitator than a bare-knuckled negotiator. As a result, the review will generally be more open and accommodating. In summary, the seller will be more inclined toward disclosure, less inclined toward salesmanship, and willing to endure a more extended period of disruption. Although this tolerance cannot be expected to be limitless, it would generally result in greater access to management and company books and records for a longer period of time. These conditions do not diminish the need for the acquirer to focus on validating key strategic assumptions; but they do provide an environment that may make it easier to do so.

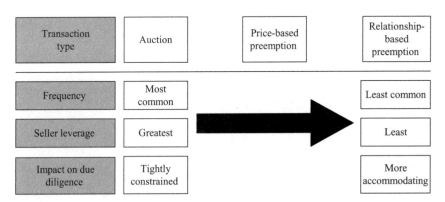

EXHIBIT 5.2 Characteristics of Sales Transaction Types

Summary of Transaction Characteristics

The characteristics of these different transaction types and their potential impact on the conduct of the due diligence review are summarized here and illustrated in the Exhibit 5.2.

Auctions are the most commonly occurring type of sales transaction and they yield the greatest degree of seller leverage in the diligence process. Access is tightly controlled and a competitive environment is fostered. Price-based preemptive bid transactions are less common and, to a limited degree, leverage is sacrificed for the sake of speed and confidence that the transaction can be consummated at a price sufficiently attractive to the seller. Relationship-based preemptive bid transactions, decades ago a common occurrence, are now fairly rare. When they do materialize, the seller's leverage and the attendant motivation to maximize purchase price is generally subordinated to other objectives, with a positive impact on the environment in which the acquirer conducts its diligence.

COMPONENTS OF THE DUE DILIGENCE REVIEW

The due diligence review has two primary components: interactive discussion between the due diligence team and the management team responsible for the business being sold; and a detailed review of the target company's business, legal, and financial documents. It may also entail a tour of the seller's facilities. The importance of observing operations is largely dependent on the type of business being reviewed. For example, there is probably considerably less to learn about a service organization than there is about a manufacturing operation where hard assets and production processes are important aspects of the company being reviewed.

The interaction between reviewers and the target's management team generally takes the form of a management presentation by the latter group to the former, followed by interviews and follow-up discussions. Document review occurs in a physical or electronically accessible data room, which houses a broad array of company information. From the buyer's perspective, the diligence process should be approached with the intent of continually narrowing its focus as the review proceeds—initially casting its net broadly to ensure that it has a fundamental understanding of the business, but quickly homing in on the issues with the greatest impact on the transaction's value. (This top-down approach is discussed in more detail in the section "Due Diligence Reviews: An Objectives-Driven Approach.")

Management Presentations

Presentations by senior management of the business being acquired (typically, the CEO, CFO, and other key executives) generally initiate the due diligence review process. If there has been an *offering document* (OD) prepared and distributed by the seller, the management presentation will mirror the basic contents and message of that document and expand upon it. If an OD has been made available, the acquisition team should use it, in conjunction with its own plan to create value, to prepare for the management presentation. The OD will generally contain a description of the business, its market(s), and its products/services, as well as a discussion of its organizational structure, its historical financial performance, and its development potential. A thorough review of these documents should enable the review team to approach the presentation more efficiently by ensuring that the presentation confirms its understanding of the business and by focusing discussion on those areas it considers most important.

The due diligence team should understand that these interactive presentations will undoubtedly be well-rehearsed, are likely to be supported by a slick PowerPoint slide show, and almost surely to be tightly managed by the seller's advisors. Although they are intended to inform the audience of the dynamics of the business, its past performance, and future strategies and goals, the acquisition team should know that management presentations are an integral element of the target company's *selling process*. Accordingly, they will focus on the positive aspects of the business, its favorable position in its market, and its strategic potential. At the same time, they are likely to attempt to side-step discussion of areas of weakness and risk.

Given the nature and tenor of the presentation, the acquisition team's objectives for the management presentation should be twofold: to confirm or modify its understanding of the business and its position in its market(s); and to evaluate its management team. With regard to the former, the team should answer the following questions:

- Did the presentation alter the team's understanding of the business?
- What impact did the presentation have on the team's view of the business' growth prospects, future profitability, potential synergies, and risk profile?
- What important information was missing, or not adequately addressed?

The answers to these questions would determine whether the scope and focus of the due diligence review is appropriate as planned or whether it should be expanded or altered. That, in turn, would influence the nature of follow-up interviews and discussions and the focus of the data room review (discussed in detail in the "Document Review" section).

The presentation should also be seen by the reviewers as an opportunity to evaluate the management, both individually and as a team. In making these evaluations, the acquisition team should attempt to answer the following questions:

- Do presenters have command of the facts?
- Can they answer questions about the business and the market confidently and convincingly?
- Do they have a firm grasp on the financial dynamics of the business?
- Do they project an image of leadership?
- Do they have a unified vision of the business' potential and its future strategic direction?

As noted, members of the management team will generally have been rehearsed and they will realize that the management presentation is also an audition for continued management of the business. In light of the importance of the event, uncertainty about key issues, or repeated statements, such as "I'll have to get back to you on that," or an excessive tendency to route reviewers' questions to one individual, can usually be read as a lack of command and should alert reviewers to potential weakness. Similarly, starkly differing views on the market or the strategic direction for the business may imply a lack of team cohesiveness and potentially a lack of leadership. Although the acquirer may be enamored of the property being offered for sale, rarely can the value of the management team be disassociated from transaction. Accordingly, the perceived strengths and weaknesses of the management team should be an important element of the due diligence review and should be documented in the team's findings and recommendations.

Another important aspect of the management presentation relates to the fact that, for the management team, there are consequences associated with the information that they present. Not only are they effectively auditioning for their next jobs in many cases, they are also presenting a view of a business and its prospects—views for which they will have responsibility if the transaction is consummated. Even though the presentation is part of a sales process, the reviewers should recognize that there is a countervailing force at work that should temper presenter hyperbole, that is, *the presenters will have to stand behind their representations* of the business as it exists and of its prospects for the future. As a result, reviewers should be inclined to probe core issues aggressively and with a reasonable degree of skepticism. They should not sit back passively or be reticent to put presenters on the spot and challenge their assumptions and conclusions. Legitimate, aggressive questions can be effective in revealing potential risks and weaknesses in the business.

Management Team Interviews

At various points in the due diligence process, the reviewers will have opportunities to question individual members of the management team, either in formal break-out sessions (usually by functional area) or in more informal discussions. The advisors to the seller will make every effort to control the extent and the form of that access. That, in itself, is a strong indicator that these opportunities to drill down into greater detail can be effective vehicles for discovery for the due diligence team members. Advisors may require written questions for vetting in advance, or may limit access in other ways. However, the leaders of the diligence effort should demand as much face-to-face time with the management team as they need to adequately address all areas of concern. The formal management presentation will involve a large number of participants over a relatively short period of time. Typically, it will be limited to three or four hours and include several presenters and a greater number of reviewers. These follow-up sessions enable the reviewers to get much more detailed and nuanced information about specific areas of concern and they should be approached with clear objectives and targeted questions.

Document Review

A major component of the due diligence is document review, a process that takes place in the data room. The data room has historically been a physical site where a large volume of business, legal, and financial documents are housed for review by potential acquirers. In recent years, technology has enabled sellers and their representatives to provide electronic access to documents via "virtual" data rooms. The relative merits of physical and virtual data rooms are discussed in the section titled "Technology Trade-Offs." From a content perspective, the data room contains comprehensive documentation of key aspects of the business that is being sold, organized, and indexed into categories such as those listed below. (A list of typical data room documents appears in Appendix 5B.)

- Finance and accounting
- Product or service
- Intellectual property
- Legal
- Insurance
- Litigation
- Sales and marketing
- Customer service
- Employee matters
- Information systems
- Research and development

Review of the information contained in the data room is a critical aspect of buyer due diligence. It is an opportunity for potential buyers to assess the data underlying representations that have been made by the seller in the OD, the management presentation, and follow-up discussions with business unit executives. Furthermore, key elements of this information will support representations and warranties that will be incorporated into the purchase and sale agreement in the form of schedules to that contract, and data room access will be the first opportunity for buyers to scrutinize this information.

As the due diligence team approaches the document review phase of the process, it must determine two things: whether the documents provided contain the information needed to validate the representations of the buyer and the assumptions embedded in their organization's plan to create value; and how it plans to deploy its resources to validate those representations and assumptions. With regard to the former point, the team should be sensitized to the fact that the seller will be inclined to provide information that substantiates its selling points and disinclined to showcase data that might undermine those points. Therefore, it is incumbent upon the diligence team members to take a proactive approach to ensure that documents critical to their review are made available. To this end, the due diligence team typically funnels requests for additional information to the seller's representatives during the course of its work.

Insofar as resource allocation is concerned, team leaders should ensure that there is a clear and coordinated plan for document review and analysis, one that focuses reviewers on the deal's key value-drivers. The data room will contain a large volume of documents of varying importance. A common pitfall of reviewers, especially first-time members of the team, is to treat all documents as equal and endeavor to look at everything made available. As discussed in "Components of a Due Diligence Review," in most due diligence settings such a checklist approach is an extremely poor use of time and, instead, the team should employ an objectives-driven approach.

Tour of the Facilities

Touring the target business's facilities has a number of benefits. Rather than being an abstraction, the business takes on more meaning when one sees it in operation. It also provides those evaluating operations and technology with concrete information about their areas of review and the potential for realizing assumed cost synergies. This is particularly the case when the acquisition involves companies with manufacturing facilities, complex operations, and large inventories. In addition, a firsthand view of the operations often provides meaningful impressions of whether the business is well run or poorly run. Needless to say, such impressions should not be confused with validation but, as a supplement to the other elements of the review, they often support conclusions about the quality of the operation under evaluation and opportunities and challenges associated with postacquisition integration.

Technology Trade-Offs

Information technology provides acquirers and sellers alike with tools that enhance the efficiency of the acquisition process. From the seller's perspective, virtual data rooms, in particular, enable simultaneous access by multiple potential buyers, enable the monitoring and measurement of information usage by potential buyers, and establish a secure and orderly environment for the information provided. From a strategic perspective, virtual sites allow the seller to better control the diligence process, accelerate the pace of the sales process (via simultaneous access by multiple buyers), and heighten the sense of competition among potential buyers.

Teleconferencing and access to virtual data rooms also enhance the efficiency of buyers. Virtual data rooms enable due diligence team members with specialized skills and expertise to participate in the due diligence review from remote locations. Virtual data rooms also allow immediate access to the same data by different members of the due diligence team, thereby obviating problems of overlapping interest in the same documents. Although these capabilities make the team more efficient, that efficiency can come at the price of reduced effectiveness. It can aggravate the natural tendency toward myopia and compartmentalized behavior (discussed in Chapter 1). A critical component of the due diligence review is the cross-functional interaction of team members who look at much of the same information from different perspectives. One of the benefits of close physical proximity of team members is the ease with which these perspectives and review findings and recommendations can be shared and discussed regularly. In the absence of such proximity, a silo mentality among team members can result, with specialists losing perspective of the big picture. To mitigate this risk, team leaders should ensure that there are regular, periodic (daily) meetings involving *all* team members. If there are team members who are participating remotely, it is particularly important that they be included via conference call and that there is a conscious effort to tease out the potential impact of specialists findings on other aspects of the review. The importance of cross-functional coordination is discussed further in the "Cross-Functional Coordination and Analysis" section.

DUE DILIGENCE REVIEWS:
AN OBJECTIVES-DRIVEN APPROACH

Overview

This section discusses the due diligence review from two perspectives: that of the *operation of the specific business function* or process under review, and of the *impact of that function on the transaction's value*. By tasking each functional team to address some aspect of the valuation, the acquirer can ensure that reviewers maintain their focus on those items of greatest importance to the transaction. These items include the validation of the strategic purpose and value drivers that motivated the acquirer to pursue the transaction in the first place. They also include the assessment of potential major risks identified prior to or during the diligence process. As noted, there are natural constraints of time, access, and resources inherent in the due diligence review process. It is almost invariably short in duration; there are limits to the willingness of the seller to endure intrusion in and disruption to its business; and the acquirer's ability to dedicate staff (most reviewers have other, full-time responsibilities) and attention (this project is likely to be one of many that the organization is managing) is finite. In this environment an effective review must be highly focused and a preponderance of time and resource should be dedicated to confirming assumptions and assessing risks that impact the value creation potential of the combination and, by extension, determining whether and on what basis the transaction should be executed.

The alternative to this top-down type of review is a checklist or compliance approach that ascribes equal value to virtually all aspects of discovery. This approach results in reviewers adopting an administrative attitude and focusing on completeness and efficiency at the expense of effectiveness, often failing to penetrate past the initial layers of inquiry on issues of critical importance. This form of review can be seductive, especially to those not practiced in the diligence process, because it provides comfort in the knowledge that all items on the checklist were looked at and all steps on the due diligence program were addressed. The optimal result from this approach is the ability to provide negative assurance—that is, that nothing emerged that would cause the reviewer to recommend that the transaction not be pursued. Unfortunately, negative assurance is a necessary, but not sufficient, diligence finding. This may indicate that the company under review is a solid company, but it by no means validates that it is a good investment.

Therefore, it is critically important that the review team adopt a top-down, objectives-driven approach, accompanied by an investor mentality that intensely focuses its attention on the strategically important aspects of the transaction.

However, a top-down approach cannot be effective until and unless the members of the due diligence team truly understand the business under review. Prereview analysis will have enabled the team to establish a preliminary understanding of the dynamics of the business and its operational strengths and weaknesses. That understanding should be confirmed or modified during the initial stages of the review, that is, management presentations and initial follow-up discussions with management. It is the foundation that will enable it to make informed judgments about the entity's inherent growth and profitability characteristics and the acquirer's assumed synergies and potential risks. An effective diligence effort is one where the net is initially cast broadly and narrows quickly as the team confirms or modifies its preliminary view of the business. This is accomplished via a review of business operations by function (i.e., accounting, sales and marketing, information technology, etc.). By the time the team has reached the intermediate and later stages of the process (document review and confirmatory diligence), the effort should be heavily weighted toward the validation of the assumptions that underpin the rationale for the acquisition.

The remainder of this section discusses the application of a top-down approach to due diligence. It focuses on the following topics:

- The central role of *due diligence objectives* in the assessment process
- The nature of *integration risks* and their potential impact on the transaction
- Business and transaction *assessment by functional area*
- The importance of *cross-functional coordination* of assessment, findings, and recommendations

Due Diligence Objectives

The central role of the due diligence objectives is illustrated in Exhibit 5.3. They are the lynchpin between the organization's plan to create value and the findings and recommendations that guide its decisions, its negotiating posture, and its postacquisition action plans.

The team endeavors, first, to confirm their understanding of the business, as it exists. This consists of a detailed survey of each of the functional

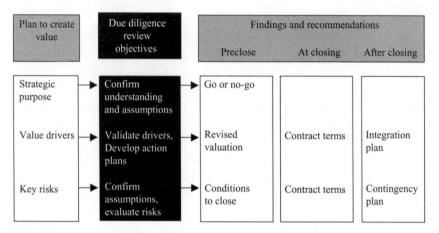

Plan to create value	Due diligence review objectives	Findings and recommendations		
		Preclose	At closing	After closing
Strategic purpose	Confirm understanding and assumptions	Go or no-go		
Value drivers	Validate drivers, Develop action plans	Revised valuation	Contract terms	Integration plan
Key risks	Confirm assumptions, evaluate risks	Conditions to close	Contract terms	Contingency plan

EXHIBIT 5.3   Due Diligence Continuum

areas (e.g., finance and accounting, sales and marketing, human resources, and information technology) by the team members assigned to those functions. That aspect of the review provides the basis for further analysis. That analysis results in the confirmation (or modification) of key assumptions reflected in the organization's valuation model and its value creation plan. These assumptions relate to:

- The fundamental soundness of the business, as measured by its capacity to sustain growth and profitability
- The potential for the combined entity (buyer and seller) to create value
- The risks associated with the plan to extract that value

Accomplishing these objectives is discussed in the context of integration, individual functional reviews, and cross-functional coordination.

Integration

The issue of postacquisition integration permeates M&A transactions, presents potential risks at multiple levels, and should be considered in virtually every aspect of the review. Integration falls into three distinct categories, namely, operational integration, synergy integration, and cultural integration. Operational integration refers to the effort to normalize operations of the combined entity to ensure that "the trains run on time." It includes the harmonization, or standardization, of all manner of systems, consolidated policies, and unified procedures, as well as common image and identity. It generally has no revenue enhancement and cost savings associated with it. In fact, in some instances, it may result in significant one-time costs. The risks associated with poorly planned and executed operational integration are those of distraction, business interruption, customer alienation, and lost revenue and profits.

Synergy integration refers to the execution of the measures necessary to extract value, as well as the timing of the implementation of those measures. Synergy integration risks, therefore, relate to execution and timing. If redundant activities or personnel are not eliminated, or not eliminated in a timely manner, the related savings are foregone. Similarly, if revenue synergies are not exploited or are delayed, the assumed benefits (increased sales and profits) will not materialize.

Cultural integration refers to the merging of two entities' organizations, attitudes, and behaviors. It can be viewed on two levels, that of the entire entity and that of individual departments or functions. At the entity level, it deals largely with attitude and style. Friction arises when significantly different corporate cultures are combined. A typical example is the marriage of a mature, conservative, administrative organization to an entrepreneurial, risk-taking one. Clashing organizational cultures will almost certainly derail integration, but even in situations in which corporate cultures may be largely compatible, there is the potential for dissonance at the functional level. Differences in training, methodology, or philosophy in critical functions, such as IT or R&D, can also occur. Culturally dissonant departments or segments of the new entity will surely impede the acquirer's integration plans and diminish its ability to extract value.

Given the pervasive nature of integration issues, all members of the team should incorporate steps to evaluate integration risk into their reviews. In addition, specific team members should be assigned responsibility for aggregating findings relative to operational, synergistic, and cultural integration (see Exhibit 5.4).

Assessment by Function

The due diligence team is composed of specialists and each is charged with the responsibility of assessing the business from the perspective of their discipline or function. Although it is critical that these specialists share their perspectives with other team members (this aspect of the review is covered in the "Cross-Functional Coordination and Analysis" section), it is entirely natural and appropriate that they focus their attention on their respective areas of expertise in advance of doing so. Although the objectives and procedures for each due diligence review are situation and transaction specific, the basic approach described in the following sections provides general guidance on an objective-driven examination.

Finance and Accounting   Finance and accounting is one area of the due diligence that, by its very nature, lends itself to looking at the business under review in a comprehensive manner. The financial review provides a perspective that encompasses virtually every aspect of the business. In addition, the senior financial reviewer is generally one of the leaders of the due diligence team and, as such, should be thinking holistically about the transaction. The previously discussed objectives-driven approach provides the framework for these specialists to confirm their understanding of the business, evaluate its stand-alone potential, validate assumed value drivers of the combined businesses, and assess integration risks.

- *Functional assessment.* The operational component of the financial review includes confirming or modifying the reviewers' understanding of
  the business, historically and as it presently exists. This entails a detailed
  review of the company's business model, its financial dynamics, and its
  historical financial performance. It also requires an understanding of
  the accounting policies it employed and how they impact such things as
  revenue and expense recognition, as well as how they compare to the
  acquirer's accounting policies and those of the industry as a whole. This
  review and confirmation process is substantially aided if the company
  has audited financial statements. Audited statements provide a high
  level of comfort with the reported results. In addition, the associated
  disclosures may provide important insights into areas of exposure not
  otherwise considered. The review of audited financials is particularly
  valuable when the reviewers have access to the company's auditor, especially if accounting issues arise that warrant further elaboration and
  discussion. (It should be noted that, in an auction sale environment, this
  access may not be provided until the process reaches the confirmatory
  stage.) If the statements are not audited, the scope and depth of the

review would have to be substantially expanded to provide the acquirer with adequate confidence in the reliability of reported results. Given the time constraints under which due diligence is generally conducted, this means that the review would require significantly more resources and suggests the need for the involvement of an independent accounting firm to assist in the process.

In addition to financial accounting and reporting issues, the reviewers would spend a significant amount of time understanding the company's internal control processes and reviewing related documentation, management accounting systems and reports, and finance practices such as credit and collection policies, banking, and other creditor relationships. Additional valuable insight into the company's historical performance will result from reviewing the budgeting process, tracking recent year's budget to actual results, and any explanation of material variances.

- *Impact on the valuation.* An area of considerable risk for the acquirer is to "get it wrong" on the fundamental financial soundness of the company being acquired. A way to address this risk is to understand the financial characteristics of the business as it should perform *under the acquirer's ownership*, by assessing its "quality of earnings" and "quality of assets." In other words, the team should review the historical financial statements with an eye toward quantifying any one-time, unusual, or other nonrecurring events that should not be expected to impact future results, either positively or negatively. Such items might include nonmarket salaries and owner expenses, accounting adjustments or differing accounting practices, or one-time gains or losses. The financial reviewers should aim to confirm or modify the baseline view of historical growth, profitability, and cash conversion embedded in the valuation model and plan to create value. This baseline is the prologue to expected future performance of the business. It reveals underlying trends and the potential for the company to sustain profitable growth. Based on this assessment, the acquiring company's reviewers then validate or alter assumptions about the potential future performance of the business on a stand-alone basis.

This historical data should also be analyzed by reviewers (both financial and marketing specialists) in the context of the competitive environment. In addition to absolute growth, reviewers should evaluate the company's historical performance in relation to the market and to the competition. If the company has underperformed the market (i.e., if the market overall has grown at a faster rate than the company), reviewers have to consider the implications of that underperformance. More specifically, if the company has grown at a slower pace than the overall market, it is clear that either some competitors have exceeded market growth rates or there are emerging competitors taking market share. In either case, the reviewers must consider the cause of this loss of market share and the implications for *future growth and profitability*.

The conclusions and findings of the financial members of the team regarding the foundational growth and profitability of the target company are critical to the validation (or modification) of the acquirer's valuation model and value creation plan. Any apparent erosion of that foundation certainly suggests a need to revisit the valuation, and possibly the transaction.

Layered on top of the growth potential of the stand-alone business are the synergies that are derived from the combination of buyer and seller, and the presumption that the additional financial returns that will result would not have been realized if the businesses had operated independently. These synergies take two general forms, revenue synergies and expense efficiencies. If they truly exist and if they are properly harnessed, these synergies are *potential* value drivers for the combined entity.

Insofar as synergies are concerned, assessment and validation fall primarily to those functions that would be responsible for their execution. This not only provides a sound basis for evaluation (it is made by those with the appropriate expertise), it also establishes ownership on the part of the evaluators (those who will have to deliver on the promise). The validation of expense synergies generally falls across multiple functional areas, essentially wherever there are redundancies in personnel, facilities, and systems, and they are usually relatively easy to quantify. As a general rule, that quantification should be the responsibility of each functional area, with the accounting and finance team applying a reasonableness test to those calculations and developing consensus around any changes.

Similarly, the validation of revenue synergies would fall to the functional area responsible for their execution (such as product development or sales and marketing). Validation of the magnitude of revenue synergies is considerably more difficult than determining the size of expense synergies. It requires an in-depth understanding of market dynamics and, even then, is usually based on multiple variables. More specifically, this requires *layering* additional growth on an already *assumed* growth rate, based on *assumptions* about combined capabilities. While it is the role of the product and market specialists on the due diligence review team to validate these assumptions, the finance and accounting reviewers should not be passive participants in that assessment process. This is an area where the financial specialists should challenge those assumptions and moderate the enthusiasm of their product and market counterparts when it appears to be excessive. Such enthusiasm is not uncommon, since the product and market reviewers are often among the champions of the transaction.

Equally important, the financial specialists will have to aggregate the results of these validated (and frequently modified) calculations and determine whether they, in combination, still create value. That is to say, the mere existence of synergies does not guarantee value creation. Value creation only occurs when returns exceed the acquirer's internal hurdle rate of return, a rate directly related to purchase price. If the financial team finds that the projected yield from synergies materially decreases as a result of this validation process, they must determine the potential impact on valuation. If the valuation cannot be supported by newly projected synergies, either the purchase price must be revisited or the acquirer should disengage from the transaction.

This group will also consider integration risk, within the accounting and finance function, as well as companywide. They should first determine whether there are any risks associated with assumptions made about the integration of accounting personnel and systems. In addition, this group is generally the logical choice for the consolidation of all cross-functional inputs on integration and other transaction risks. (See the discussion of cross-functional coordination in the section "Cross-Functional Coordination and Analysis.")

Human Resources HR reviewers also look across the entire business, albeit from a significantly different vantage point than that of the finance and accounting colleagues. Operationally, their focus is on compensation and organizational issues. In terms of the valuation, their attention should primarily be focused on integration issues.

- *Functional assessment.* The HR specialists on the review team must establish a firm understanding of the company's personnel policies, benefit plans, employee compensation structure, human resource information systems, and organizational structure, as well as union agreements if applicable. Most organizations have documented company policies and procedures in the form of HR policy handbooks or company Intranet sites that would facilitate this aspect of the review. Similarly, they will have developed summary benefit plan documents that outline the major aspects of health coverage, pension plans (defined benefit plans), defined contribution plans (e.g., 401(k) plans), tuition assistance plans, life insurance plans, and any other benefit plans it may offer. These policies, plans, and procedures should be benchmarked against those of the acquirer, as well as the industry as a whole. Also, the team should assess the soundness of the organizational structure (i.e., whether it facilitates or impedes effective management) and should analyze compensation profile of the company. The compensation review should include an examination of salaries by functional category and the details of management incentive and sales commission plans. These, too, should be compared to industry standards and the acquiring company's practices. Particular attention should be paid to executive compensation contracts and conditions, such as severance or change of control terms, which may trigger material payments.

Additional areas that warrant scrutiny would generally include data dealing with employee turnover, merit increases, employee surveys, employee litigation, and the company's severance experience. If the seller employs union labor, contracts and any record of grievances should also be examined. In addition, reviewers should determine whether the company has complied with any applicable governmental programs by examining any reports to or correspondence with organizations such as the EEOC, NLRB, and OSHA (discussed in "Legal and Insurance Reviews"). These steps provide reviewers with indices of employee satisfaction and may identify areas of risk.

The HR specialists should also solicit input on perceived managerial strengths and weaknesses from other members of the review team. In this regard, the HR professionals can establish criteria (such as experience, expertise, leadership, and integrity) upon which to make this assessment. This starting point for this type of evaluation is during management presentations. As the review progresses these impressions will generally be confirmed or modified. As noted in "Management Presentation," the evaluation of the management team can be a critical aspect of the review. Accordingly, it is important that these inputs are documented and made part of the HR specialists' findings.

■ *Impact on the valuation.* Human resource reviewers should initially focus on HR departmental integration and any associated synergies. These typically relate to staff and systems integration. The objectives should be to validate any assumed efficiencies and identify any unanticipated opportunities or potential risks. On a broader scale, they should assess all assumed expense synergies resulting from the transaction and determine their impact from a human capital perspective. In evaluating assumed personnel efficiencies (i.e., staff reductions) across the organizations (both the company being acquired and their own organization), the HR professionals are able to bring a degree of objectivity to the analysis. There often will be those on the team who will be very aggressive in favoring the reduction in the size and cost of the combined entity's personnel infrastructure; and, there will be those on the team who will have responsibility for specific operations after the acquisition who will be inclined to be very conservative in their approach to staff reductions. The role of the HR specialist in these cases should be to provide a balanced perspective that considers the ongoing needs of the combined business, as well as the need to optimize efficiencies in creating value.

These reviewers can also provide valuable input in analyzing the cost basis of the personnel component of the business. Having benchmarked the cost of compensation and benefits against the market and their own organization, they can provide valuable input in determining whether those costs should be materially adjusted after the acquisition. Normalizing these costs can change the profitability profile of the business both retrospectively and, more importantly, prospectively. This is particularly true if the company being evaluated is labor (versus capital) intensive and compensation and benefits comprise a large percentage of overall operating expense.

An important, if not central, concern of HR specialists should be the assessment of the corporate culture of the company being reviewed and a determination of the degree of difficulty in harmonizing it with the culture of the acquirer. In many acquisitions this aspect of due diligence does not get sufficient attention. It is a critical component of the review (and subsequent integration activities) and it is ignored at great potential cost. To the extent that the acquirer does not have the requisite skills to evaluate cultural differences and plan for their harmonization, it should enlist the assistance of HR consultants that do. In comparing and contrasting organizations' cultures, the reviewers will look at qualities, such as attitudes, styles, and behaviors, and how these qualities manifest themselves in policies, procedures, and internal communication and interactions. Dissonance can occur on the overall organizational level. For example, the acquisition of an entrepreneurial organization by a more conservative and structured company may result in management confusion and frustration. On a departmental level, differences in training, policies, and procedures may result in conflicting approaches to everyday operations. Unaddressed, these types of distractions come at the price of substantially reduced productivity for an extended period of time. Assessing cultural differences requires HR reviewers to work closely with all members of the due diligence team to identify significant impediments to harmonization, to assess the degree of risk, and to craft a plan to mitigate that risk.

Sales and Marketing   The operational aspect of the sales and marketing review should be primarily focused on the business' existing products or services, how they are priced, distributed or delivered, and supported. With regard to the valuation, the emphasis should be on assessing the ability of these products to retain their strength or durability in the market, as well as on the revenue synergies assumed in the acquirer's value creation plan.

- *Functional assessment.* Sales and marketing specialists on the due diligence team should first establish a thorough understanding of the company's offerings, specifically the nature and characteristics of the products or services; the segments of the market that they serve; the extent of their market penetration; and their pricing history and the philosophy or rationale behind it. With regard to products and markets, reviewers should assess product differentiation, market demographics and market growth, and the price/volume dynamics of that growth. In addition, reviewers should obtain an understanding of customer attitudes and satisfaction levels (through customer service records and any customer surveys that may exist), the nature of product sales and distribution, and the attributes of sales and marketing systems support. The nature of the sales and distribution process should be thoroughly explored and, to the extent that there are arm's length agreements with distributors, the team should understand the nature of those agreements, as well as any limitation they place on the company's ability to sell directly to customers.

■ *Impact on the valuation.* The sales and marketing reviewers should focus on the validation of key assumptions made by the acquirer about product strength and synergy potential. They should also assess integration risks associated with their area of responsibility. Product strength should be examined in terms of the sustainability of revenue growth. More specifically, reviewers must determine whether the team's assumptions about stand-alone growth are supportable. They must explore such factors as where products are in their life cycle and the implications for growth, the extent to which historical revenue growth has been driven by price or by volume, and whether their market positions can be maintained over time; and the sensitivity of the offerings to exogenous factors such as macroeconomic fluctuations, demographic trends, and globalization.

A critical element of the sales and marketing review is the assessment of assumed revenue synergies. More often than not, revenue synergies are the single most important factors influencing the pursuit of the target company, and it is in the sales and marketing arena that that these perceived benefits might be extracted. Synergies typically take the form of complementary strengths, such as matching superior products with strong distribution capabilities. The reviewers must validate the complementary nature of these capabilities, as well as the assumed magnitude of their benefits.

Another key aspect of this assessment is the evaluation of any downside risk associated with efforts to extract the value of the potential synergies. This risk can take a number of forms. For example, when the marriage is between two organizations that have competed in the same market for an extended period, critiques of the competitive products may have become embedded in their respective cultures. As a result, sales and marketing personnel may have to be re-trained to ensure that there no lingering sense of the ex-competitor's product inferiority. Also, when a company is acquired to penetrate an adjacent or foreign market, there is a risk of incomplete or superficial understanding of the market by the acquirer. Those evaluating synergies should be sensitized to the need to look at downside risks as well as the magnitude of the opportunities.

Research and Development　In many acquisitions, research and development is a key area because it is an important engine of future growth. Those tasked with evaluating the R&D function should first establish a detailed understanding of the processes involved and then determine whether the target company's approach and output are sufficiently robust to yield products that will sustain revenue growth over time.

- *Functional assessment.* The R&D function can be a somewhat opaque area leading up to the due diligence review. Opportunities along the research and development continuum being considered for commercialization are unlikely to be identified in specific terms in selling materials (particularly in an offering document, which is widely distributed to competitors and potential competitors). As a result, the due diligence review is likely to be the first time that the acquirer is able to establish an understanding of the nuts and bolts of the R&D operation. The objectives of the functional review should be to understand the process employed to bring products from the concept stage to market introduction, the benchmarks used to determine go/no-go product development decisions, and the function's success quotient in identifying and introducing successful offerings.
- *Impact on the valuation.* A quantitative assessment of R&D activities can be a tricky proposition. The objectives of this phase of the review should be to determine if the process can provide a healthy pipeline of new products that are capable of sustaining future revenue growth at rates assumed in the acquirer's value creation plan. These determinations are dependent on two factors: the function's historical track record and the projected success of specific planned new product introductions presently in the pipeline. The degree of historical success can be measured relatively easily. This is a factor of the number of new products introduced over time and the contribution that those products have made to revenue and profits. The evaluation of the present pipeline may be a more difficult undertaking. Organizations are frequently reluctant to share information about new product introductions that are not imminent, especially with competitors. The seller may choose not to reveal this information until very late stages of diligence, when there is a high probability that the transaction will be consummated. In such situations the information may be initially presented in very generic terms and only revealed in detail in the confirmatory stage of due diligence.

Because this can be an important aspect of the evaluation, the acquirer should make it clear to the seller that final valuation could be materially impacted by the results of that review and analysis.

Integration of R&D operations may also present challenges. R&D can be a discipline that spawns its own unique culture within an organization. The reviewers must determine whether any differences in approaches and cultures are an impediment to value creation. For example, to avoid compromising the ability of the newly combined entity to introduce new products on a timely basis, it may be necessary to delay the integration process and sacrifice some of the assumed cost efficiencies. Alternatively, the organization may choose to proceed with integration despite the risks. In that event, the acquirer should assess the potential impact on its effectiveness and quantify its potential cost.

Information Technology Review   Information technology permeates all aspects of modern business. IT lubricates operational activities and, in many organizations, enables product development and delivery. The IT review should be designed to ensure an understanding of the company's IT infrastructure, validate assumptions about any underlying technology-related synergies, and provide expert support to the other functional teams.

- *Functional assessment.* The IT functional assessment should include a survey of hardware, software, operational support systems, Web sites, and technology-related intellectual property (IP) assets. The reviewers should determine whether systems are current or antiquated and, if the latter, whether and at what cost upgrades should be implemented. The reviewers should also determine ownership rights: issues such as whether software licenses are current or whether the entity being acquired holds title to IT and IP assets being transferred. These issues can be complex if the sale involves the divestiture of a division or segment of a larger corporate entity. In such cases, title may be held by the larger entity or licenses may be in its name. If so, the reviewers must determine the impact on the transaction and the need to identify any steps necessary to ensure that the entity being purchased possesses the assets and capabilities assumed by the acquirer. Also, one of the most important objectives of the IT review is the assessment of operational integration issues and challenges. IT operational integration is generally a high priority and issues of compatibility and plans for harmonization, including timing and any associated costs, should be addressed by the team during due diligence.

- *Impact on the valuation.* The extent to which the IT team will focus on valuation issues is directly related to the synergistic benefits the acquirer has assumed the combination will provide. In the case of technology-based businesses, such as software, communications, information, and Internet companies, these benefits will generally be central to the acquirer's plan to create value. Additionally, IT plays a crucial cross-organizational role in support of the other due diligence team members, as most other functional areas (e.g., accounting and finance, human resources, etc.) of the target business probably have systems aspects that require joint evaluation to determine the costs and benefits of integrating those functions.

Operations/Production Review   Those involved in the non-IT operations review generally look across the organization to understand areas such as facilities management and maintenance, purchasing, inventory management, customer service, order entry, fulfillment, and security. In cases where the acquisition involves a manufacturing business, the reviewers will focus on production and process efficiencies. These reviewers will also play an important role in validating and identifying cross-company efficiencies and in the postacquisition integration process.

- *Functional assessment.* Operational reviewers should establish a good understanding of the supporting infrastructure of the target company. Areas of review would be specific to the company and industry but might include such items as real estate and lease arrangements, service agreements, supplier contracts, and policies and procedures relating to purchasing, manufacturing processes, inventory management and control, and product fulfillment. Reviewers would work closely with all other functional reviewers in identifying operational efficiencies and often take a leadership role in consolidating that information. In a manufacturing environment the reviewers should also focus on duplication of assets and economies of scale. In service environments the focus would be on efficiencies that would result in material reductions in duplicated infrastructure costs.
- *Impact on the valuation.* As noted, the operational team would normally play a central role in the integration process. Typically, the area

of greatest impact is likely to be combining or co-locating overlapping or redundant facilities. In addition to rationalizing the real estate footprint of the combined organization, these reviewers may also be tasked with harmonizing operational practices of the target business with those of the acquirer. As a result, their review efforts should entail validating expense synergy assumptions (e.g., consolidation of space and the elimination of process and staff redundancies) made prior to due diligence, as well as identifying unanticipated opportunities to reduce costs. An output of that process should be a plan for postacquisition integration.

Legal and Insurance Review   Legal and insurance aspects of due diligence are essentially oriented toward risk avoidance. By their very nature they focus on actual and potential exposures.

- *Legal.* Those attorneys leading the legal review are usually engaged in the transaction process from its early stages and play a key role if the transaction proceeds past the due diligence stage. Their involvement in the due diligence review and their interaction with their peers on the due diligence team will also provide them with a detailed knowledge of the business under review and the ability to provide valuable input during the negotiation and contracting stages of the transaction. However, their main focus during the review stage of the process should be to assess and mitigate transaction risk. Consistent with that objective, they would typically review the following:
    - *All material agreements.* This would include assessing and reporting contracts with employees, lessors, customers, suppliers, contractors, licensees and licensors, and distributors, as well as any business agreements (e.g., prior acquisitions, nondisclosure, or noncompete agreements) that may limit the range of the target company's commercial activity. If the transaction being contemplated is to take the form of an asset (versus stock) purchase, the reviewer should determine whether contracts are assignable and, if not, the potential impact on the transaction.
    - *Regulatory requirements.* Compliance with government and regulatory reporting requirements with organizations, such as the Environmental Protection Agency, the Internal Revenue Service, the Occupational Safety and Health Administration, the Equal Employment Opportunity Commission, the Federal Trade Commission, and the

Department of Justice, and related correspondence should be reviewed, analyzed, and reported on.

- *Litigation.* All claims, pending and threatened, and assessments, as well as any judicial, administrative or regulatory rulings and pending proceedings should be evaluated and relevant findings and recommendations should be provided.

- *Ownership.* Ownership of all material tangible and intangible assets should be confirmed and irregularities noted. This would include such items as deeds and title reports for real property, ownership records of other major assets, and filings for trademarks, trade names, patents, and copyrights.

- *Organizational status.* If the transaction involves a stock (versus asset) purchase, records relating to the ownership and capitalization of the company should be reviewed and documented. This would include certificates of incorporation, bylaws, board minutes, jurisdiction in which the company would be acquired, and the outstanding shareholders and their ownership and voting rights.

- *Insurance.* The review of insurance coverage is a critical aspect of the team's risk assessment. It may be conducted in conjunction with the legal or the operations review, but in any case would require the involvement of a specialist with insurance expertise. This specialist's objective is to ensure that all areas of significant exposure are addressed by the target company and, if self-insured for any risks, the degree to which the company is exposed. The insurance specialist would also review premiums to determine whether they are competitive, as well the history of losses and claims. Importantly, the insurance reviewer would try to determine whether the company is exposed to any pending or potential liability and, if so, to quantify the extent of that exposure.

Cross-Functional Coordination and Analysis

Specialists conduct due diligence reviews and see the company under review through the prism of their individual expertise. The resulting perspectives are critical to an effective review. However, these views do not provide sufficient insight, in and of themselves. For a due diligence review to be effective, cross-functional coordination and analysis is a necessity. Absent such coordination and analysis, a silo mentality can result where there is no comprehensive or overarching view of the business being considered for purchase. With shared and synthesized perspectives comes the proverbial "whole" that is more than the sum of its parts. A process that fosters cross-functional team coordination and analysis provides is described next. It has the following characteristics.

- *Prereview identification and communication.* This refers to the identification and communication, by team leaders, of key issues to be understood and strategic objectives to be accomplished. These issues and objectives are those that are articulated in the acquirer's value creation plan and reflected in the valuation model used to justify the acquisition price. These issues and objectives should be enunciated in advance of the review and understood by all reviewers.
- *Regular and frequent communication during the review.* Once the review process begins, the team should meet early and often. Team leaders should initiate meetings of the entire team periodically, at least daily. Provision should be made to include those specialists who may be participating from remote locations (as in the case when there is a virtual data room and team members are not in physical proximity). The inclusion of remote participants is particularly important because that very remoteness can foster the silo mentality referenced above. Meetings among subgroups on an as-needed basis should be encouraged. The focus of all exchanges should be on the key diligence objectives, specifically the validation or modification of prediligence assumptions and the identification and sizing of risks.
- *Assignment of responsibilities.* Individual specialist groups should be assigned responsibility for specific key objectives. That responsibility should include taking the lead position in accomplishing that objective, documenting the findings relevant to that objective of all team members, synthesizing those findings, and making recommendations for the postdiligence phase of the transaction. Exhibit 5.4 illustrates an approach to the assignment of strategic objectives to an appropriate functional team. The exhibit characterizes objectives in generic terms and is meant to provide general guidance. All transactions are different and the strategic objectives for any individual due diligence are specific to that transaction. That said, this illustration provides what we believe is a useful example of how responsibility among members of the due diligence team can be assigned.

EXHIBIT 5.4 Assignment of Due Diligence Objectives

Objective	Lead Specialists	Support Specialists	Comments
Confirmation of stand-alone potential	Sales and marketing	Finance and accounting	The extent to which the business can sustain stand-alone growth and profitability is a determination that is usually best made by the sales and marketing specialists on the team. Those specialists should opine on assumptions about the strength of product offerings and the business' ability to maintain sales volumes and pricing power in the face of competition. Financial specialists should play a strong supporting role in challenging underlying assumptions and in modeling past and future performance.
Validation of revenue synergies	Sales and marketing	R&D, production, finance, and accounting	Revenue synergies generally fall within the purview of the sales and marketing function. These synergies are usually the product of complementary capabilities, possessed by the target company and the acquirer, that would expand or deepen market penetration. Sales and marketing reviewers are usually in the best position to validate assumptions about the revenue potential associated with such capabilities. The input of other functions in the product development and delivery continuum, such as R&D and production, should also be provided. The finance and accounting team should also play important role in challenging growth assumptions and modeling projections.

Validation of expense synergies	Operations	Expense synergies generally result from the elimination of redundancies. Redundancies generally take the form of personnel and facilities duplication. These redundancies are usually in multiple functions throughout the company. The operations specialists on the due diligence team are generally the most appropriate choice to take the lead in this area. This is particularly the case because they will almost certainly be in a lead position in developing and executing the resulting integration plan. Key support should come from production, HR, accounting and finance, and any other area for which there are anticipated expense synergies.
	Production, HR, finance, and accounting	
Coordination of systems integration	IT	Information system or IT function supports virtually every individual function or department in most organizations. In addition, cross-company information technology systems, such as networks, permeate the typical business environment. Although these systems support the activities of these various functions, they themselves are typically supported by a central IT function. The IT specialists on the team are invariably the clear choice to champion the integration of the acquirer and target company systems. However, their efforts must be closely coordinated with all elements of the due diligence team.
	Specialists in all functions affected	

(Continued)

EXHIBIT 5.4 Assignment of Due Diligence Objectives (*Continued*)

Objective	Lead Specialists	Support Specialists	Comments
Coordination of nonsystems integration	Operations	Specialists in all functions affected	There are a wide variety of nonsystems integration initiatives that must be addressed postacquisition. The operations specialist on the team will generally be the manager tasked with implementing these initiatives. Accordingly, the operational specialists should be assigned responsibility for coordinating the due diligence discovery aspect of that effort with all reviewers of affected areas.
Assessment of cultural integration risks	Human resources	Due diligence team leaders	Cultural integration is clearly the domain of HR specialists. They are best equipped to evaluate the risks and options associated with this aspect of the review. In doing so, they would need the input of a wide variety of other team members and their findings should be thoroughly discussed with and evaluated by the due diligence team leaders.
Assessment of transaction risk	Finance and accounting	Legal, insurance	There are a wide range of transaction risks that may arise throughout the diligence process. The finance and accounting specialists are natural leads in collecting, assessing, documenting, and quantifying the potential impact of these risks. Legal and insurance, and other specialists who identify risks, should provide perspectives and input.

CONCLUSION

This chapter has presented an approach to due diligence that recognizes the natural constraints on that process and optimizes the efforts of those conducting the review in light of those constraints. A diligence review is constrained by time, resources, and the predisposition of the seller. Neither buyer nor seller is willing to commit to an open-ended process that will tie up valuable resources and disrupt the operation of the respective companies. These constraints place a premium on planning (described in Chapter 4) and purposeful execution, the central topic of this chapter. We believe that the most effective use of time and resources by a buyer is the implementation of an objectives-driven approach, one that is:

- Intensely focused on the issues of greatest impact on the valuation
- Informed by a thorough understanding of the business, its operation, and its markets
- Buttressed by cross-functional cooperation among team members

Key Points

1. The sale process is influenced by the type of transaction the seller wishes to employ. The objectives of the seller determine whether the business will be sold via an auction or some sort of preemptive bid. ("Overview of Transaction Types")

2. The characteristics of different types of transactions (auctions or preemptive bids) influence the conduct of the due diligence review. Leverage shifts between seller and buyer and can result in a more or less restrictive review, depending on the nature of the transaction. ("Summary of Transaction Characteristics")

3. The due diligence review has two primary components: interactive discussion between the due diligence team and the management team responsible for the business being sold; and a detailed review of the target company's business, legal, and financial documents. The diligence process should be approached with the intent of continually narrowing its focus as the review proceeds—initially casting its net broadly to ensure it has a fundamentally sound understanding of the business, but quickly

homing in on issues of greatest strategic importance. ("Components of a Due Diligence Review")

4. Information technology enables buyers to enhance the efficiency of their due diligence review. It enables those in remote locations with specialized skills to participate. However, that efficiency can come at the price of reduced effectiveness if behavior is compartmentalized and cross-functional exchanges are limited. ("Technology Trade-Offs")

5. There are natural constraints on time, access, and resources inherent in the due diligence review process. Therefore, the review should be highly focused and a preponderance of time and resources should be dedicated to confirming assumptions and assessing risks that may impact the value creation potential of the transaction. ("Due Diligence Reviews: An Objectives-Driven Approach")

6. The issue of postacquisition integration permeates M&A transactions, presents risks at multiple levels, and should be considered in virtually every aspect of the review. Given the pervasive nature of integration issues, all members of the team should incorporate steps to evaluate integration risk into their reviews. ("Integration")

APPENDIX 5A: ILLUSTRATIVE FINAL PROCESS LETTER OUTLINE

This document is provided for illustrative purposes. It provides an overview of the procedures for the second round of an auction process. It also provides guidance for the contents of the "best and final" offer of those bidders that will participate.

Invitation

Broker is inviting recipients to participate in the second and final round of the process for the sale of [Selling Corporation's] ___ business unit.

Description of Transaction Process

The selected parties will be provided access to due diligence materials and sent a draft purchase agreement to enable them to formulate their final proposals. Due diligence will include meetings with management and access to a data room that will contain customary financial, operational, and legal information. [At the end of a defined time period], potential acquirers will be asked to submit final proposals including a copy of the draft purchase agreement marked up to show requested changes. Final offers should be submitted [when] [how] [to whom].

Guidelines for Final Offers

- *Best and final offer.* Offers should be best and final. Bidders should not expect to have an opportunity to revise the offer, though the Broker may contact them to seek clarifications or revisions to the offer.
- *Purchase price.* Fixed price for 100 percent interest in the [assets or stock].
- *Purchase agreement mark-ups.* Offers should be accompanied by a copy of the purchase agreement that was distributed by the Selling Corporation, marked up to show any requested changes.
- *Financing.* State sources and confirm that the deal has been financed without any remaining contingencies.

APPENDIX 5B: ILLUSTRATIVE DATA ROOM INFORMATION LISTING

This document is provided for illustrative purposes. It is not meant to be comprehensive. It identifies the major categories of potential data room documents, but the actual data provided in the data room is dependent upon the specifics of the transaction being executed, particularly the nature of the business being divested.

Financial Data
- Historical financial statements
- Management reports (monthly, quarterly, and annual)
- Accounting policies
- Internal control processes and related documentation
- Budgets
- Budget versus actual reports and analysis
- Tax returns

- Bank statements and reconciliations for major bank accounts
- Accounts receivable and aging information
- Inventory records
- Fixed asset records
- Analysis of trade accounts payable and accrued expenses
- Analysis and support for other material asset or liability accounts
- Support for bank loans or other third-party debt
- Carve-out audit
- Bridge schedules (analysis of differences between audited and pro-forma financials)

Product/Service Information
- Product/service descriptions
- Product/service sales histories
- Product and product line P&Ls

Intellectual Property Information (Actual and In-process)
- Copyrights
- Trademarks and service marks
- Patents
- Internet domains

Legal Matters
- Customer agreements
- Supplier agreements
- Lease agreements and amendments
- Contractor agreements
- Agent agreements
- Employee agreements (employment, severance, and incentive)
- Proof of ownership of material assets
- Resolved, threatened, or pending litigation
- Any communication regarding noncompliance with laws or governmental regulations

Insurance Information
- Details of insurance coverage
- History of insurance claims
- Workers' compensation reports

Sales and Marketing Information
- Description of sales and marketing process
- Description of sales and marketing department (headcount and responsibilities)
- Documentation of agreements with agents, resellers, and distributors
- Monthly sales by product (units and dollars)
- Reports on sales by channel
- List of top XX customers
- Analysis by sales by geographic region
- Descriptions of pricing and discounting policies
- Marketing budgets for last three years

Customer Service Information
- Customer information and order system description
- Customer inquiry and complaint database
- Customer surveys for the last X years

Employee Matters
- Current organization chart
- Copies of position descriptions
- Salary, bonus, profit sharing, and merit increase information
- Sales compensation plans
- Details of employee benefits and retirement plans
- Company policies for vacation, sickness, bereavement, work schedules, and performance reviews
- Quantification of accrued leave time
- Terminations for cause within the last five years
- Retention agreements

Information Systems Information
- Listing of major information system providers and vendors
- Detailed description of phone system
- Detailed description of all major information systems hardware and software (data centers e-mail, network, accounting, customer service, production, sales, CIM)

Real Estate and Facilities
- Listing of all business locations

- Size of facility, business units, or functions supported
- Ownership status or lease terms
- Key vendors and contract terms

R&D Information
- Major research projects for the last X years
- Products/services presently under consideration for development
- Product plans and designs presently under development
- Competitive tracking information

CHAPTER 6

Reporting on Due Diligence

Deliverables and Decisions

INTRODUCTION

In discussing the results of the due diligence review, we return to the exhibit that illustrates the relationship between the organization's plan to create value and the findings and recommendations that result from the review (see Exhibit 6.1). The plan to create value establishes the strategic purpose of the acquisition and identifies potential risks and the assumed value drivers of the transaction. The diligence review is designed to confirm, validate, or modify those assumptions and risks and present findings and recommendations regarding the potential transaction. Those findings and recommendations then become the basis for the acquiring organization's decisions and action plans. This chapter describes the form for reporting findings and recommendations, and discusses the decisions that the prospective acquirer makes based on the results of the due diligence review.

Outcomes of the Due Diligence Review

The due diligence review can result in a number of outcomes. In an auction sale, a potential acquirer may simply be an unsuccessful bidder that is eliminated from the field of potential buyers. In other situations the prospective acquirer may discover during the review that the transaction presents an unacceptable level of risk or it was based on seriously flawed assumptions—discoveries that are material enough to cause the acquirer to disengage from the transaction. In yet other circumstances, the acquiring company may identify serious risks or inaccuracies in its assumptions

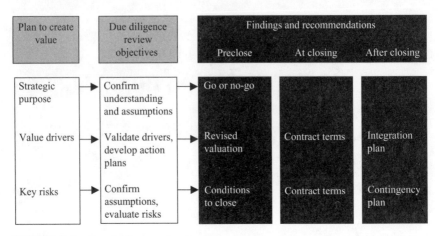

EXHIBIT 6.1 Due Diligence Continuum

that impair the target's perceived value, necessitating the renegotiation of purchase price and/or other basic terms of the transaction. Finally, the review may result in a recommendation to proceed to the contract negotiation stage. This does not mean that no impediments exist to finalizing a deal; it means that the acquisition team believes any issues it has identified can be negotiated as part of the purchase agreement. It also means there is a high probability that a transaction allowing the organization to realize its value creation objectives can be consummated. These outcomes and their accompanying outputs are the topics discussed in the rest of this chapter.

The Importance of Backup Planning

In Chapter 2, we outlined a strategic assessment process that we believe establishes the foundation for an effective value creation plan. It links an organization's growth strategy to its investment objectives and those objectives to the choice of the most appropriate investment vehicles for accomplishing those objectives. That choice is typically made after a thorough comparative analysis; that is, the organization evaluates alternative investment initiatives—whether it is better to build, buy, or ally—and arrives at what it believes is the optimal choice. This evaluative process not only provides the organization with the framework for a sound investment strategy, it also establishes the basis for nimble backup planning in the event factors emerge that require course correction.

As discussed, if an organization identifies an acquisition as the best vehicle to accomplish certain of its investment objectives, it should not turn a blind eye toward other alternatives that had been considered during the assessment process. Acquisitions, after all, are not pursued in a static environment. Transactions may be derailed in the bidding stage of an auction-based sale (an eventuality discussed in detail in "The No-Go Decision"). Also, in the course of a transaction, perhaps during due diligence, information may come to light about the target company and its market that alters the acquiring company's perspective on the pending deal. Therefore, it is important that the acquirer revisit its alternatives to the acquisition when a transaction is terminated or if there are major changes in its view of the risks and opportunities associated with it. If the transaction is derailed, the organization should be positioned to consider its next-best alternative to accomplish the investment objective(s) underlying the transaction.

Not only does a backup plan provide the organization with its next-best option in the event that the transaction being pursued doesn't materialize, it also provides the organization with a negotiating benchmark if it decides to proceed. Absent alternatives, the acquiring company is left with a binary go/no-go decision. This can result in extraordinary pressure to get a deal—even a bad deal—done. As discussed in "The No-Go Decision," the initiation of an acquisition transaction results in a process and environment that can make withdrawal a difficult decision. If the organization has an alternative vehicle to accomplish its investment objective, clear-eyed assessment is considerably easier when important assumptions are called into question or unacceptable risks are identified. In the following sections of this chapter, the desirability of having a backup plan is further discussed in the context of the scenarios described earlier in "Outcomes of the Due Diligence Review."

ELIMINATION IN THE AUCTION PROCESS

As described in Chapter 5, the auction process is a competitive one that typically involves a number of potential buyers. Only one aspiring acquirer emerges from that process. All other bidders, having made their best and final offers, will have been eliminated from the process and will then have to determine how to proceed. That decision will largely be driven by a company's approach to the transaction, specifically, whether the transaction was approached from an opportunistic or a strategic perspective.

If the approach was opportunistic, the organization will have been focused on the acquisition of a *company* and the follow-on decision-making process is very likely to be binary. The acquisition effort was unsuccessful, so the acquisition team would disengage and inform the appropriate executives within its corporate hierarchy that their company had been eliminated from the process. Under these circumstances, the unsuccessful acquirer is left with a failed transaction and little else. Any assessment of alternatives is likely to occur after the fact. However, if the decision to pursue the acquisition was rooted in the company's strategic planning process, the acquisition is more likely to have been sought because it possessed strategically desirable *capabilities*, not just because a seemingly attractive company suddenly became available. In addition, in advance of the transaction, the company would have evaluated all options available to it (i.e., internal development, partnering with a strategic ally, or even other potential acquisitions) to add those capabilities. That evaluation provides the basis for a backup plan in the event the acquisition did not materialize.

Outputs/Reports

When a company is eliminated from an auction process, the acquisition team reports that information through the transaction sponsor (e.g., the operating division's CEO) to the corporate decision makers. Much of the information provided in such a report will be known by the transaction sponsor, since he or she would have been closely monitoring the progress of the transaction and have been intimately involved in the related decision-making process. This report would also provide the corporate hierarchy, who are removed from the details of the acquisition, with an explanation of how and why involvement was terminated. In doing so, it is also advisable to provide an outline of the plans of the company in the wake of the unsuccessful transaction. Such a report enables knowledge transfer (clear communication of all the relevant facts and circumstances to present and future interested parties) and provides an end point for the deal.

The report should provide an overview of the transaction process, a discussion of the underlying valuation and its drivers, as well as a discussion of the company's bid (i.e., how it arrived at its upper limit on price). It might also provide preliminary observations about the winning bidder, if known, and the impact that this acquisition may have on the market and its own business. An outline of such a report appears in Exhibit 6.2. As noted, the organization should also provide its corporate parent with its

EXHIBIT 6.2 Report Outline: Elimination from an Auction

Introduction
- A statement that the company has been eliminated from the bidding process for (name) Company in a competitive auction process
- An indication that the company bid (amount) based on its valuation and found it inadvisable to increase that bid in light of due diligence performed

Background
- Brief description of (name) Company
- A description of the strategic rationale for the pursuit of the transaction
- A description of the specific synergies and benefits assumed

Description of Due Diligence
- Identification of those who performed due diligence
- A summary of the procedures performed
- An indication of when and where the review took place

Factors Influencing Final Bid
- The fundamental soundness of the business or lack thereof
- The potential for synergistic benefits
- The major risks that would have to be mitigated

Market and Competitive Impact
- The effect of the elimination on acquirer's market position
- The impact of the prospective transaction on competitive structure of the market

Backup Plan
- An explanation of if and how the capability gap left by the failed transaction would be filled
- A description of the options available (i.e., either build, buy, or ally) to fill that gap
- A determination of whether it is more desirable to pivot to another investment objective that offers better potential to increase shareholder value

planned response to having been unable to acquire the company in question. This is especially the case if the corporate organization was provided a compelling rationale for the transaction, to justify a significant investment. By implication at least, the acquisition would have been framed in terms of an important, if not critical, need. If the acquisition effort failed, the natural question the corporate parent would pose is: What is the company going to do to fill that important or critical need? This suggests that, at the corporate level, there is the expectation of some degree of backup planning on the part of its operating company management. As noted in "The Importance of Backup Planning," if the decision to acquire is based on a thoughtful strategic assessment process, alternative initiatives will have been considered during that process. More specifically, the acquisition would have been measured against other options, such as internal development, strategic alliances, or even alternative acquisitions. Or the organization may have considered the acquisition a unique opportunity and, if it did not materialize, that the next-best alternative would be to focus on a different investment objective. In any event, the analysis associated with that strategic assessment provides a good basis for the development of a backup plan in the event the acquisition gets derailed.

THE NO-GO DECISION

The no-go scenario is one in which the due diligence team discovers during its review that the transaction presents an unacceptable level of risk or that its value creation plan was based on seriously flawed assumptions, or both. As a result, the team would have disengaged from the transaction after having made its case and gotten the concurrence of the transaction sponsor.

There is a strong relationship between the potential for a transaction to be derailed in this manner (i.e., a flat-out no-go decision) and the level of pre-transaction planning and candidate evaluation. If the transaction was rooted in a proactive approach such as described in Chapter 3, the prospective acquirer is likely to have had the benefit of prereview analysis and is less prone to enter into a transaction that did not meet its expectations. Although a transaction that is seller-driven and is reactive in nature is by no means guaranteed to result in a no-go decision, it is considerably more likely than one that is based on proactive pursuit. In any event, when the due diligence team reaches the conclusion that the transaction process should be terminated, it should recommend withdrawal, and do so in a decisive manner.

As we have noted, acquisition transactions take on a life of their own. Individuals and organizations become invested in them and that investment manifests itself in the form of enthusiastic support, optimistic expectations, and broad-based company involvement: (1) A decision would have been considered and made at the executive level of the company pursuing the transaction; (2) corporate approval had probably been sought and given; (3) a cross-functional team would have been formed and deployed at some significant cost (both actual expense and opportunity cost) to the organization; and (4) expectations at various levels of the overall organization would have been raised. As a result, many of the forces at work would mitigate against "pulling the plug" on the transaction. Regardless, the acquisition team should have the discipline to recommend, quickly and unequivocally, that the process be discontinued if obvious "deal killers" have surfaced during the review. Any temptation to continue the review and to justify the transaction is usually a triumph of hope over good judgment and should be strongly resisted. Prior staging and evaluation efforts should be seen for what they are—sunk costs—and expectations should be dealt with sooner rather than later, before further expenditure of time and resources are incurred.

No-Go Discoveries

The discoveries that can trigger a decision by the due diligence team to disengage are specific to a given transaction. However, typical deal-breaking issues can generally be categorized as strategic, valuation, or risk issues.

Strategic Issues   These issues relate to situations where the acquirer's central strategic assumption driving the acquisition proves to be inaccurate. The acquirer's plan to create value is generally based on a belief that the target company possesses strategically important capabilities that will enable the combined business to result in a sum that is greater than its parts. For example, this might take the form of complementing the acquirer's product development prowess with the superior distribution capability of the target or complementing the acquirer's market position and brand strength with the target's superior processing capabilities. If the due diligence team determines that assumptions about the target company's capabilities are largely inaccurate or unrealistic, the primary rationale for the transaction would be irretrievably undermined and the team would recommend withdrawal from the transaction.

Valuation Issues Valuation issues that can derail a transaction arise when the acquirer realizes that the transaction is unlikely to create value and, in fact, is more likely to destroy value. At the margins, there is often ample room for renegotiation when the diligence team realizes that growth and profitability assumptions are too aggressive. However, there are situations where these assumptions prove to be so aggressive as to lead to the conclusion that "One just can't get there from here." Examples of such situations are discussed in the following:

- *Historical growth or margins, as represented by the seller, are not supported by the data.* This situation can arise if the review team discovers that the business has been packaged for sale and that historical margins and growth are overstated when they are closely scrutinized. That realization can result from a number of factors. As a result of its quality of earnings assessment, the team may conclude that unsustainable below-market costs (e.g., labor costs or owner manager compensation) or expense recognition policies have masked the true historical expense run rate and overstated margins. Similarly, historical top-line growth may not withstand close scrutiny. Extraordinary items or revenue recognition policies may have overstated revenue growth and operating margins, altering baseline assumptions and future projections of growth and profitability.

  In other cases, upon close scrutiny, the due diligence team may discover that overall market growth is slowing at an unanticipated rate, due to factors such as demographic, regulatory, or technological change. This may occur when the acquisition involves a company in an unfamiliar market, one that is tangential or new to the acquiring company. Because of that unfamiliarity, the market weakness may have gone undetected until the due diligence team got deeply involved in its review.

  If any of these factors materially affect underlying assumptions about the stand-alone potential of the business, they may substantially alter the acquirer's valuation and seriously undermine its value creation plan. When that is the case, the acquirer is generally well advised to disengage.
- *The absence of anticipated synergies.* The value creation plans of an acquirer are strongly, if not primarily, influenced by assumptions about some combination of the revenue and expense synergies that the

transaction can yield. When those assumptions are seriously called into question, the acquirer will often have no choice but to withdraw from the transaction.

Insofar as revenue synergies are concerned, the due diligence team may discover that assumed synergies are impeded by unforeseen factors such as contested ownership rights, the nontransferability of important customer contracts, or the recent loss of a major customer or customers. With regard to ownership, assumptions about revenue synergies may be based on the belief that the target company owns the rights to intellectual property that will enable rapid and effective product development or to a process that will enable significant cost reduction. As far as customer relationships are concerned, the loss of a major account or accounts can not only create basic revenue and profitability shortfalls, they may seriously impair the ability of the acquirer to leverage customer relationships and impede the exploitation of assumed revenue synergies. If the value creation plan hinges on such assumptions, and those assumption prove to be inaccurate, the ability to create value may be seriously impeded.

The due diligence team may also find that assumptions about expense synergies prove to be flawed or invalid. Items such as union contracts that inhibit the ability of the acquirer to eliminate redundancies, prohibitive lease terms that do not allow for the elimination of unnecessary facilities costs, or supplier agreements that have locked in unfavorable operating costs can materially impact expense synergy potential. While any one of these items may not be sufficient to materially impact an acquirer's value creation plan, in combination with other factors, they can constitute an impediment to the attainability of that plan.

Risk Issues   Occasionally, a due diligence review may uncover an unacceptable level of unanticipated risk. Examples of situations in which this can be the case are discussed in the following paragraphs.

- *Irreconcilable management issues.* Deal-breaking management issues can take a number of forms. Occasionally, the management styles and personalities of the two organizations may simply be incompatible. In the due diligence stage of the transaction, it may become apparent that personality differences or the cultural divide is unbridgeable. Or, the principals or executives of the target company may be rigid or

contentious and clearly resistant to the type of change necessary to realize synergistic potential. Evidence of these types of issues can frequently
be identified in the review process. A lack of cooperation, an unwillingness to respond to reasonable requests for information, or, worse yet,
factual misrepresentations are troublesome indicators for postacquisition behavior. If the cooperation of these individuals is necessary for an
extended transition period, the due diligence team may conclude that
it would not be possible to integrate the new business or that the risks
associated with that integration (in the form of business disruption, employee confusion, and lost revenue and unrealized efficiencies) would
be too great to bear.

Similarly, the due diligence team may conclude that the involvement of the target company management team would be critical to the
successful integration of the companies, but the management team is
weak and not up to the task of leading and managing that effort. This
is a particular risk in situations where the business being acquired is a
segment of a larger business (i.e., when the transaction involves a corporate divestiture). In such situations, the seller may be predisposed to
retain that business' strongest managers and divest the segment led by
a weakened executive team.

Unacceptable risk may also be encountered when the business being
sold has not lined up key revenue generators, such as salespeople, with
retention plans. If there is evidence that such key personnel have, or are
likely to, defected to a competitor, assumptions about growth may be
seriously flawed. This is a particular problem if the target company is a
service business that relies on strong personal relationships.

■ *The inability of the business to function as a stand-alone entity.* More
than one-third of M&A transactions involve corporate divestitures, that
is, sales of a segment (such as a subsidiary, a division, or a product line)
of a larger corporate entity. These types of transactions can introduce
a level of complexity and risk not experienced when an entire enterprise is sold. That complexity and associated risk stems from the fact
that the property being sold may not be a stand-alone business. These
transactions commonly involve businesses that have received infrastructure support (typically, in the areas of accounting, human resource,
and information technology) from the larger corporate entity or parent
organization that is the seller in the transaction. As a result, the business being sold may not have the ability to function as an independent,
stand-alone entity. In many instances, the acquirer will have the ability

to fill those gaps. However, there are circumstances in which the absence of sufficient infrastructure poses a substantial risk to the buyer. This might include situations where the business to be acquired is large in relation to the acquirer, or located remotely or in another country. In such cases, the due diligence team may conclude that the level of risk is unacceptably high and may recommend disengagement from the transaction.

Outputs/Reports

When the due diligence team identifies risks it deems unacceptably high or factors that are inconsistent with prereview assumptions about profitability, growth, or overall organizational compatibility, it formally reports its findings and recommendations to the transaction sponsor who, in turn, uses it to inform the appropriate individuals in the corporate chain of command. Team leaders and the sponsor will have undoubtedly been in close contact and the decision to disengage would have ultimately been that of the transaction sponsor. However, it falls to the due diligence team leaders to provide the document outlining the original rationale for pursuing the transaction, the reasons for withdrawing, and any related action plans going forward.

The resulting report should provide background on the transaction, specifically the going-in assumptions that were anticipated to drive value creation. It should also summarize the measures taken by the due diligence team to evaluate the candidate company and to validate assumptions and identify any unanticipated risks. It should then provide its findings and recommendations, specifically identifying the nature and impact of the factors that it believes were serious enough to derail the transaction. In addition, and as noted in the discussion of deals terminated as a result of elimination from an auction sale (see the section "Elimination in the Auction Process"), the report should include a discussion of alternative courses of action to fill the capability need (either explicitly detailed or implied) to pursue the failed transaction. Exhibit 6.3 contains an outline of a model report.

RENEGOTIATIONS OF MAJOR TERMS

It is not uncommon for the due diligence team to identify serious risks or inaccuracies in its assumptions that may not rise to the level to justify

EXHIBIT 6.3   Report Outline: Decision to Withdraw

Introduction
- A statement that the company has decided to terminate the pursuit of the acquisition of (name) Company
- An explanation of the rationale for withdrawal

Background
- Brief description of (name) Company
- A description of the strategic rationale for the pursuit of the transaction
- A description of the specific synergies and benefits assumed.

Description of Due Diligence
- Identification of those who performed due diligence
- A summary of the procedures performed
- An indication of when and where the review took place

Factors Influencing Withdrawal
- The fundamental soundness of the business or lack thereof
- The potential for synergistic benefits
- The major risks that would be incurred

Market and Competitive Impact
- The effect of withdrawal on acquirer's market position
- The impact of withdrawal on the competitive structure of the market

Backup Plan
- An explanation of if and how the capability gap left by the failed transaction would be filled
- A description of the options available (i.e., either build, buy, or ally) to fill that gap
- A determination of whether it is more desirable to pivot to another investment objective that offers better potential to increase shareholder value

outright withdrawal from the transaction. However, these risks and inaccuracies may be significant enough to necessitate renegotiation of some of the basic financial terms of the deal agreed to prior to the review. This includes renegotiation of purchase price, or the structure of the transaction (an asset versus a stock deal), or a contingent purchase price (i.e., an earn-out) to share originally unanticipated risk might be built into the deal.

The findings of the due diligence team prompting renegotiation may be similar in nature, but not degree, to those that trigger a withdrawal. For example, inherent growth rates or margins may have been modestly overstated or synergies may not be in the anticipated order of magnitude as originally projected or may be more difficult to extract than originally believed (and less timely in their execution). This type of situation may leave room for modification of terms that might be acceptable to the seller, yet sufficient to enable the buyer to meet its value creation objectives.

If the due diligence team identifies concerns that necessitate the renegotiation of basic deal terms, it should communicate those concerns to the transaction sponsor immediately. However, the appropriate timing of the initiation of discussions with the seller and its representatives is less obvious. While there are no guarantees that such discussions will result in finding common ground, the potential to do so would be sharply diminished if *all* salient issues did not surface in those discussions. To ensure they do, the team should identify all major issues before the transaction sponsor initiates or delegates the renegotiation process. Otherwise, the seller may perceive a series of negotiations that pick away at individual issues as a technique to whittle away at its position. In addition, the transaction sponsor and the acquisition team leaders should formulate their position on those issues in advance of those discussions and obtain corporate concurrence for the proposed restructured deal, if appropriate, before proceeding. Once there is internal concurrence on renegotiation positions, the outline of a new framework for the deal can be presented to the seller. Although this may not guarantee success, it is likely to expedite renegotiations and do so in the spirit of good faith.

Clearly, unsuccessful renegotiation can bring the transaction to an end. In contrast, successful renegotiation can be seen as a detour on the path toward consummation of the transaction. Obviously, there must be a willingness on the part of the seller to engage in renegotiations and ultimately accept new terms that enable the buyer to realize its value creation goals if the transaction process is to be put back on track. If agreement is reached on new basic terms, the transaction would proceed to the detailed negotiation stage (discussed in the section "Decision to Proceed to Contract Negotiations").

Outputs/Reports

Any effort to renegotiate terms of the transaction necessarily require the input and approval to do so by the transaction sponsor. If those efforts were unsuccessful, the due diligence team leader(s) would generally document the salient aspects of the failed transaction to establish a permanent and accurate record and may be used to communicate the transaction's termination to those in the corporate hierarchy. The resulting report is similar in content to that described in the "Outputs/Reports" section of "Elimination in the Auction Process" and "The No-Go Decision" and contains the following information:

- An *introduction* recommending the termination of the transaction
- *Background on the transaction,* specifically outlining the rationale for pursuing the acquisition
- A *summary of evaluative measures* taken by the due diligence team during their review
- The team's *findings and recommendations,* with particular attention to the nature and extent of the factors they determined were serious enough to bring the process to a close
- A description of any *efforts made to restructure the transaction* by the team, and the seller's response to those efforts
- A discussion of any potential *impact on the market and competition* of terminating the transaction
- A *backup plan* outlining the steps the acquiring organization intends to pursue to fill the strategic need that initiated the failed transaction

If renegotiation efforts appear to be successful, it may or may not be within the purview of the transaction sponsor to approve the renegotiated terms. In any event, the due diligence team leaders would draft an interim report that outlines the new terms of the transaction, along with a revised valuation model. These documents form the basis for communicating these new terms (and obtaining approval, if needed) to the appropriate individuals in the corporate hierarchy. This interim report provides an overview of the original terms of the transaction, the nature of the changes to those terms, the impact of those changes on valuation and on the plan to create value, and a recommendation or request for approval to proceed under these revised terms.

DECISION TO PROCEED

Frequently, a due diligence review results in a recommendation to proceed to the contract negotiation stage. This does not mean that there are no impediments to finalizing a deal. It simply means that the acquisition team believes that there is a high probability of being able to negotiate a contract and finalize a deal that would allow the organization to realize its investment objective(s). In fact, the fieldwork performed by the due diligence team will have undoubtedly uncovered numerous items that are called out in their report that should be addressed in the preclosing, contract, and postacquisition phases that follow. These items are discussed in detail in Chapters 7 and 8.

Outputs/Reports

A successful due diligence review, that is, one that results in a recommendation to proceed, will generate a number of documents that shape transaction decision making, negotiations, and postacquisition planning. These include:

- A comprehensive due diligence report
- A summary due diligence report
- A corporate approval document
- An integration plan
- A contingency plan

These documents are described in detail in this section.

In addition, it is also important that those who will be handling negotiations be armed with a backup plan; that is, a plan that provides a benchmark against which the benefits of the transaction can be compared. As noted in "The Importance of Backup Planning" section such a plan describes the next-best alternative to the pending transaction. As negotiations proceed, such an alternative establishes boundaries for the terms of that transaction. Without those boundaries, the negotiators would be left with a simple go/no-go decision, one that can have a material impact on negotiating leverage.

Comprehensive Due Diligence Report   The reviewers should produce a full, detailed, and complete report that contains a record of all fieldwork and analysis performed and conclusions reached. The size of that report can vary, depending on the size and complexity of the business being reviewed, but will be voluminous, and in hard-copy form would consist of binders containing work papers, exhibits, spreadsheets, analysis, observations, commentary, and recommendations. The very extensive and detailed nature of the report makes it very unlikely that most interested parties will read it cover to cover. It serves more as a reference document that various interested parties (such as negotiators and line managers involved in postacquisition integration) may access to get specific information. Senior executives will almost undoubtedly rely on abbreviated versions of this report (discussed here) or approval documents (discussed in the next section) that contain distilled versions of the information presented in summary form (the *summary due diligence report*) or in the broader context of the entire transaction (the *approval document*).

Summary Due Diligence Report   The summary report should provide the reader with an overview of the process, its major findings, conclusions relative to the review's objectives, and a recommendation to proceed with the acquisition. The summary report should be directed at the transaction sponsor as well as any other individuals in the corporate hierarchy who have approval authority, or who have input to the approval process (e.g., corporate financial or business development professionals staff), for the transaction. An annotated outline recommending the form and content of the summary report appears in Exhibit 6.4 and a description follows.

- *Background and introduction.* This section of the report should discuss the circumstances leading up to the acquisition, the value creation opportunity the acquisition presents, and the terms under which the organization proceeds with the transaction. Frequently, those who have the approval authority or input to the approval process are not close to the transaction. In large corporations there are generally many initiatives being considered by these individuals, so the document should provide sufficient context for these individuals to evaluate the merits of the transaction.
- *Due diligence team.* This section should describe the makeup of the due diligence team and team member review responsibilities. This information provides insight into the coverage and quality, as well as the credibility, of the review.

EXHIBIT 6.4 Report Outline: Summary Due Diligence

Background and Introduction
- A description of circumstances leading up to the pursuit of the acquisition
- A description of the business being pursued
- A brief description of the value creation opportunity the acquisition presents

The Due Diligence Team
- A listing of those who participated in due diligence
- An account of team member responsibilities and qualifications
- An explanation of the involvement of specialists (e.g., local counsel for a cross-border transaction) or significant external resources (e.g., an accounting firm)

Due Diligence Objectives
- An articulation of the primary objectives of the review
- A discussion of major assumptions that were validated or modified
- A discussion of major exposures revealed

The Review Process
- An indication of when and where the review was performed
- Commentary on the quality of the information provided
- An indication of the level of cooperation of the seller
- An assessment of the effectiveness of the review

Major Findings
- A declarative indication of whether there were any issues uncovered that would preclude moving forward with the transaction
- The review team's assessment of the quality of the business
- The review team's assessment of the quality of the management team
- Identification of major items that must be addressed prior to closing and in the definitive purchase agreement
- Identification of major items that must be addressed subsequent to closing

Conclusions
- A declarative indication that the acquirer should proceed with efforts to acquire the business, subject to satisfactory resolution of key issues identified in the team's findings

- *Due diligence objectives.* This section should articulate the primary objectives of the review and the areas of opportunity and risk on which the review focused. Material opportunities, such as revenue and expense synergies, and major exposures, such as integration risk, should be thoroughly discussed.
- *Review process.* This section should indicate when and where the review was performed. It should comment on the quality of the information supplied by the target company and indicate the level of cooperation of management. And it should comment on the effectiveness of the review; that is, that all major issues were addressed to the satisfaction of the review team.
- *Major findings.* This section should identify those issues that came to light that must be addressed before moving forward with the acquisition. Findings should also include observations about the inherent quality of the business and the quality of its management. Whereas the comprehensive report described above will detail all findings of any significance, this document should focus on those major issues that should be addressed before, during, and after contract negotiations.
- *Conclusions.* This section should contain a recommendation to proceed with efforts to acquire the business, qualified by the need for satisfactory resolution of key issues identified in the *findings* section of the document.

Corporate Approval Document   In addition to the due diligence report, those leading the acquisition process normally draft a final report (sometimes referred to as a board paper, because it is the document sent to the board of directors for final approval in some organizations), to obtain formal approval to negotiate and execute definitive agreements to consummate the acquisition. This paper is an enhanced and updated version of the document drafted to support the initial decision to pursue the acquisition (i.e., the position paper described in Chapter 3). This document contains an extensive discussion of all important aspects of the transaction and should indicate whether and to what extent the preliminary assumptions relative to risk and opportunity were validated or modified. The written document (outlined in Exhibit 6.5) contains a discussion of the following items:

- *An executive summary.* This should be a synopsis of the key points covered in the body of the document and, if appropriate, a request for

EXHIBIT 6.5 Report Outline: Corporate Approval Document

Executive Summary
- A synopsis of key points covered in the body of this document
- Brief indication of the target company's market position and capabilities
- Linkage of the acquisition to growth strategy
- Indication of recommended purchase price, structure of the transaction, and comparable transaction metrics, if available
- A declarative indication that the acquirer should proceed with efforts to acquire the business, subject to satisfactory resolution of key issues identified in the team's findings

Business, Organization, and Management
- A brief overview of the business
- Size
- Recent history
- Ownership structure
- Significant principals
- Location(s)
- A description of its major products and services

The Due Diligence Team
- A listing of those who participated in due diligence
- An account of team member responsibilities and qualifications
- An explanation of the involvement of specialists (e.g., local counsel for a cross-border transaction) or significant external resources (e.g., an accounting firm)

Strategic Rationale
- A discussion of the link between the target company, the acquirer's investment objectives, and growth strategy
- A discussion of major assumptions that were validated or modified in due diligence
- A discussion of major exposures revealed in due diligence and the manner in which they would be mitigated

Market and Competition
- A description and sizing of the relevant market segment(s)
- A characterization of the forces driving the market segment(s)
- A description of the segment(s) growth and profitability characteristics
- Identification of major or emerging competitors in the segment(s)
- A discussion of how the transaction may reshape the market

(*Continued*)

EXHIBIT 6.5 Report Outline: Corporate Approval Document (*Continued*)

Business Infrastructure
- A description of key aspects of infrastructure support specific to industry (e.g., technology, manufacturing capabilities, distribution capabilities)
- An assessment of the adequacy of the target company's infrastructure support to maintain competitive standing

The Due Diligence Review
- A brief description of the due diligence review process
- Highlights of the findings and recommendations resulting from the due diligence review
- Reference to the Summary Due Diligence Report and the Comprehensive Due Diligence Report for additional detail

Postacquisition Integration
- A brief account of the salient points of the Integration Plan [key milestones]
- Reference to the complete Integration Plan for addition detail

Financial Discussion
- A description and quantification of the historical financial performance of the business
- Projections of postacquisition revenue, expense, profitability, and cash conversion
- A discussion of purchase price, deal structure, and anticipated returns

Valuation
- A discussion of the assumptions and methodology used to arrive at the valuation that supports the purchase price
- A discussion of upside and downside valuations based on more optimistic and more conservative growth and profitability assumptions, respectively

Other Options Considered
- A discussion of other investment options (build, ally, or alternative acquisitions) considered
- The rationale for pursuing the acquisition under discussion

approval to proceed. It should establish the link between the acquirer's strategic plan and the capability gap that the target company will fill. It should also characterize the target company's position in the market and its key capabilities, as well as the synergistic benefits it will provide. Finally, it should identify the nature of the transaction (i.e., whether a stock or asset purchase) and the purchase price recommended. If available, that purchase price should be supported by comparable multiples from other, like transactions.

- *The business and its organization and management.* This section of the document should provide a snapshot of the business, its history, its ownership structure, its major principals, and location(s), as well as a brief description of its major products and services.

- *The strategy underlying the acquisition.* This is the place in the document that the link between the company and its capabilities is made to the acquiring company's growth strategy and investment objectives.

- *The market and competition.* This section should describe the market in which the target company operates, and its drivers, and its growth and profitability characteristics. In addition, it should provide an overview of the major competitors and the position of the target company in that market, as well as how the combination will enable market penetration.

- *Key infrastructure elements supporting the business.* In many industries, the supporting infrastructure of a company should be measured against standards within those industries. In industries such as communications, information, and entertainment, technology capabilities are often of paramount importance. In manufacturing industries, state-of-the-art processes and supporting assets may be critical. Although the key supporting infrastructure may differ from industry to industry, they can be capabilities that are crucial to the maintenance of competitive advantage. To the extent that this applies to the target company, it should be fully discussed in this section.

- *The results of due diligence.* This section provides the highlights of the major findings and recommendations resulting from the due diligence review. It also references the due diligence review documents described above to provide addition detail.

- *The postacquisition integration plan.* This section outlines the integration plan developed as a result of the review. The elements of the plan are described next in "An Integration Plan"), and the plan itself is discussed in detail in Chapter 8.

- *The financial dynamics of the acquisition.* This section discusses the historical financial performance of the business and postacquisition projected revenue, expense, profitability, and cash conversion. It also discusses purchase price, deal structure, and anticipated returns.
- *Next-best option.* The document generally also contains a discussion of other investment options (build, ally, or alternative acquisitions) considered by the acquiring company, and the rationale for pursuing the acquisition under discussion.
- *The valuation analysis.* This discussion focuses on the assumptions and methodology used to arrive at the valuation that supports the purchase price. Many firms use a discounted cash flow model to determine value and rely on other metrics such as industry or recent transaction multiples of revenue and income to support their value. This section of the document generally also provides upside and downside valuations based on more optimistic and more conservative growth and profitability assumptions, respectively.

This report is used to obtain final approval to acquire, subject to finalization of open contract issues, and advance the process to the negotiation of the purchase agreement.

Integration Plan   Development of an integration plan is a central element of the due diligence review. Best practice strongly suggests that integration planning start well in advance of the due diligence review process, and substantially accelerate during that phase of the transaction. The rationale for this level of attention to integration is twofold. First, valuations rely heavily on the extraction of value from the synergies that result from the combination of buyer and seller. Failure to extract those benefits, or failure to do so in a timely manner, result in lost revenue, profit, and cash, and ultimately value. Second, integration is a complex process that requires extensive planning and effective execution. If planning is deferred until late in the transaction process, the likelihood of identifying difficult issues and challenges is substantially reduced. It is during the due diligence review that the acquirer is best able to unearth such issues and challenges.

Integration is discussed further in Chapter 8. The objective here is to highlight the most important aspects of the plan. It should:

- *Address the three major aspects of postacquisition integration.* These are operational integration, synergy-related integration (both revenue and expense), and cultural integration. These aspects of the integration process are discussed in Chapter 5 and further in Chapter 8.
- *Assign leadership responsibility.* There are a number of ways to approach the assignment of authority and responsibility for the integration process. Some large and acquisitive firms have gone so far as to assign an individual full-time responsibility for the integration process. This approach has merit if the organization has the resources to do so. In the absence of an integration "czar," the acquirer must select a number of individuals to manage distinct and separable aspects of the integration and ensure a mechanism exists to coordinate their efforts. These individuals must have the authority to make day-to-day decisions and the support of senior management within the sponsoring organization.
- *Clearly define objectives.* The objectives of the integration plan should be explicitly articulated and clearly understood by all those affected. In addition, the organization as a whole should understand the importance of those objectives. They are generally critical to creating value sufficient to justify the transaction.
- *Establish timelines and milestones.* In the integration business, an opportunity missed, more often than not, is an opportunity foregone. It is therefore imperative that deadlines are established for each specific initiative and that progress on those deadlines is tracked through a series of interim milestone accomplishments.
- *Establish feedback and reporting mechanisms.* Those in charge of various aspects of the integration effort should meet regularly with managers involved in the implementation of integration efforts and keep themselves apprised of developments. While missed milestones and deadlines should be considered major failings, those that are unanticipated or unexpected should be considered inexcusable. Those charged with integration management should also meet periodically with the transaction sponsor and report in detail on progress.

- *Establish a communication plan.* The postacquisition phase of a transaction (the first one to two years) can be a very traumatic period for
  employees. Positions are eliminated, many employees report to new
  superiors, and cultures clash. The period is marked by change and uncertainty. These factors naturally manifest themselves in the form of
  disruption and reduced productivity. The goal of the integration team
  should be to limit this uncertainty in both the duration and degree. A
  tool for doing so is a communication plan that ensures that employees
  are kept abreast of changes.

Contingency Plan　　We believe that a postacquisition contingency plan,
sometimes referred to as an *enterprise risk management plan*, should be
one of the deliverables of a review which results in a recommendation to
proceed with the transaction. A contingency plan provides the team's best
thinking about "over-the-horizon" potential changes in the business or the
market that could affect postacquisition performance of the combined entity, and measures to mitigate any associated risks. By their very nature
these items would be potential threats that are not imminent and may, in
fact, never materialize. The objective of the plan is to induce the organization to think outside the box to ensure that it has looked beyond what it
considers the most likely case scenario and that it is not caught flat footed
in the event one or more of these threats does materialize.

The contingency plan, discussed more fully in Chapter 8, includes consideration of some or all of the following items:

- Critical dependencies on vendors or business partners
- Concentration of customer base
- Seminal (emerging) competitive threats
- Potential weaknesses in internal processes
- Legal/regulatory developments

Key Points

1. The diligence review is designed to confirm, validate, or modify those
   assumptions and risks, and present findings and recommendations regarding the potential transaction. Those findings and recommendations

then become the basis for the acquiring organization's decisions and action plans. ("Introduction")

2. The due diligence review can result in a number of outcomes. The acquirer may be eliminated (in an auction), withdraw, renegotiate major terms of the transaction, or proceed to the contract negotiation stage. ("Outcomes of the Due Diligence Review")

3. The acquirer should routinely develop a backup plan in the event the transaction gets derailed. Such a plan also provides the acquirer with a negotiating benchmark if it decides to proceed. ("The Importance of Backup Planning")

4. The no-go scenario is one in which the due diligence team discovers during its review that the transaction presents an unacceptable level of risk or that its value creation plan was based on seriously flawed assumptions, or both. As a result, the team would have disengaged from the transaction after having made its case and gotten the concurrence of the transaction sponsor. ("The No-Go Decision")

5. It is not uncommon for the due diligence team to identify serious risks or inaccuracies in its assumptions that may not rise to the level to justify outright withdrawal from the transaction. However, these risks and inaccuracies would be deemed significant enough to necessitate renegotiation of some of the basic financial terms of the deal preliminarily agreed to prior to the review. ("Renegotiation of Major Terms")

6. Frequently, a due diligence review results in a recommendation to proceed to the contract negotiation stage. This does not mean that there are no impediments to finalizing a deal; it simply means that the acquisition team believes that there is a high probability of being able to negotiate a contract and finalize a deal that would allow the organization to realize its investment objective(s). ("Decision to Proceed to Contract Negotiations")

Three

Execution

CHAPTER 7

Optimizing Value

Translating Due Diligence Findings into Action

ACTING ON DUE DILIGENCE FINDINGS

Preacquisition vs. Postacquisition Issues

In Chapter 6, we addressed a range of potential outcomes and decisions facing the prospective acquirer following completion of its due diligence review, including the critical decision to terminate or continue acquisition discussions. We noted that a decision to continue discussions and proceed with the transaction does not signal a clear path to closing. Instead, it often requires the resolution of an array of issues identified during the due diligence review. This chapter presents options for dealing with those issues.

Typically, in the course of due diligence, exposures of various types and magnitudes are identified, and the prospective acquirer must address the more significant ones at some point. The nature of each due diligence finding dictates whether it is best addressed before or after the closing. For example, some findings may alter preestablished assumptions about future growth and profitability prospects and therefore affect the perceived value of the target business. Similarly, other issues might involve the discovery of legal or regulatory concerns that place the target business at risk for future liability. Issues such as these may result in the need to renegotiate the value, structure, or terms of the acquisition transaction. They would be assigned to the team charged with negotiating the definitive purchase agreements, which must obviously address them prior to the closing. Other issues, alternatively, may flag potential risks to the combination of the acquiring and acquired businesses. Those issues should be considered by a separate team tasked with the postacquisition integration and contingency planning.

The process of channeling the resolution of due diligence findings to preclosing or postclosing activities is illustrated in Exhibit 7.1. In this chapter we focus on the preclosing tasks and issues confronting the acquisition team, including:

- Resolving issues raised in the due diligence review through actions such as:
    - Revisiting the valuation and renegotiating the purchase price
    - Reviewing and potentially modifying the transaction structure
    - Sharing risk with the seller through contractual terms and conditions
- Reviewing and marking up the draft purchase agreement
- Managing the contract negotiations
- Managing the transaction toward closing

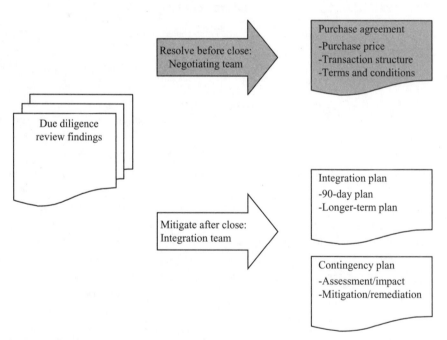

EXHIBIT 7.1   Resolution of Due Diligence Findings

We discuss activities following the closing of the transaction, including the integration and contingency plans, in Chapter 8.

Revisiting the Valuation and Purchase Price

As discussed in Chapter 4 (Key Aspects of the Due Diligence Program), a fundamental purpose of the due diligence review is to validate or modify the key assumptions underlying the acquirer's plan to create value. In Chapter 6 (Renegotiation of Major Terms), we outlined a scenario where the team identifies issues that alter the value of the acquisition, requiring the team to revisit the economics of the transaction. This section and the one that follows elaborate on this scenario and discuss approaches to preserve the value of the transaction.

The acquisition team typically synthesizes and aggregates the due diligence findings of the various functional representatives and prepares an updated financial forecast and valuation of the target business in order to determine if the combined value of the acquisition (i.e., stand-alone value plus synergies) has changed. If the combined value is lower than that in the acquisition's pre–due diligence business case, the team's first steps should be to understand the magnitude of the impact on the organization's value creation objective, and to identify which value drivers are causing the decline (whether it relates to reduced prospects for growth and profitability of the stand-alone business, or to smaller magnitude and delayed timing of expected synergies). Exhibit 7.2 illustrates such a case.

In this case, the pre–due diligence valuation portrays a win-win situation for both acquirer and seller. The purchase price exceeded the stand-alone value of the target business, so the seller was presumably receiving a value higher than other alternatives (certainly higher than continuing to own the stand-alone business). Additionally, the combined value of the acquired business to the buyer exceeded the purchase price, so the deal would also have created shareholder value for the acquirer.

The post–due diligence valuation, conversely, points to a win-lose situation. The stand-alone value of the target (in the opinion of the acquirer's due diligence team) is lower than previously thought, suggesting that a much larger purchase premium has to be paid. Further, the value of projected synergies is also lower than expected. The result in this case is the combined value of the target to the potential acquirer is now lower than the originally

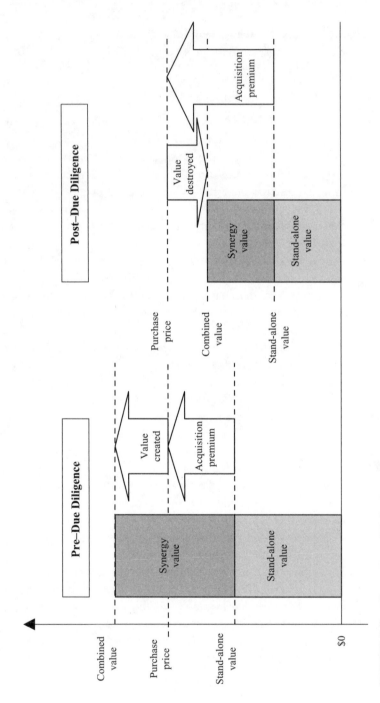

EXHIBIT 7.2 Illustration of Value Impairment

discussed purchase price. In this scenario, the prospective acquirer faces a difficult choice:

- Renegotiate the purchase price
- Terminate discussions because, absent a reduction in the purchase price, shareholder value would be destroyed if the deal proceeded

A middle-ground scenario can also be envisioned where the combined value is lower than originally projected but still remains higher than the purchase price. In this case, the prospective acquirer can choose to accept a lower, albeit still positive, level of value creation if it is unwilling or unable to renegotiate the price. The decision as to whether the deal should still proceed with a lower return depends on what alternatives are available to the acquirer. At a minimum, it should revisit its options, namely, alternative acquisitions, building the capability itself, or allying with a strategic partner, before deciding to proceed with the deal, to ensure that this transaction remains its best option. This is exactly the kind of situation where a corporation will benefit from developing and sustaining strategic alternatives to a particular acquisition as discussed in previous chapters.

If the prospective acquirer decides to renegotiate the purchase price, it should first gain a clear understanding of the assumptions that have changed and how much each has impacted the valuation, so that it can speak credibly about specific aspects of the stand-alone business as the rationale for any proposed reduction in price. Exhibit 7.3 outlines how a comparison of assumptions and their impact on value might be summarized.

Most prospective acquirers utilize relatively sophisticated and flexible financial models that facilitate sensitivity analysis, making the direct linkage of changes in assumptions to present value a straightforward calculation (e.g., a reduction in the forecasted compound annual revenue growth rate growth by X percent would lead to a $X reduction in the acquisition's present value). The most important distinction is to understand the changes impacting the stand-alone business versus the changes in expectations for synergy. If due diligence indicates that realistic prospects for future growth, profitability, or cash generation do not align with representations made by the seller throughout its marketing process, the prospective acquirer can make a specific and credible argument for proposing a reduced purchase price. If due diligence points, instead, to faulty assumptions about the deal's

EXHIBIT 7.3   Value Drivers Pre– and Post–Due Diligence

Value Drivers	Pre–Due Diligence Assumptions	Post–Due Diligence Assumptions	Increase (Decrease) in Present Value
Stand-alone business	–Revenue growth rate –Profit margin –Margin expansion –Working capital –Capital expenditures –Operating cash flow –Income taxes	–Updated assumptions	+ / (−) $X million
Synergies: Revenue synergy	Specified revenue initiatives: –Cross-selling existing products/services –New products/services	–Updated assumptions	+ / (−) $X million
Cost synergy	Specified cost initiatives: –Shared infrastructure –Elimination of redundancy –Economies of scale	–Updated assumptions	+ / (−) $X million
Total			+ / (−) $X million

potential to generate synergies, it may well be characterized as the acquirer's problem.

Of course, any discussions with the seller about reducing the purchase price are influenced by the context of its alternatives. In a preemptive sale, the seller may face the binary decision of selling at a lower price or pulling the business off the market, which is why they tend to prefer competitive auctions. In a competitive auction that generates strong interest from multiple parties, even if all prospective acquirers arrive at similar conclusions regarding the impairment of the target business, the seller needs to convince only one of them to stay with the original price. Considering the time, effort, and cost an organization has likely expended by the second round of bidding, there is often internal pressure within prospective acquirers to get the deal done; and absent sufficient discipline or viable alternatives, an unacceptable return on investment may be the cost of "winning" an auction.

Reviewing the Acquisition Transaction Structure

Contingent Purchase Price In the previous section, we presented a scenario where a perceived decrease in the value of a targeted business prompts an attempt to renegotiate the "headline" purchase price of the transaction. In other cases, however, things may not be so black or white. Rather than perceiving an outright impairment, the prospective acquirer may emerge from its due diligence review with a fundamental disagreement with the seller about the level of risk involved in achieving the projected results of the stand-alone business. This may lead to an impasse in the price negotiations. A technique to bridge such differences, to share the risk for areas of uncertainty, is to keep the total purchase price the same, but make a portion of it contingent on the occurrence of future results or events. Two basic alternative approaches include:

1. *Earn-out.* This type of transaction structure divides the purchase price into two components: part of it is paid to the seller at closing, and the other part is made conditional, paid over a period of several years based on formulae applied to future revenues or profits. Earn-outs probably make the most sense when management and ownership of the selling organization overlap, creating a convergence of interest in maximizing the sale proceeds, and when that management team is viewed as instrumental in delivering the projected results.

   That said, the acquirer should be aware of two aspects of earn-outs: accounting treatment and operating guidelines. Under recently released accounting guidelines, acquirers in the United States will need to record earn-outs at their "fair value," and then periodically remeasure them, charging any changes to the income statement. While this would not impact the cash impact of the arrangement, it could introduce significant volatility to the reported earnings of the acquirer, something most corporations seek to avoid. Additionally, earn-outs typically include operating guidelines to govern how the business will be managed following the sale, to allow the seller to maximize its opportunity, unimpeded by interference from the acquiring organization, increasing the potential for postclosing conflict. Consequently, earn-outs should be structured carefully and defined in detail, in close consultation with accounting and legal advisors.

   From a business standpoint, earn-outs do not make as much sense for acquirers when significant synergies are projected because the operating guidelines may preclude major changes to the acquired business, thereby limiting the acquirer's ability to maximize synergies. Therefore, determining whether an earn-out is optimal requires a trade-off based on where the most value is expected postacquisition: from the efforts of the management/owners of the seller, or from the integration plan executed by the acquirer.

2. *Hold-back*. If the acquirer's concerns relate to the occurrence of specific events (e.g., securing a key contract renewal) within a reasonably short time after the closing, it may propose holding back a portion of the purchase price. Timing in these cases tends to be much shorter than for earn-outs, typically ranging from a few months to a year. Because of the short time frame and the binary nature of the contingency, these arrangements tend to involve placing an agreed amount of the purchase price into escrow, with instructions to release it to the seller upon occurrence of the specified events, or to the buyer if the events do not transpire. See "Purchase and Sale" in the section "Key Sections of the Purchase Agreement" for further discussion of escrow agreements.

Acquiring Assets vs. Stock The seller's preferred transaction structure (e.g., whether it is selling assets or stock of the target business) is normally communicated up front to prospective acquirers in an auction and is presumed as part of their initial bids, and acquirers normally solicit guidance from their tax advisors before the initial bids are submitted. The reason we address the transaction structure here is that the acquirer may want to revisit it in light of the due diligence findings, especially if a stock transaction is being contemplated and the due diligence team has identified specific unwanted assets or liabilities. Additionally, the transaction structure itself is a value driver, as discussed in Chapter 1, because of the significant tax advantages afforded to some types of transaction structures, so this is an area that due diligence team members should at least be conversant with. The following are general considerations concerning the purchase of assets versus stock, the two most common transaction structures:

1. *Purchase of assets*. For the acquirer, structuring the transaction as a purchase of assets has two major advantages. First, as mentioned, in an asset purchase, the transaction can be structured to include or exclude specific assets and liabilities. Consequently, this structure would

be preferable if the due diligence review revealed undesirable lines of business or contractual commitments that the acquirer has no interest in taking on. Additionally, an asset deal could allow potential liabilities for past actions (e.g., tax, regulatory, or contractual compliance) of the seller's corporate entity to remain with the seller. One potential drawback is that an asset purchase might introduce hurdles to closing if there are any constraints on the transferability or assignability of specific assets or contracts.

From a U.S. tax perspective, a purchase of assets provides the acquirer with the benefit of a "step-up" in the basis of the assets acquired. In other words, the acquirer's tax basis in the business can be increased to the amount of the purchase price, and the excess of that price over the book value of the net assets acquired (the excess purchase price can be a large number) can be deducted from taxable income over a period of time. This has the effect of lowering the acquirer's after-tax cost below the cost of acquiring stock, where step-up is not normally available (with one exception described in *Purchase of stock*, below), allowing the acquirer to pay more for the assets at the same after-tax cost.

2. *Purchase of stock.* When the acquisition is structured as the purchase of shares of the target company's stock, the acquirer normally assumes ownership of the entire legal entity, with all of its assets and liabilities, contracts and agreements, and, generally speaking, liability for the entity's past actions. Any concerns, on the other hand, about the transferability or assignability of assets or contracts are usually mitigated by structuring the transaction as a stock sale.

From a U.S. tax perspective, the purchase of stock does not ordinarily provide the acquirer with the benefit from a step-up because the selling corporation's tax basis in the divested business carries over to the buyer. This difference in tax treatment should lower the price the acquirer is willing to pay for the stock, compared with the price of the assets. An exception to this tax treatment is if both parties jointly agree to make an election under Internal Revenue Code Section 338(h)(10), a stock sale can be treated for tax purposes as if assets were sold. This means that the acquirer would receive the benefit of step-up. However, under a Section 338 election, the acquirer would still have to contend with unwanted assets and liabilities. If that were a significant issue for them, they might still want to structure the deal as an asset purchase.

Sharing Risk: Contractual Terms and Conditions

Certain due diligence findings do not rise to the level of the overall valuation of the target business and, because of the attendant tax consequences for both buyer and seller, the transaction structure may be a somewhat "blunt object" for dealing with specific acquirer concerns. For example, the due diligence team may identify a concern about the target company's prior level of compliance with certain laws or regulations, and in a stock deal, does not want the acquirer to assume a future liability for possible preacquisition violations. The most common way to resolve concerns such as this is to share risk with the seller through the terms and conditions of the legal contracts for the acquisition, namely, the purchase agreement and its related disclosure schedules, and the transition services agreement.

Because of the importance and complexity of these legal agreements, we discuss them in some detail in the following section, highlighting the areas where due diligence findings are most often resolved.

MARKING UP THE DRAFT PURCHASE AGREEMENT

Contract Drafting and Revision

Before reviewing the components of the purchase agreement, we will first provide an overview of the typical contract drafting and revision process in a competitive auction. In a competitive process (and in many preemptive sales), the seller usually creates the first draft of the purchase agreement and distributes it to one or more potential acquirers. The exact timing of distribution can vary, but sellers usually wait to expend the legal fees on a draft until a relatively late stage, when they are confident that a transaction looks likely. A competitive sale process usually results in a first draft that adopts "seller-friendly" terms on most issues, with some amount of negotiation of terms expected by both seller and buyer. In an attempt to limit the extent of proposed changes, the seller may distribute the draft to auction participants while they are in the process of conducting their due diligence reviews, requiring submission of contract drafts "marked up" with desired changes as an integral part of second-round bids. The nature and extent of proposed markups would then be a consideration (along with the purchase price) in the determination of the winning bidder. We further discuss the process of negotiating changes to the contract in the section "Managing Contract Negotiations."

Key Sections of the Purchase Agreement

The purchase agreement and its related disclosure schedules comprise what is generally referred to as the "definitive agreement" for the acquisition transaction. In addition, closing documents may also include a transition services agreement, if the transaction involves the acquisition of a division, subsidiary, or business segment of another corporation. The purchase agreement sets forth the financial terms of the transaction, establishes the legal rights and obligations of the parties, lists required activities prior to and following the sale, provides a detailed description of the business being acquired, determines remedies if that description is materially inaccurate, and, importantly, allocates risk between the seller and buyer. The purchase agreement is organized into sections addressing specific issues. While individual contracts may be assembled differently to address issues relevant to specific transactions, most contracts for U.S. transactions cover in some form the points that are outlined in Exhibit 7.4 and described in the discussion that follows.

Purchase and Sale The *purchase and sale* section identifies the parties to the agreement and the general structure of the transaction. This section also describes and defines the business being acquired. Three issues require particular focus in this section:

1. *Parties to the agreement.* It is important that the acquirer understand who the seller (i.e., the person or legal entity) is, since that entity bears any liabilities resulting from the purchase agreement. In cases where the seller is an individual or individuals, the acquirer needs to be comfortable that the seller has the capacity to honor the obligations defined in the agreement and may solicit personal guarantees to stand behind any commitments made in the agreements. Even when the seller is a large, multitiered organization, with multiple corporate organizations within its structure, the acquiring company will similarly want to have confidence that the selling entity has the capacity to honor its obligations or ensure that the parent organization is the guarantor of those obligations.

EXHIBIT 7.4   Purchase Agreement—Illustrative Outline

Purchase and Sale
Defines the business being acquired, outlines the deal structure, and identifies parties to the agreement.

Closing
Sets the location and mechanism of the close: what is exchanged and when, the purchase price, and any price adjustments.

Representations and Warranties of the Seller
Seller represents its ability to enter into the transaction and describes in detail the state of business being sold.

Representations and Warranties of the Buyer
Buyer represents its ability to enter into the transaction: e.g., availability of funds/financing.

Covenants
Governs conduct of both parties leading to and following the close. Usually includes a covenant for the seller not to compete with the acquired business.

Employment Matters
Specific agreements and covenants regarding employment matters. Can be included within *Covenants* or in a separate section, depending on extent of issues to be addressed.

Conditions to Close
Conditions that must exist to obligate each party to close the transaction.

Termination
Conditions that must exist to allow for termination of the agreement.

Indemnification
Level of financial protection each party offers the other against losses arising from breaches of representations, warranties, covenants, or other performance obligations.

Tax Matters
Specific agreements and covenants regarding taxation matters. Can be included within *Covenants* or in a separate section, depending on extent of issues to be addressed.

General Provisions
Includes definitions and interpretations, and addresses procedures regarding making claims.

---

2. *Structuring the transaction as an asset or stock purchase.* As noted in "Acquiring Assets vs. Stock," the purchase of assets versus shares of stock can have significant tax as well as legal implications for both the seller and acquirer, impacting value and price, as well as other important aspects of the purchase agreement. Accordingly, the acquirer's tax advisors should work closely with their legal counsel in reviewing the purchase agreement.

3. *Defining the business being acquired.* This section is particularly relevant when the transaction is structured as an asset deal because it would specify in detail the assets and liabilities included or excluded from the transaction. Even in a stock deal, the definition of the business being acquired should be written with precision because its breadth or narrowness, depending on how the agreement is drafted, may impact the scope of the noncompetition covenant, as further described later in this section.

Closing   The *closing* section of the agreement specifies the location and timing of the closing, the purchase price, and any purchase price adjustments. Several points are worth highlighting in this section.

- *Timing of the close.* A key consideration is the length of time between signing the purchase agreement and closing the transaction. In many cases, both parties prefer to sign the agreement and close simultaneously. Often, however, it is necessary to delay the closing to allow the acquirer to secure financing, or the parties to obtain consents from shareholders, third parties, or governmental agencies. If there must be a delay between signing and closing, it should be kept as short as possible. This is a period during which the business can be rudderless, and undetected impairment can occur. A short delay quickly gets the business under the control of the acquirer and reduces the possibility of impairment.

- *Purchase price and adjustments.* This section specifies the purchase price, including the form and mechanism of consideration received, and any anticipated price adjustments. The type of consideration received (e.g., cash, shares of stock, assumption of debt, guaranteed consideration vs. contingent) determines the ultimate value of the transaction. We discussed two typical contingent purchase price arrangements in the section "Contingent Purchase Price." Additionally, the purchase price may be adjusted for the amount of working capital required at closing, and for any portion of the proceeds to be held in escrow.

- *Working capital adjustment.* The purpose of a working capital adjustment is to balance the competing interests of the parties to the agreement. The seller is interested in removing any excess working capital prior to the sale, while the acquirer expects the business to have a level of working capital sufficient to fund operations following the close. The working capital section should specify a reference amount, the level above or below which the purchase price will be increased or decreased, and include a predefined process for settling disputes (e.g., third-party arbitration). It should also define working capital precisely, with specific accounts listed (e.g., to include or exclude cash, or intercompany accounts), and describe the accounting policies and practices that govern the calculation of the amounts. The due diligence review, specifically the work performed by the accounting and finance professionals on the team, should provide the acquiring company with the insights necessary to identify an adequate level of working capital and its components.

- *Escrow agreement.* An escrow agreement is a vehicle for appointing a third party to hold part of the purchase price until specified uncertainties (e.g., the expiry of the survival period for representations and warranties, or the occurrence of specified events) are resolved, at which time the amount is released to the seller. The acquirer may seek to require an escrow agreement to ensure there is a funded account to access in cure of a contractual breach, especially if the seller is an individual(s) and there are any concerns about the ability to recover any claims against the seller. The intensity with which the acquirer pursues an escrow agreement, as well as its size, should be a function of the nature and extent of the risks it identifies as a result of the due diligence review.

Representations and Warranties of the Seller   The primary function of the representations and warranties of the seller is to provide the buyer with a snapshot of the business at particular points in time, typically as of the date of the agreement and then again on the date of the closing, if they do not occur simultaneously. Representations and warranties of the seller generally cover its ability to enter into the deal and disclose the state of the business being sold. Typical representations and important considerations for this section of the contract are described in the following points.

- *Seller's ability to enter into the agreement.* The seller makes a number of representations concerning its ability to legally close the transaction. These representations tend to be relatively uncontroversial in the negotiations. Typically, they cover several standard areas, all of which should have been validated in due diligence.
  - The seller is a valid organization authorized to enter into the deal.
  - The deal will not conflict with any contracts, laws, or regulations.
  - There is no litigation that would affect the seller's ability to close the transaction.
  - The seller has valid title to the assets (or shares) being sold.
- *State of the business being sold.* These representations are some of the most important aspects of the entire purchase agreement. In this section, the seller makes detailed representations concerning the state of the business being sold and, importantly, discloses any exceptions to those representations in the schedules to the purchase agreement (see "Disclosure Schedules"). The acquirer will have the right to make a money damages claim for any items not accurately represented or disclosed in this section. Acquirers should closely review this section to verify that its contents are consistent with their understanding of the business, in particular ensuring that the seller has made explicit representations about any areas of concern flagged during the due diligence review (e.g., compliance with contracts, laws, or regulations). Some commonly seen representations and warranties are illustrated by the following examples:
  - The financial statements disclosed to the acquirer are properly stated.
  - The contracts being transferred are valid, and the parties to them are not in breach.
  - Business permits are in full force.
  - Tax returns have been properly filed and there are no outstanding claims.
  - Employee benefit plans have been properly managed and regulations complied with.
  - Environmental regulations have been complied with.
  - Assets are sufficient to conduct the business.
  - There are no undisclosed liabilities.

Representations and Warranties of the Buyer   This section lists the representations the acquirer makes about its ability to enter into the agreement. Unlike the seller, the acquirer makes just a few representations and warranties in the purchase agreement. Following are some examples:

- The acquirer is a valid organization authorized to enter into the deal.
- The deal will not conflict with contracts, laws, and regulations.
- There is no litigation that would affect the acquirer's ability to close the transaction.
- The acquirer has sufficient funds to execute the transaction, or has secured financing to do so.

Covenants   Covenants govern the relationship between the seller and acquirer over a period of time. Certain covenants apply from the signing of the agreement until the closing date and provide assurance that the proper actions are taken to facilitate the closing of the transaction and preserve the business pending the closing. These normally include a list of actions allowed, or prohibited, without the buyer's consent. Other covenants survive the closing for a certain length of time, such as covenants requiring the cooperation of the parties with respect to the postclosing transition of the business, or the sharing of facilities or of support operations. Additional covenants can include such things as access to information, rights to use the seller's names and trademarks following the close, and agreements to keep the negotiations exclusive and confidential. If the acquirer is relying on third-party financing for the transaction, covenants may require it to perform certain activities between signing and closing to secure the financing. Several points are worth noting.

- *Preclosing covenants create an awkward relationship between the seller and acquirer.* Covenants are largely intended to increase the acquirer's comfort that the seller will not take major actions to change the business prior to closing, and that they will be cooperative regarding the transition following the close.

  There is an inherent awkwardness in the period between signing and closing. During this time, the seller still retains the benefits and the risks in owning the business, but is made answerable through the covenants to the acquirer to act or not act in certain ways. If there will be an antitrust filing, the legal advisors must review this part of the contract to ensure that the acquirer is not perceived as assuming effective control of the business before the transaction has been approved by the appropriate governmental agencies.

These are additional reasons why the time between signing and closing should be minimized. From the perspective of the buyer, few good things can happen between signing and closing.

- *The noncompetition covenant.* The covenant made by the seller not to compete with the business it is selling is another very important section of the purchase agreement, and can be one of the most difficult to negotiate. The acquirer, from its perspective, needs assurance that the seller will not enter into competition with the business it has just sold. The seller, conversely, expects that the sale will not unreasonably limit its commercial options in the future. These concerns are generally more acute when the seller is a large corporation selling a portion of its business (i.e., a corporate divestiture) and will remain active in related segments of the market.

  Negotiation of this section requires the involvement of the acquirer's operating management with in-depth knowledge of the markets the business operates in. This is one of the sections of the contract requiring extensive involvement of the acquirer's senior management, as it needs to determine how much latitude, if any, it can tolerate to satisfy the seller's concerns.

  The covenant not to compete is composed of four elements, each of which can be fiercely negotiated, with the selling corporation looking to narrow each term, and the acquirer seeking to broaden its definition:
  - Definition of competitive activity
  - Geographic area
  - Specified period of time
  - Exceptions

    The seller may look to list certain areas, known as exceptions, or "carve-outs," where the terms of the noncompetition covenant would not apply. Each carve-out, then, can bring several additional definitions and percentage or dollar thresholds into the negotiations, another example of how detailed the contract discussions can get.

Employment Matters This section addresses representations, warranties, and covenants of both parties specifically relating to employment matters.

While these items can also be incorporated into the other contract sections, organizing them in a separate section facilitates review by the employment experts on both sides of the transaction. In order to ensure that its former employees are treated fairly in the transition of ownership, the acquirer may be asked by the seller to make commitments about how employees transferring with the deal will be treated. For example, it may be asked to specify which employees will or will not transfer to the acquirer, or to sustain equivalent levels of salaries and benefits for a period of time following the closing. The acquirer may also commit to certain actions, to support the transition of employees to the acquirer's plans, and to ensure a smooth transition of plan administration.

Conditions to Close   This section outlines the conditions that must be met in order for the parties to be legally obligated to consummate the transaction. If one party fails to satisfy a condition by the date of the closing, the other party has the right to terminate the agreement and walk away from the transaction. This section should address any open issues from due diligence that rise to the level of a "deal breaker" for the acquirer (e.g., if a major customer or supplier contract can be terminated in the event of a change in control, the acquirer may demand to make that party's commitment to continue to do business with new ownership a condition to closing). Typical conditions to close may include the following items:

- Receiving governmental approvals such as antitrust clearances
- Obtaining key third-party consents
- Having no judgments or restraints
- Having no litigation
- No material adverse change occurring in the business
- Performance by either party of specific actions (such as obtaining financing)

There is a natural tension associated with the respective parties' approach to these conditions. The acquirer will not want to legally obligate itself to commit the funds to close until it is comfortable that the things it views as most important are in place. This will tend to lengthen the list. Conversely, the seller wants to have as few conditions as possible to increase its certainty of closing.

Termination   This section defines the conditions under which the agreement can be terminated. The parties might agree that the contract can be terminated prior to closing upon mutual agreement, or if specific conditions are present. This section normally outlines the effect of termination, for example, specifying the terms of the purchase agreement that would survive termination (e.g., confidentiality, publicity, jurisdiction, or governing law). The section should also list any penalties or specific performance obligations that would be required upon termination.

There are circumstances when the agreement should be terminated, and the acquirer will want to have provisions built into the contract to allow it to do so. The seller, on the other hand, will want to establish a very high threshold for an event that allows termination. Having progressed to the contract stage, the last thing the seller would want is to have to restart the sale process from the beginning. If the seller has the leverage, it will try to make termination as distasteful as possible, by including disincentives such as breakup fees or other termination penalties.

Indemnification   Indemnification requires the parties to pay damages in the event of a breach of their respective representations, warranties, and covenants. Indemnification provisions also serve to allocate specific post-closing risks associated with the transferred business. Even after all of the representations, warranties, and covenants are agreed, the parties will often continue to hotly debate the indemnification section of the contract, since this section sets both the floor and the ceiling amounts for any damage claims that can be made under the contract. There are three typical elements of the indemnification section:

1. *Caps: placing a limit on the maximum exposure.* This section defines the aggregate level of each party's obligations and the allocation of legal and financial risk in the contract, through caps or limitations of the aggregate amount of claims that can be made. These aggregate obligations directly impact the ultimate value of the deal.
2. *Survival: establishing an end date for claims.* Survival represents a specified period of time during which claims can be made. The acquirer will generally want to extend that period as long as possible and the seller will want to shorten it. Often, separate survival periods are established for tax and environmental representations (based on statutes of

limitation), while some representations (e.g., incorporation, title, ownership) may survive indefinitely.

3. *Deductibles, baskets and* de minimis *amounts.* Minimum dollar amounts can be established to ensure that only substantive claims for breaches of the agreement are made. A deductible would be an amount that the acquirer would be at risk for, since they would only be able to make claims for amounts in excess of the deductible. A "basket" would be a threshold amount that claims must surpass, but is recoverable from the selling corporation. Having a *de minimis* amount would indicate that a claim cannot be made unless it exceeds a certain minimum dollar level, to mitigate the possibility of spending time and legal fees disputing minor items.

Tax Matters   This section addresses representations, warranties, and covenants of the seller and buyer specifically relating to tax matters. It normally addresses the purchase price allocation, assigns responsibility for transfer taxes, tax filings, and tax liabilities, and outlines procedures for making tax claims. This section also may include a separate tax indemnification with its own survival and limits. While these items are sometimes incorporated into the other contract sections, organizing them in a separate section facilitates review by the tax experts on both sides of the transaction.

General Provisions   This section addresses some of the specifics of dispute resolution, in addition to matters not covered elsewhere. It also includes definitions and interpretations of terms used in the purchase agreement.

- *Fundamental importance of definitions.* Definitions and interpretations can often be overlooked, but are critical to establishing how broadly or how narrowly statements made elsewhere in the contract are interpreted. The definitions and interpretations section is an important indicator of how seller-friendly or buyer-friendly the entire agreement is or, in other words, how the legal and financial risk is allocated between the parties to the agreement.

For example, if the "business" being purchased is defined in this section, it has direct relevance to how restrictive the noncompetition covenant is to the seller's ability to operate another "competitive" business after the transaction has been consummated. Similarly, to the degree that representations and warranties are qualified to the extent of the "knowledge" of the seller, this sections' definition of knowledge will broaden or narrow the risk assumed by the seller and the buyer and seller will negotiate the wording accordingly. Other key definitions requiring careful reading include "materiality" and "material adverse effect," both of which are used to modify many of the representations, warranties, or covenants. This section needs to be read carefully and in conjunction with the applicable section of the purchase agreement where the terms are utilized.

Disclosure Schedules

The schedules to the agreement list all the disclosures the seller has made and itemize any exceptions to the representations and warranties. Items included in the disclosure schedules are keyed to the appropriate contract section. Inclusion of an item on a schedule has the effect of *modifying* the relevant section of the agreement. For example, a representation may be made that there is no litigation *except* as disclosed in the schedules to the agreement. Another typical representation might say that the acquirer has been provided with a copy of every contract over a certain dollar amount, and that the selling corporation is not in breach of any, except as disclosed in the schedules. Exhibit 7.5 illustrates some additional items often included in the disclosure schedules.

The disclosure schedules are prepared by the seller and are reviewed by the acquirer. Much of what is contained in the schedules should agree with the information and documents provided in the data room. The due diligence team should thoroughly review the schedules and ensure that there are no inconsistencies or, if there are, that they are satisfactorily explained.

Transition Services Agreement

When a sale involves the divestiture of a segment or division of larger corporation, the purchase agreement will generally include a commitment from the selling corporation to provide certain support and back office services to the acquirer for a limited period as the buyer transitions the unit to its ownership. This commitment is captured in the *transition services agreement* (TSA). TSA terms normally include the definition of included services, time period, pricing, and terms of billing and payment. The scope of the TSA is determined by two factors: the extent to which the divested business

EXHIBIT 7.5 Disclosure Schedules to the Purchase Agreement: Illustrative List

Organization and Good Standing
Jurisdictions where qualified to conduct business

Company Subsidiaries

Included and Excluded Assets and Liabilities
Specified assets and liabilities transferring (or not) to the buyer in an asset sale

Real Property
Details of owned and leased properties

Permits

Insurance
List of policies, premiums, coverage limits, claims

Intellectual Property
Lists of copyrights, patents, and trademarks

Contracts
List of all contracts above a defined dollar amount; agreements where consents are required in a change in control; agreements containing noncompetes or other restrictive covenants.

Financial Statements
Copies of financial statements the seller is making representations about; description of any departures from GAAP (especially for interim statements)

Litigation
Threatened or pending claims

Compliance with Laws or Permits
Exceptions

Environmental Matters
Any issues

Employment Matters
Employee lists, bonus and benefit plan descriptions

Related Party Transactions
Contracts with owners or affiliates; related party receivables and payables

Indebtedness
List of all debt or loans; description of restrictive covenants

Taxes
Outstanding audits; tax claims or liens

possesses a back-office infrastructure that can support stand-alone operations, and the nature and scale of any back-office infrastructure owned by the acquirer. The more dependent the divested business is on the selling corporation for back-office services functions (such as customer service, accounting, human resources, facilities, and information technology) and the less capability owned by the acquirer, the more likely it is that the TSA will have a broad scope and an extended transition term.

MANAGING CONTRACT NEGOTIATIONS

Effective and Efficient Negotiations

Both buyer and seller are significantly invested in the transaction by the time it reaches the contract negotiation stage, and management expectations on both sides are heightened, resulting in pressure to get the deal done. If both parties are negotiating in good faith and the acquirer is satisfied that there are no deal breakers, what remains is the negotiation of the details of the definitive agreement. This does not mean that there are not major issues to be resolved (or even that the deal is guaranteed to close), but it does mean that those issues relate more to the allocation of risk than with fundamental disagreements on the basic framework of the deal.

Under these circumstances, both buyer and seller will be motivated to get the deal done as quickly and effectively as possible. To do so relies heavily on an efficient and effective negotiating process. Major elements of that process include empowered leadership of the principal negotiator; strong support of legal counsel; support of internal and external experts; a well-structured mechanism for review and feedback; and a commitment on the part of negotiators to getting the deal done. From the perspective of the acquirer, these principles should be operationalized as described in the remainder of this section.

Empowered Leadership

The negotiating lead is the single face of the buyer for the transaction. That individual should be appointed by the transaction sponsor and should be vested with a visible level of authority to make binding decisions. Generally, that individual has headed up the acquisition team from the early stages of the transaction and had led the due diligence effort. As a result, he or she would have in-depth knowledge of the target company.

It is critical that this individual is recognized (both internally and externally) as the person who communicates the definitive position of the buyer on key issues throughout the negotiation of the contracts and agreements. The transaction sponsor must clearly communicate to all relevant parties that the team leader has both the responsibility *and the authority* to negotiate on the part of the acquirer. While such authority cannot be a "blank check," it must be defined broadly enough so that the negotiating lead need not continually seek approval to make commitments on behalf of the organization. Effective negotiation also requires timely and structured access to the transaction sponsor. A predetermined mechanism for communication must be established to assure seamless management of negotiations when issues arise that exceed the decision-making authority of the negotiating lead. Thus empowered, the negotiating lead is positioned to aggressively and efficiently negotiate on behalf of the acquirer.

Support of Legal Counsel

Depending on the size of the transaction and scale of the organization involved, the legal team can be comprised entirely of in-house counsel or supplemented with external legal resources. Smaller organizations, faced with more limited resources, may choose to hire a law firm specializing in mergers and acquisitions to manage all aspects of the transaction. The legal team's role in contract negotiations includes supporting negotiations, drafting and revising agreements, and advising on issues in areas such as antitrust, intellectual property, employment, or securities law. The legal team should also coordinate the internal review and sign-off of the various sections of the agreement.

A single individual should direct the transaction from a legal perspective. This individual will support the negotiating lead and be the primary interface with the seller's legal team. Preferably, that individual would have been involved in the transaction from its earliest stages and would have led the legal review of the due diligence effort. As a result, he or she will have established a strong basis for providing legal and business inputs during the contacting phase. In addition, a good legal advisor will orchestrate an efficient and effective negotiation by clearing many of the more routine contract points directly with the seller's legal team, allowing the negotiating lead to focus on a limited number of important pivotal issues.

Support by Experts

There are a number of areas involved in negotiating the transaction that stretch beyond the technical knowledge of the negotiating lead. As a result, the negotiating lead must have easy access to subject matter experts responsible for covering specialized areas such as finance, accounting, tax, human resources, real estate and facilities, and technology. These individuals will generally have been those lead reviewers responsible for conducting due diligence in the respective areas of expertise. Major support will come from the following:

- *Finance and accounting.* The senior financial executive such as the acquirer's chief financial officer, vice president of finance, or controller will play a major role in the negotiation process. Throughout the process, the senior financial executive will coordinate the input of finance, accounting, and tax specialists and will advise and oversee the other subject matter experts to ensure that the financial ramifications of all issues are understood. In this respect, this executive is an integral member of the negotiating team, serving not only as technical advisor, but also as a link the various functional experts.
- *Human resources (HR).* The HR specialist, along with the legal team, is responsible for reviewing all contractual issues relating to employee matters. The employment matters section of the purchase agreement generally covers significant legal and operational ground. It identifies the employees who will transfer with the business and under what terms, how changes in benefit plans will be handled, and issues such as severance and vacation policy. These items can be complex and require substantial coordination with the seller.
- *Operational management.* Managers responsible for functions such as sales and marketing, information technology, real estate, and facilities management provide the operational knowledge to review and comment on sections of the agreement dealing with such issues as contracts, competitive matters, real property, environmental matters, fixed assets, insurance, and intellectual property assets. Their involvement in the negotiation phase is important to identifying and advising on technical issues and is often critical to effective postacquisition implementation. Involvement helps shape certain terms of and definitions in the agreement and knowledge of what is contained in the final contract can significantly impact their approach to postclosing activities.

Review and Feedback

The previous sections described the team—its character and configuration. A well-structured and well-directed team ensures that the acquirer has an *effective* approach to negotiations. These characteristics are essential to successful negotiations but, of themselves, not sufficient. The negotiators should also have in place a review and feedback mechanism to ensure that negotiations are also *efficient*. Such a review and feedback model is illustrated in Exhibit 7.6 and discussed in the paragraphs that follow.

- *The initial draft.* As mentioned in "Contract Drafting and Revision," the initial draft of the agreement is traditionally created by the seller and its counsel and submitted to the prospective buyer(s). In a competitive sale process, the draft can be expected to be favorable to the seller on all issues of risk. This is a reflection of the leverage the seller creates and tries to maintain, using competition to limit markups as well (i.e., the more substantive the markup, the greater the potential to be eliminated from the bidding process).

- *Review and markup by the acquirer.* In a nonauction situation, the attorneys from both sides may clear some of the more noncontroversial issues before engaging the principals (the negotiating leads on both sides of the deal) in the process. In auction sales, that luxury will generally not exist and the initial markups will include these noncontroversial items in addition to more substantive issues. Regardless of the nature of the transaction (whether in an auction environment or not), the critical issues that the acquirer should address are largely informed by the findings of the due diligence review and relate mainly to transaction risk, as described throughout the section "Marking up the Draft Purchase Agreement."

- *Lawyer-to-lawyer discussions.* Seasoned legal advisors (on both sides of the transaction) will normally speak after the buyer's marked-up draft

Additional markups

EXHIBIT 7.6 Contract Negotiations: Process Flow

has been returned to the seller's attorney. In the initial conversations, the legal advisors for the buyer will articulate the buyer's underlying concerns. Ideally, they will then prioritize the major open issues to help focus the discussions between the principals.

A good legal team can actually play a much more valuable role than simply clarifying and resolving technical matters. The better and more experienced legal advisors have likely been involved in dozens, if not hundreds, of similar transactions, and have a nuanced understanding of the human dynamics of negotiations that can facilitate negotiations immeasurably. They know, for example, when to call for a break in the conversations to allow parties to cool off if negotiations become too heated. And they know how to orchestrate the trading of points to advance the negotiations, and precisely when and how to take a strong stand on an issue.

- *Principal-to-principal discussions.* Face-to-face discussions between principals are most effective when legal advisors have organized and prioritized issues, allowing the principals to focus on resolving a limited number of items of significant importance. Items agreed on are sent back for redrafting, the revised agreement then being recirculated for review.

  The negotiating lead, as noted in the section "Empowered Leadership," should be invested with some predetermined level of negotiating authority to get the deal done. For example, the lead may have the authority to make price concessions up to a defined percentage of the preliminary bid; or to negotiate a contract survival period up to a certain number of years; or to set limitations of liability up to some dollar amount. Setting a level of quantifiable limits makes the entire team more efficient by allowing the lead to act decisively in this critical part of the process. Knowing that every contract point cannot be anticipated in advance, a mechanism should also be established for obtaining corporate approval of items exceeding the negotiating lead's authority. This internal approval process should be kept as seamless as possible, to minimize any lags in responding to offers and counteroffers made in the negotiating process. To facilitate quick and informed review and approval, the negotiating lead should report regularly and frequently to the transaction sponsor on the status of negotiations and key issues.

- *Reaching the final agreement.* The above process iterates until all issues have been negotiated and resolved to the satisfaction of both parties, with a succession of marked-up contract drafts exchanged between the parties, followed by a series of calls or face-to-face meetings. In the case of an auction sale, this will happen sometime after the completion of the acquirer's confirmatory diligence in order to ensure that all issues have been included in the contract.

The amount of time it takes to get a deal done is routinely underestimated by corporations in setting timing expectations for the sale process. While it is not unheard of for motivated and cooperative parties to negotiate an agreement in a few days to a week, it is more reasonable to expect the negotiations to span several weeks, and in more complex or contentious cases, negotiations can last well over a month. A good rule of thumb is that each iteration of the contract draft can extend the negotiations by approximately a week. This underscores the need to minimize the number of iterations by resolving as many issues as possible during each negotiating session.

Commitment to Getting the Deal Done

A very real but more amorphous aspect of the negotiation process is the commitment of the parties to closing the deal. This is reflected in a number of ways. From the acquirer's perspective, it requires an understanding of the subtle nature of contract negotiations, a willingness to dedicate the resources necessary to get the transaction done, and the confidence to be able to stand firm on the most important issues and to compromise when circumstances allow.

Contract negotiations are an exercise in optimization. A rigid approach that treats all issues equally is almost guaranteed to result in a protracted process and one that increases the potential for failure. The negotiating team's focus should be on the issues of greatest importance and they should be willing to be accommodating when compromise makes sense. The due diligence findings provide the road map when making those judgments.

CLOSING

Shepherding the Transaction toward Closing

In some transactions, the closing is effective immediately upon signing the purchase agreement. A simultaneous signing and closing can simplify smaller transactions, where there is no externally required waiting period. It benefits both the acquirer and the selling corporation by eliminating the risk of unforeseen events occurring during this period. More often, however, it is necessary to separate, or "bifurcate," the signing and the closing, establishing an intervening period in order to conduct certain activities. The most common reasons to delay closing are:

- To obtain regulatory approval
- To allow buyer financing to be finalized
- To obtain consents from third parties

Regulatory Approval

Once the contracts are negotiated and signed, frequently there is a significant hurdle to contend with before the deal can close: regulatory review and approval. In the United States, the Hart-Scott-Rodino Antitrust Improvements Act of 1976 (HSR) requires premerger filings and a waiting period for transactions over a certain size. Since the federal government under HSR can either request additional information before approving a transaction—a time-consuming and expensive prospect—or choose to contest the transaction, careful planning, and consultation with antitrust experts from both sides of the transaction should be initiated early in the acquisition process.

For transactions outside the United States, the team needs to consider not only antitrust, but any other laws or regulations unique to the country or region that may affect the transaction. For this reason, the acquisition team should engage counsel for each country or region of operations to guide the team through the local compliance process.

Hart-Scott-Rodino (HSR) Act HSR requires parties planning certain mergers and acquisitions to notify the Federal Trade Commission (FTC) and the Department of Justice (DOJ) of the impending transaction via a notification and report form with information about their businesses and wait a specified period of time, usually 30 days, before consummating the transaction. The objective of the Act is to prevent transactions that the federal government would view as anticompetitive. (The Appendix contains a comprehensive overview of the HSR program.) Following are a few points about the HSR requirements and their implications.

- *HSR affects a significant number of transactions.* An HSR filing is generally required for transactions with an aggregate value above $65.2 million, an amount that is adjusted upward annually. Clearly, many transactions fall above the filing threshold. The acquisition team, in conjunction with the seller, should consider whether an HSR filing is a possibility early in the transaction process, and should retain expert antitrust counsel if a value anywhere near the filing threshold is anticipated.
- *The FTC Notification and Report Form is the required filing document.* If a transaction does meet the criteria for HSR, then both the buyer and the seller must submit information about their respective business operations via the Notification and Report Form. This form requires disclosure of the following items:
  - Identity of the parties involved and structure of the transaction
  - Financial data and certain documents filed with the Securities and Exchange Commission (SEC)
  - Certain planning and evaluation documents pertaining to the proposed transaction
  - Revenues by industry segment and geographic area, previous acquisitions or assets engaged in business in overlapping segments

    The requirement to provide certain planning and evaluation documents, sometimes referred to as the "4C request" after its section on the Notification and Report Form, is quite broad. It includes copies of studies, surveys, analyses, or reports prepared by or for officers or directors that evaluate or analyze the proposed transaction with respect to markets or market share, competition or competitors, potential for sales growth or expansion into product or geographic markets. Typically responsive documents include memoranda prepared by seller, and documents submitted to management including studies and presentations. It is not just formal documents or presentations that would be included. Even informal communications, as seemingly innocuous as notes to the file or e-mails, can be viewed as responsive documents if they contain competitive or market analysis for the transaction and are prepared by or for the corporation's officers or directors.
- *The government can approve the transaction, contest it, or ask for more information.* Once the Notification and Report Form is filed, the agencies begin their review, focusing on whether the target company and the

acquiring firm are competitors, or are related in any way such that the transaction might adversely affect competition. They analyze the submitted materials, but also may consult publicly available information as well as their prior experience with either the markets or the organizations involved in the filing. After analyzing the information within the initial 30-day waiting period, the government can choose to approve the transaction, contest it in court by requesting injunctive relief, or ask for more information before making a decision.

- *Getting a "second request" is a very big deal.* If either agency determines that further inquiry is warranted, it can request additional information via a second request. The second request extends the waiting period, and the clock on the additional waiting period does not start until all parties are deemed to have complied with the request. The acquisition team should understand that getting a second request is a very big deal as a practical matter. Depending on how much information the government is asking for, the entire team could easily be faced with multiple months of internal and external effort, and potentially millions of dollars of additional legal fees, to comply.

- *Planning for the HSR filing.* While the prospect of a second request can never be prevented, the team can certainly make the initial submission as complete and high quality as possible, to lower the likelihood of anything in the submission itself triggering the second request. If a transaction is projected to have a value anywhere near the $65.2 million threshold, guidance should be given to the entire acquisition team at the outset of the process to ensure there is a consistent understanding of the requirements of HSR, and that 4C documents in particular are assembled and reviewed during the course of the transaction so that time is not lost rushing through this critical process once the deal is signed. In preparing all forms of documents and communications related to the divestiture, the team needs to be precise and consistent in characterizing markets, and in explaining the rationale for the deal. Any such documents should accurately characterize the market position of the target business based on a consistent set of market measures. Documents should be written factually, free of the hyperbole that can sometimes make its way into corporate documents and presentations concerning the effect of the strategic alternatives under evaluation, to avoid any ambiguities or misunderstandings once these documents are subject to governmental review.

Buyer Financing

If the acquirer intends to use third-party debt to finance the transaction, it will normally need a period of time after the purchase agreement is executed to finalize the financing. Even though the acquirer should have obtained a bank commitment letter (and perhaps provided certain additional guaranties to the seller) for the financing prior to signing the purchase agreement, it must then negotiate the definitive loan agreements and satisfy any conditions set by its bank. Additionally, depending on the magnitude of the transaction and the specific plan for financing the deal, the acquirer's bank may also choose to syndicate the acquisition debt to other participating institutions. These activities normally lead the acquirer to request that a several-week period exist between signing and closing.

Third-Party Consents

In some cases, third parties other than the government are asked to provide their consent before the close of the transaction. For example, if the transaction is structured as an asset purchase, and if certain material customer contracts are not assignable to another corporation without the customers' prior consent, the acquirer may request that those consents be obtained before the closing. Given the potential for third parties to upend an otherwise successful transaction, the seller will normally attempt to negotiate a relatively soft commitment to use "best efforts" to obtain the consents. However, if nonassignable contracts are material to the value of the business, the acquirer should attempt to make its legal obligation to close the transaction conditional on obtaining those consents.

Closing the Transaction

Considering how intense the acquisition process can be, the actual close can seem anticlimactic in comparison. The closing itself, while technically taking place at the office of either the seller's or the acquirer's attorney, is usually accomplished remotely between the two legal advisors, with the (electronic) exchange of signature pages of the agreements and with the confirmation of the wire transfer of the purchase price. The acquisition team has little to do at this point—it may simply receive an e-mail from the legal counsel informing it that the transaction has closed. In some respects, the "real" work of the acquirer about to begin, with the integration and management of the newly acquired business, a topic we discuss in Chapter 8.

Key Points

1. Due diligence findings are channeled to preclosing or postclosing activities, depending on the nature of each issue. Resolving issues prior to closing requires action such as:
   - Revisiting the valuation and renegotiating the purchase price
   - Reviewing and potentially modifying the transaction structure
   - Sharing risk with the seller through contractual terms and conditions

   ("Preacquisition vs. Postacquisition Issues")

2. The most common way to resolve concerns that do not affect the overall valuation of the target business is to share risk with the seller through the terms and conditions of the legal contracts for the acquisition, namely the purchase agreement and its related disclosure schedules, and the transition services agreement. ("Sharing Risk: Contractual Terms and Conditions")

3. Both buyer and seller are significantly invested in the transaction by the time it reaches the contract negotiation stage, and management expectations on both sides are heightened, resulting in pressure to get the deal done. To do so relies heavily on an efficient and effective negotiating process, whose major elements include:
   - Empowered leadership of the principal negotiator
   - Strong support of legal counsel
   - Support of internal and external experts
   - A well-structured mechanism for review and feedback
   - Commitment on the part of negotiators to getting the deal done

   ("Effective and Efficient Negotiations")

4. The most common reasons to separate, or "bifurcate," the signing and the closing are:
   - To obtain regulatory approval
   - To allow buyer financing to be finalized
   - To obtain consents from third parties

   ("Shepherding the Transaction toward Closing")

CHAPTER 8

Integration

Extracting Value and Mitigating Risk

DUAL FOCUS OF THE INTEGRATION EFFORT

The integration of the acquired business is the culmination of the holistic acquisition approach described in this book. Thus far, we have seen how this approach is guided by a dual focus on the creation of value for shareholders and the mitigation of the transaction's various risks. We have also seen how the phases of the acquisition tie together, from planning to investigation to execution:

- The plan to create value established the acquisition team's road map, documenting the transaction's strategic purpose, value drivers, key assumptions, and initial risk assessment.
- The due diligence review validated and modified the plan to create value, supporting the acquirer's decisions concerning whether, or how, to proceed with the transaction, and produced informed plans to extract value and mitigate risks.

In this chapter, we address the integration of the acquired business, which involves implementing the plans mentioned above, monitoring the results, and adapting to changing circumstances.

With their expectations buoyed by the transaction's announcement, the acquiring corporation's stakeholders do not wait long to see evidence of the deal's promised strategic and financial benefits. At the same time, none of the parties with an interest in the transaction wants to hear about significant negative surprises. The level of inherent risk is, unfortunately, often perceived as an internal matter to be managed by the transaction team. The common expectation of all the other parties is to see successful results. Consequently, a dual focus on value and risk must continue to guide the postacquisition activities and deliverables of the team as it begins the integration of the acquired business.

Extracting Value

Successfully extracting value places a premium on the timeliness of execution for several reasons. First, even a delay in generating benefits can reduce the financial return on the acquisition investment (i.e., the value created by the deal). To illustrate this point, consider the following two scenarios described below and illustrated in Exhibit 8.1:

> *Scenario 1* assumes that synergies generate $1 million of additional after-tax cash flows annually beginning immediately after acquisition, increasing by 5 percent per year.

> *Scenario 2* assumes that there is a delay in generating the synergy benefits in the first two years, but higher levels of annual benefits are generated in the third through fifth year, so that the cumulative (undiscounted) results match those in Scenario 1.

Despite generating a significantly higher run rate of cash flow in three of the five years following acquisition, Scenario 2 still results in a reduction of

		Year 1	Year 2	Year 3	Year 4	Year 5	Cumulative Results
Scenario 1:							
	After-tax cash flow	$ 1,000	$ 1,050	$ 1,103	$ 1,158	$ 1,216	$ 5,526
	Present value	$ 4,151					
Scenario 2:							
	After-tax cash flow	$ —	$ 750	$ 1,250	$ 1,720	$ 1,806	$ 5,526
	Present value	$ 3,855					
Change in present value		$ (295)					
Discount rate		10%					

EXHIBIT 8.1 Present Value Effect of a Delay in Synergies ($ thousands)

the present value of cash flows over the five-year period of nearly $300 thousand, or 7 percent, compared with Scenario 1. Depending on the magnitude of the other value drivers (i.e., the purchase price and the stand-alone performance of the acquired business), this delay in generating benefits could have a measurable impact on the deal's rate of return. Many corporations utilize similar discounted cash flow methodologies to calculate the value created by their acquisition investments. Therefore, the timing of returns must be considered along with the magnitude of the returns.

A second factor supporting timely integration relates to the financial results reported by the acquirer. Recently released U.S. financial reporting standards make integration costs and benefits much more transparent in acquirers' financial statements, because most expenditures incurred for "restructuring" (e.g., severance, plant closing costs, or other expenditures related to combining the operations of the acquired business with that of the acquirer) will have to be treated as an expense in the income statement when incurred, rather than capitalized to the balance sheet as part of the accounting for the acquisition transaction. This requires greater care in setting expectations for when such restructuring expenses will appear in reported results, and then in meeting those expectations. A delay in integration activities might thus attract the attention of those relying on the acquirer's financial statements (such as investors and securities analysts), and potentially raise doubts about the successful integration of the acquired business. Revealing the costs of integration may also result in the need to explain and rationalize the expected level and timing of the returns (savings) that these costs will generate.

Finally, from an operations perspective, opportunities deferred can become opportunities lost. Experienced managers guard against delays in the integration process, knowing that they can foster an environmental sense of uncertainty, paralysis, and employee disaffection, conditions that can lead to a loss of momentum and underperformance of the business versus expectations. We are not advocating speed so much as timeliness. The goal is not to act rashly, but purposefully and decisively, leading to greater predictability of results.

Mitigating Risk

While the acquiring corporation cannot always prevent unfavorable developments from occurring, there are a number of steps that can be taken to mitigate risk. A logical starting point is to make full use of the findings from the due diligence review, as discussed in Chapter 7 and illustrated in Exhibit 8.2. While this may sound like common sense, different teams may sometimes be tasked with the due diligence review and the integration as the acquirer pivots from a transaction mode to a management mode. So there is a risk of knowledge sitting unutilized unless the due diligence team is formally debriefed by those tasked with the integration.

Specifically, the due diligence team may have discovered vulnerabilities in the acquired business that should be factored into the integration plan for certain functions (through additional oversight, quicker integration, utilizing experts, or having backup plans ready). For example, suppose the due diligence team notices that a key system of the acquired business is dependent on heavily customized and unsupported software. The integration team may decide to undertake an accelerated conversion to the acquirer's system to reduce the risk of failure, prioritizing it ahead of other systems judged to be more stable.

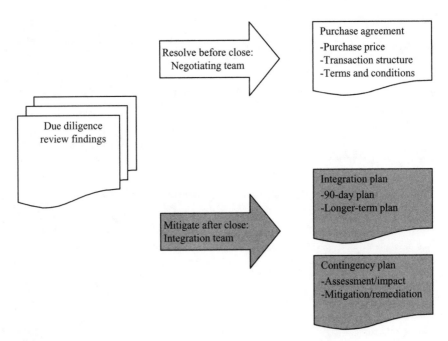

EXHIBIT 8.2   Resolution of Due Diligence Findings: Postclosing Issues

As another example, the due diligence team may note that the acquired business is dependent on a single supplier for a critical product or service. While this may not present an immediate integration issue, the acquirer should use this knowledge to anticipate potential future problems, developing a contingency plan to deal with the possibility of an unanticipated interruption in supply from that vendor.

In addition to utilizing due diligence findings, the acquirer can manage the integration itself in a way that mitigates risk, through close monitoring, frequent updates, decisiveness, and a flexible and adaptable posture. In the next section of this chapter, we discuss these and other aspects of the integration process that enable the acquirer to extract maximum value while mitigating risk, including:

- The integration team
- Details of the integration plan
- The management of the integration process
- Contingency planning
- Human factors

INTEGRATION TEAM

Early Formation

Timely execution of the integration is predicated on having the plan complete and ready to go before closing. This is the reason that we advocated making the identification of integration risks an objective of the due diligence review (see Chapter 5), and the drafting of the integration plan a deliverable of the diligence process (see Chapter 6).

In order to facilitate rapid implementation of the plan, the acquirer should also give early, serious consideration to the integration team. Ideally, the nucleus of the integration team should be named at the time the due diligence team is formed, and those individuals should participate in the due diligence review. In other organizations, the same functional experts performing the due diligence review may be responsible for the integration of their respective business functions. Integration planning is one reason corporate acquirers tend to send large teams to conduct due diligence, especially compared with "financial" buyers such as private equity firms that do not always look to integrate acquisitions with their other portfolio businesses.

Whatever approach is taken regarding the due diligence review, the nucleus of the integration team must be established early enough that it can become familiar with the target business, understand the due diligence findings, influence the finalization of the integration plan itself, and assess the types of internal and external resources required to implement the plan.

In the following sections, we discuss the characteristics required for the leadership of the effort in addition to the structure and composition of the integration team.

Leadership

Acquisitive companies tend to develop and adapt best practices through trial and error and thoughtful retrospective analysis of past transactions. One practice that has been proven effective is the assignment of a single individual to lead the execution of the postacquisition integration. Because integration spans many functions and processes, and interrelationships link many of these, the acquirer cannot afford a diffusion of responsibility (and authority), a condition likely to lead to poor decisions and delay. This individual leader should be empowered with a defined level of decision-making authority, provided with a clearly established approval path for decisions exceeding his or her limit, and be able to call on a cross-section of functional resources from across the organization for assistance.

As far as individual characteristics are concerned, the challenges of integration are such that the skills required for managing the process are extremely varied and often difficult to find embodied in one individual. That said, individuals with an optimal mix of skills should possess most of the following:

- *Comprehensive knowledge of the acquiring company.* Unquestionably, a seasoned and knowledgeable insider would have the advantage of a deep understanding of the acquiring company's operations, its key personnel, and its culture. Effective management of the process would be much more difficult under the leadership of someone, no matter how talented, who comes from outside the organization.
- *Strong project management skills.* Integration is extremely process-oriented and built around objectives, milestones, and concrete accomplishments. Consequently, an operational mentality is a key requirement. The leader should be results-oriented, and operations/logistical management should be a significant strength.

- *Adaptability.* The integration process will inevitably present unforeseen obstacles, resource constraints, or other situations that do not follow the course of the integration plan. The leader should possess the flexibility necessary to adjust direction when circumstances dictate, rather than rigidly adhering to a plan that requires modification.
- *Effective communication skills.* There are multiple stakeholders, both internal and external, with an interest in the progress of the integration. The leader's written and verbal communication skills need to be first rate.
- *Business sense.* The integration process will challenge the leader to exhibit a strong business sense, applying a value orientation to help prioritize the team's efforts and avoid getting trapped in the minutia of day to day details.

Structure and Composition

The integration team is typically composed of individuals who are expert in a specific functional area, but who have other day-to-day operational responsibilities. Many of them will not have the luxury of spending more than a portion of their time on the integration process. Nevertheless, the team members should be held responsible for delivering their part of the plan and encouraged to bring in, or request, the resources necessary to meet their commitments, utilizing external consultants to supplement employee efforts where possible. The exact structure and composition team will vary from case to case, but, generally speaking, it should have the following characteristics:

- *Address every major business function.* Even if a given function's systems or business processes are not slated to be combined, there are probably acquisition-related tasks to be done, such as conforming the two organizations' policies and procedures, or establishing organizational reporting relationships. Additionally, the integration team, if it covers every function of both organizations, could become an effective communications channel to reinforce the acquiring organization's messages to employees. Finally, this structure would offer every part of the acquired business a voice in the integration, providing essential feedback on progress and flagging issues that might otherwise be overlooked. For these reasons, an integration task force should be established for every major operational function.

- *Jointly staffed.* Each functional team should include members from both the acquirer and the acquired organizations. Including the acquired organization provides access to a depth of knowledge about its functions and is an excellent vehicle through which to foster "buy-in" to the integration plan. Having both organizations on the team is also an efficient way to exercise a span of control over combined operating resources, especially during times when management responsibility is transitioned from one organization to the other.
- *Led by unit assuming responsibility for function.* While each function should be jointly staffed, a single individual should be responsible and empowered with decision-making authority for the details of that function's integration. Depending on the integration plan for the function, this may or may not be an employee of the acquirer. Ideally, it should be a representative of the organization (preferably, the individual) who will ultimately be responsible for managing the combined function.
- *Clear individual accountability.* In even the most straightforward integration, there are too many moving parts for team members to have any level of uncertainty about their individual responsibility. Accountability for each team member should be clearly defined, down to the level of tasks, due dates, and deliverables.

INTEGRATION PLAN

Plan Components

In Chapter 5, we described three general aspects of the integration plan:

1. *Operations.* Represents the effort to normalize operations of the combined entity, including the harmonization or standardization of such things as systems, policies, and procedures (e.g., employee compensation and benefits), and corporate/brand identity. It should also involve establishing the organizational and management reporting structure. The goal for the operations aspect is the optimal performance of the acquired business as a stand-alone concern. Note that we are using the word *stand-alone* to refer to the expected rate of growth and profitability of the acquired business *excluding the benefits of combination with the acquirer.* We recognize that most acquired businesses are combined operationally with their acquirer in some ways. Still, as a conceptual

distinction, it is useful to separate the benefits expected from managing the continuing business functions of the acquired business from those additional benefits expected to derive from synergies.

2. *Synergy.* Involves the execution of the measures necessary to extract value as a direct consequence of the combination of the acquiring and acquired entities, either in the form of additional revenue growth or cost reductions.

3. *Culture.* Refers to the meshing of two entities' organizational attitudes and behaviors. We address culture as a separate topic in the section "Human Factors."

In practice, these aspects are not separated, but instead represent the business objectives driving certain steps within the integration plan. A typical integration plan is a logistical document outlining the goals, participants, objectives, tasks, and timing for the postacquisition period, as illustrated in Exhibit 8.3 and described in the following discussion.

- *Overall objectives.* The integration plan's key strategic and financial success factors are a restatement of the original goals for the acquisition as spelled out in the plan to create value, presented here so that their attainment can be objectively tracked. The acquirer should be able to determine in a measurable way whether, or to what extent, it accomplished its goals for the transaction. While the quantification of financial goals is straightforward, even the strategic objectives should be portrayed in terms of key metrics (e.g., market share, customer/user statistics, customer retention or growth rates, product portfolio characteristics, innovation/product development rates). These objectives, in turn, should be explicitly articulated to, and clearly understood by, all members of the integration team.

- *Plan summary.* The integration plan, in its full form, is often extremely voluminous and detailed. To allow leadership to see how the components fit together and to facilitate prioritization, it should have a summary section which consolidates the key aspects of the detailed functional plans, generating an organizational perspective of: timeline, costs and benefits, key metrics, and potential risks.

- *Integration/transition team.* The team's leadership, structure, and functional teams create the individual accountability necessary for the plan's successful execution. The team's characteristics were discussed in the

EXHIBIT 8.3 Integration Plan: Illustrative Outline

Overall Objectives	Key Strategic and Financial Success Factors
Plan summary	Timeline/milestones
	One-time costs
	Benefits (revenue growth, cost reduction)
	Key financial and nonfinancial metrics
	Potential risks and mitigation
Integration/transition team	Leadership
	Structure
	Functional teams
Functional integration plans	Integration approach
	Operating assumptions
	Actions/steps/responsible parties
	Timeline/milestones
	One-time costs
	Benefits (revenue growth, cost reduction)
	Key financial and nonfinancial metrics
	Potential risks and mitigation
Organization and management structure	Preintegration
	Transition
	Postintegration

"Integration Team" section, including our rationale for including every key business function and jointly representing both the acquired and acquiring organizations.

- *Functional Integration plans.* Separate integration plans should be developed for each business function. Major components of the functional plans would typically include:
  - *Integration approach.* The pathway for each operational area (e.g., integrate the function into that of the acquirer, integrate into the acquired organization's function, consolidate and then outsource the functions of both organizations, conform practices to those of one of the organizations, etc.).
  - *Operating assumptions.* These explain why the approach will work, and what assumptions it is based on. Even when a detailed plan exists, there may be lingering uncertainty about key details (such as the technological feasibility of the approach, or the projected volume and

capacity requirements of a combined operation), which may influence the implementation of the plan, so those assumptions should be explicitly noted and validated as soon as practicable.

- *Actions/steps/responsible parties.* This is by far the most detailed and the most critical part of the plan because it is where each and every step of the process should be mapped out. The functional plans will likely consist of hundreds, or even thousands, of steps.
- *Timeline/milestones.* Some complex activities (such as systems conversions) may require subplans utilizing Gantt charts or other sophisticated project management tools. Any points where key decisions need to be made, or approval received, should be included in the plans so that the "critical path" is understood.
- *One-time costs.* All costs related to executing the integration plan should be itemized. They will generally fall into one of two categories: capital expenditures (where new systems or facilities are developed or built) and restructuring (such as severance or plant closing costs that are required to downsize or eliminate duplicate functions or facilities).

  The integration team should be aware that recently released accounting standards in the United States will require the majority of restructuring costs to be treated as expense charged to the acquirer's income statement as incurred (rather than recorded on the balance sheet as a part of the purchase price, as previously allowed). Under the new standards, the cost to restructure the operations of the acquired company as a result of the transaction can be capitalized as part of the acquisition accounting only if certain restrictive conditions are met (namely that the acquirer's restructuring plan be in place on the date of the acquisition: approved, communicated to employees, and facilities abandoned). As a practical matter, very few deals may be expected to meet this hurdle. As discussed earlier in the chapter under "Extracting Value," this places an added premium on setting and managing appropriate expectations with regard to the timing of integration activities.
- *Benefits.* Revenue growth and cost reductions achieved should be tracked and measured against targets for each initiative.
- *Key financial and nonfinancial metrics.* The key metrics are the variables that drive attainment of the strategic and financial goals of the transaction. They should be measurable and, therefore, controllable by the functional team. Depending on the functional area and chosen integration approach, such measures may include workforce

measures (headcount, productivity), technology-related measures (data centers, platforms, systems, capacity, compliance with standards), or facilities and physical plant measures (locations, owned versus leased facilities, square footage, occupancy and density, capacity).

■ *Potential risks and mitigation.* The functional teams should be asked to evaluate what may go wrong with the integration of the function under their responsibility. It is this part of the integration plan that should incorporate relevant findings from the due diligence review, as discussed in the "Mitigating Risk" section. For example, the due diligence team may notice that a given function is critically dependent on a key person or system. The functional team should devise a plan to reduce the likelihood of the risk happening, mitigate the impact if it does happen, and develop a backup plan to move the integration forward if the chosen approach meets unforeseen obstacles.

■ *Organization and management structure.* This section of the integration plan should document the preintegration organization, outline the postintegration organization, and describe any transition or interim structures required to effect the organizational change. This would typically be the responsibility of executive management, assisted by human resources, and would require an underlying process of talent evaluation, succession planning, and retention planning.

First 90 Days vs. Longer Term

As discussed in the section "Extracting Value," a timely integration is necessary to extract the value expected from acquisition synergies, which are often a major part of the total value created be the acquisition. The integration process must, therefore, get off to a crisp and decisive start. To facilitate this initial mobilization, the integration plan should map out its first three months in great detail. The priorities should be to immediately engage all members of the integration team, communicate frequently, closely monitor activities, and, importantly, to sustain the team's enthusiasm by celebrating early successes.

Beyond this initial period (most integration plans span 18 to 24 months), the plan should emphasize goals and milestones, rather than detailed steps. This keeps the team focused on attaining its targets, yet allows some leeway to make midcourse corrections in response to any issues encountered during the early stages.

MANAGEMENT OF THE INTEGRATION PROCESS

In the previous section, we described the various components of the integration plan, discussing *what* should be managed. In this section, we address the question of *how* the integration should be managed, focusing on two essential aspects:

1. Communication
2. Reporting and decision making

Communication

As with most corporate initiatives, effective communication is crucial to a successful integration. For the integration lead, this is a particularly complex challenge. There are normally multiple parties with a direct or indirect interest in the acquisition, each having different questions shaped by their particular relationship with either the acquiring or acquired business. In order to thoughtfully assess who the key audiences are, and what issues are most relevant to them, the integration lead should develop an explicit communication plan to guide the team's messaging. While the contents of the plan will be specific to the individual transaction, there are a number of points that can be made about its development. Following are some general guidelines:

- *Identify stakeholders.* Stakeholders usually include employees, customers, and major vendors of both parties to the transaction. When publicly traded companies are involved, shareholders and the investment community may also represent key constituencies to communicate with. Exhibit 8.4 illustrates the various parties with a potential interest in the acquisition.
- *Determine issues important to each key stakeholder group.* The critical issues for each group will differ, so the plan needs to consider each separately.
  - *Employees.* As discussed in Chapter 6, the postacquisition period can be traumatic for employees (of both acquiring and acquired organizations), marked by an atmosphere of uncertainty that can sap the enthusiasm necessary for the acquirer to accomplish its goals. The objective of the integration team, consequently, should be to reduce uncertainty to the extent that is possible. Once the transaction is closed and the acquirer is no longer internally encumbered by the

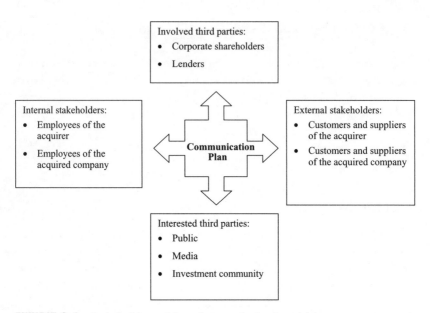

EXHIBIT 8.4 Stakeholders with an Interest in the Acquisition

deal's confidentiality requirements, it should communicate broadly about the acquisition's purpose, benefits, and goals. Communications to employees should set clear expectations for the impact of the combination on future operations and include a commitment to provide progress reports at defined intervals. Management should look to build and sustain its credibility with employees by ensuring subsequent actions are consistent with the initial communications, explaining any major changes in direction. Employees should be provided a method for voicing any questions and concerns to management. The employees of both organizations should be included in communications, because, even if integration plans will not impact the acquirer, its employees may not know that and might be subject to the same level of uncertainty as at the acquired organization.

In cases where jobs will be eliminated, it is best to approach the affected employees early with retention and severance agreements and solicit their participation in the integration process. Knowing about job losses is far less debilitating than the corrosive effect of a slow drip of leaks and rumors. And, to the extent severed employees are treated fairly (something they will discuss with retained employees regardless of confidentiality restrictions), a surprising level of goodwill can be developed.

- *Customers and suppliers.* The primary message to customers and suppliers should be that of continuity. The benefits of the business combination to customers (such as an expanded product line or enhanced service/support capabilities) are certainly worth noting, but the organization should not lose sight of the fact that the most important assurance customers can receive is that the service and product quality that has made them customers in the first place will be maintained. The message to major suppliers should be similar to that of customers, that is, one of business as usual, unless there are compelling reasons for change that affect them.

- *Third parties.* Stockholders and the investment community as a whole normally have a singular focus on the shareholder value created by an acquisition, especially in light of a mixed historical record (discussed in Chapter 1) which may invite skepticism. Accordingly, the message for these groups should focus on how the combination of the two entities will deliver increased value, and the critical follow-on message is that the key integration milestones are being met. Lenders providing financing for the deal will also be keenly focused on the achievement of integration milestones and the prospects for generating steady and increasing operating cash flow.

- *Customize communications channels.* Internal groups should be communicated with via a range of vehicles. Major written communications should be reinforced with employee assemblies (or Web casts if live events are not practical), smaller meetings for individual facilities or departments, follow-up meetings in small groups, and progress reports through e-mail or posted on internal corporate sites. Employee communications will be most effective if important messages are delivered personally, versus in writing, and if employees are provided some avenue for face-to-face interaction (e.g., with their manager or human resources) so that they can voice any concerns directly and get answers personally.

Insofar as customers are concerned, it normally makes most sense to segment the customer base, having the senior account executives meet personally with the most important customers, contacting the next largest customers by phone, and following up with standard e-mail messages to the broader customer base. Vendor communication, which is generally a lesser concern, should follow a similar pattern.

Stockholder and investment community communication is a concern when publicly traded companies are involved. Major acquisitions generally are provided significant coverage in the financial press and also routinely require a substantial amount of communication with stockholders. The integration lead would not normally have occasion to communicate directly with these groups, but may be expected to provide information in support of communications channeled through the corporation's senior executive management and its investor relations function.

■ *Provide regular updates.* Messages to key stakeholders should be updated at regular intervals to reinforce the organization's accomplishment of its goals for the transaction. The frequency should be driven by the expectations set initially.

This is particularly true of the employee population. Employees should be kept abreast of progress at regular, predictable intervals. Likewise, it is advisable to communicate progress and manage the expectations of shareholders and the investment community. Obviously, a period of silence at a time when stakeholders have been led to expect accomplishment of a key objective will erode confidence and invite speculation. Conversely, there is generally little need for ongoing communication with customers and vendors, unless there are developments that directly impact them.

Reporting and Decision Making

The purpose of any reporting mechanism for the acquisition integration is to ensure that the transaction's objectives are met. As such, formal reporting should remain in place for the full duration of key milestones outlined in the integration plan. Two aspects of reporting warrant discussion: reporting by functional team members to the integration lead, and reporting by the integration lead to corporate management.

■ *Functional team reports: Facilitate timely decisions and emphasize accountability.* Few, if any, business combinations go exactly as planned, so progress should be closely monitored during the critical first three months after closing. The integration leader should create a reporting mechanism that fosters timely updates and facilitates rapid decisions, objectives which argue against requiring voluminous reports.

Instead, the teams should meet frequently, provide information and feedback, and quickly and decisively make any necessary midcourse adjustments.

A good way to oversee the functional teams is with a scheduled weekly conference call. In advance of the call, each functional team should provide a concise one-page summary following a standard outline. The call itself should be attended by all functional leaders, who should listen in on all other team readouts, as issues arising in one function may well have implications for others. While providing an efficient vehicle for information sharing, the weekly call also serves another objective of the integration leader—to emphasize the accountability of each functional team to deliver on its commitments. The report-outs should be exception-based, focused only on issues requiring decisions, such as changes in approach, resolution of conflicting priorities, or addressing people resources or funding needs. Exhibit 8.5 illustrates an outline for the weekly team report.

On a monthly basis, each team should supplement its weekly "live action" reporting with a comparison of milestones, key metrics and financial results against targets to provide input for corporate reporting.

■ *Integration team leader reports: Emphasize results.* Corporate management tends to care much more about whether the organization's acquisition goals were achieved than how they were achieved. Consequently, the team leader's periodic report to the corporation should focus mainly on progress attained toward the acquisition's strategic and financial objectives. Depending on the frequency of the

EXHIBIT 8.5 Weekly Status Report: Illustrative Outline

Functional area	Individual in charge
Key milestones	Rolling 90-day view
Key metrics	Relating to areas under active focus
Key issues	Issues arising that might prevent accomplishment of objectives on time, delivering projected benefits
Decisions required	Approach
	Prioritization
	Resources
	Funding

corporation's other management reports, the periodic integration report may be a monthly or quarterly deliverable.

This should be viewed as more of a document of record than a decision-support tool. It should, in one place, contain all the key metrics of interest to the various parties within the corporation who are tracking the performance of the deal. It should begin with a clear indication of whether the acquisition's goals are being attained, and then drilling down into supporting financial and nonfinancial metrics. While it should discuss any major issues arising from the integration activities to date, it should indicate how each issue has been resolved, indicating the end result of any decisions made by the integration team. Exhibit 8.6 illustrates an outline for the periodic integration report.

EXHIBIT 8.6 Periodic Integration Report: Illustrative Outline

Overall status	Report on achievement of strategic and financial objectives
	Timeline and comparison of key milestones against original goals
Financial summary	Total acquisition performance compared with preacquisition projections
Financial impact of integration	Comparison of value drivers with preacquisition projections:
	–Stand-alone growth and profitability
	–Revenue synergies
	–Expense synergies
	One-time costs:
	–Capital expenditures
	–Restructuring
Nonfinancial metrics	Comparison against original goals:
	–Strategic (e.g., market, customer, product measures)
	–Financial (e.g., headcount, productivity)
Key issues	Issues and resolution

CONTINGENCY PLAN

Broader View of Risks

An acquisition is a major financial investment that, under the best of circumstances, will take years to generate a return, exposing the buyer's shareholders to a significant loss if something truly disruptive were to happen to the acquired company. As a result, we have made risk mitigation a key theme of this chapter, pointing out that relevant due diligence review findings (i.e., vulnerabilities) ought to be channeled into the integration plan, and further noting that each of the functional teams should identify potential integration risks for their areas of responsibility and develop strategies to mitigate those risks. Those are sound practices but, alone, they may still not address the full range of risks faced by the newly acquired organization. We believe that those more focused measures should be supplemented with a contingency plan, which takes a broader, enterprise-wide approach to identifying and managing risks. In an ideal situation, the contingency plan's initial development should be a deliverable of the due diligence team, as discussed in Chapter 6. Otherwise, it should be made an early priority for the integration team.

The notion of planning for enterprise-wide risks is a familiar one to many corporations, who have adopted such broad-gauge plans to supplement their more targeted internal control practices (e.g., data center disaster-recovery planning). A contingency plan provides the organization's best thinking about responses to risks that would have an impact at the level of the total business enterprise, a consequence of the acquisition itself or a characteristic of the acquired company. The focus is on threats that are not imminent and which might, in fact, never materialize. The objective of the plan is to induce the organization to think beyond what it considers the most-likely-case scenario and develop strategies to mitigate, remediate, or monitor lower-probability, but higher-impact events.

Plan Components

An outline of a typical contingency plan is illustrated in Exhibit 8.7 and described in the following discussion.

■ *Business environment.* This section describes the business environment within which the acquired company operates, establishing context for the potential internal and external risks it, by its nature, faces.

EXHIBIT 8.7 Contingency Plan: Illustrative Outline

Business environment	Description
Contingency	Description
Assessment	Qualitative impact
	Financial impact
Action plan	Mitigation
	Monitoring
	Remediation
Timing	Near term
	Longer term
Responsibility	Executive responsible

- *Contingency description.* A description is provided for each possible event judged to represent a material threat to the organization. This exercise should not try to imagine every possible scenario, but attempt to identify situations where the organization is especially vulnerable. For example, if the organization is dependent on a single vendor for a key product or service, then the contingency plan should address the organization's supply chain. Or, if it operates in a heavily regulated industry, it would benefit from considering scenarios involving regulatory compliance. Other examples might include:
  - Abrupt change in market environment
  - Competitor (existing or new) action
  - Legal action
  - Regulatory compliance issue
  - Major product failure
  - Major customer satisfaction issue
  - Failure of a mission-critical internal business process
  - Disruption of a single-source supplier
  - Employee/labor unrest
- *Assessment.* The impact of each event should be considered from both a qualitative and quantitative perspective. Both may be difficult to precisely determine, but the point is to determine each event's relative impact so that plans can be prioritized. Qualitative consequences might include damage to the organization's reputation or brand image. The financial impact would typically address revenues or costs, but might also attempt to factor in a relative probability of occurrence.

- *Action plan.* This section describes the strategies to be employed for controlling the various risks. For some items, the organization might decide to take active steps to mitigate the risk (for example, in the case of a single supplier, it might seek out and develop alternatives). In other cases (e.g., in the case of a potential regulatory change), the strategy might involve close monitoring, or periodically reviewing, the situation. A remediation plan should be outlined for each contingency in the event the situation occurs.

- *Timing and responsibility.* An individual executive should be responsible for the near-term and longer-term approaches for the management of each identified issue and update the contingency plan on a predefined, periodic basis (e.g., quarterly or semiannually).

HUMAN FACTORS

Culture

For most of this chapter, we have referred to the integration of an acquired company as the combination of its business functions. The acquired company, of course, is a lot more than a collection of functions and processes. That organization possesses a unique corporate culture, and its particular culture may or may not fit with that of the acquirer. A corporate culture is an organization's essential "personality," shaped by its assumptions, values, and behavioral norms. The impact of conflicting organizational cultures has been well chronicled in literature about mergers and acquisitions. Many otherwise successful acquisitions have ultimately failed because of the acquiring company's inability to manage the conflict caused by cultural differences.[1] For this reason, we identified culture in Chapter 5 as a separate aspect for consideration in the integration plan.

Cultural integration refers to the meshing of two entities' organizations, attitudes and behaviors. The cultural characteristics most relevant to acquisitions relate to how each organization makes business decisions:

- Is it risk-averse or aggressive?
- Does it embrace change or is it wed to existing practices?

---

[1]David M. Schweiger, *M&A Integration: A Framework for Executives and Managers* (New York: McGraw-Hill, 2002), 218.

- Does it make decisions centrally or are executives relatively autonomous?
- Is it bureaucratic or informal in style?
- Is its orientation short-term or long-term?

Those characteristics are deeply influenced by the organizations' ownership structure (e.g., privately held or publicly traded) and stage of development (e.g., an early-stage high-growth company versus a well-established, mature market leader). Given that many acquisitions tend to pair just such disparate organizations, we can see why some level of conflict is perhaps inevitable. The challenge for the integration leader is to prevent cultural conflict from becoming debilitating. While every situation will have its own particular needs, here are several general practices observed in successful business combinations:

- *Understanding cultural differences through the joint integration teams.* Cultural conflict may exist at the aggregate corporate level, but where it needs to be understood and managed is at the level of each functional team. The integration teams should take the time to share information with each other about their respective cultures so that major differences and specific points of conflict can be identified and managed. The focus, as previously mentioned, should be on the organization's decision-making process.
- *Best practice mentality.* Corporate cultures evolve the way they do for specific reasons, and different approaches may prove optimal for particular functions. The acquirer should not bring preconceived notions about the superiority of its own practices and procedures, nor create the impression that it intends to blindly impose its ways on the acquired company. The organization that exhibits excellence at that function (for example, one's R&D function may have a much higher success rate, or the other's back office operation might be more efficient) should be closely studied before finalizing the integration approach.
- *Common objectives and flexibility.* If each team is challenged with working toward a common objective, team members may be less likely to focus on differences of each organization's past practices, and adopt a more forward-looking problem-solving posture, especially if they perceive an openness and flexibility regarding how problems are solved.

- *Changing only things that are required.* There may be certain practices that are symbolically important to the acquired organization. The acquirer should consider moving more slowly to harmonize such practices unless they are deemed critical to the integration.
- *Cross-fertilization.* The acquirer should actively seek to transfer employees between (both to and from) itself and the acquired organization. These employees become invaluable sources of information and advice on dealing with the other's business culture. Over time, this practice develops a group of individuals who come to recognize and appreciate the best aspects of each organization.
- *Professional facilitation.* Sometimes the differences between organizational cultures are so vast that professional facilitation is called for. There is a broad array of professional consultants who specialize in organizational change management that can help in these circumstances.
- *Celebrating success.* There is nothing that can soften resistance to new ways of doing things like success. The integration leader should make it a priority to widely communicate and reinforce all "early wins" in the process.

Knowledge Transfer

A lot of hard-won, specialized knowledge is gained by the individuals working on the acquisition and its integration. Active acquirers should consider creating processes to capture and share this knowledge so that future transaction teams will benefit, as well as increase their organizational capacity to do future deals. Following are suggestions to optimize knowledge transfer:

- *Lessons learned.* Most every acquisition and integration team member emerges from the transaction with strong opinions about what went well or poorly, and what could have been done better. These insights could greatly benefit future transactions. The corporation should formally document the key lessons learned from each transaction and provide this information to future transaction teams. Soliciting the team's suggestions for improvement can be accomplished in a one-day debriefing.
- *Expert databases.* Acquisition and integration create the need to call upon the talents of functional experts from across the corporation. As the organization adds to the number of people experienced in

acquisitions, these individuals should be tracked in an expert database to be called on to participate in or advise teams for future transactions.

- *Formal acquisition training programs.* An organization that has an active acquisition agenda needs to consider expanding its capacity to acquire and integrate businesses. While deal-making is an expertise that can be supplemented with external advisors, organizations may be caught more off-guard with the responsibilities they face in integrating acquired organizations. Consequently, the organization should methodically build its capacity to digest transactions by conducting acquisition training programs for functional executives who may only work on transactions sporadically. Although some amount of learning inevitably happens from being on a transaction, many functional executives may only participate in narrow aspects, lacking the context and perspective that would make their future efforts much more effective. Broad-based acquisition training would shorten people's learning curve and deepen the bench of people able to participate on future deals. Alternatively, acquisition teams could be launched with an intensive seminar for a day or two before the initiating work on a transaction.

RECOMMENDATIONS FOR POSTACQUISITION MANAGEMENT

Following are some final words of advice regarding the acquisition integration process:

- *Build extra cushion into the financial targets of the functional teams.* In practice, functional integration teams often discover issues that cumulatively reduce the amount of synergy benefits or delay their achievement. In establishing targets, the integration lead should apply a "success rate" to the initiatives and build extra cushion to cover unanticipated shortfalls.
- *It is not possible to overcommunicate.* It is difficult to offer this advice without it sounding like a cliché. Yet, employees of both the acquiring and acquired organizations are hungry for information about how they will be affected by the transaction; their interest is intense and it is personal. Any information vacuums will be filled by rumor and speculation, so the integration lead should err on the side of overcommunicating.

- *Be both goal-orientated and open-minded.* This is a seeming contradiction, but the integration process will require exactly this combination of attributes. A successful integration requires a dogged focus on results, but also an agility and flexibility to identify opportunities and react to changes in circumstances.

- *Be empathetic.* The integration leader should be mindful of the human aspects of the challenge. People have limitations and will be most productive if they believe targets and deadlines are realistic. It is critically important for early actions vis-à-vis the acquisition to be successful, hopefully setting a positive tone for the entire process.

- *Don't underestimate the amount of effort involved.* Experience shows that, at any level of scale, it is extremely challenging to effect the combination of two organizations. Small acquisitions can sometimes be as or more difficult than large ones, due to a paucity of resources and, often, a lack of documentation that requires knowledge about the acquired organization to be "back-filled."

Key Points

1. The transaction sponsor must sustain a dual focus through the integration: optimize the stand-alone business performance and synergies and, at the same time, mitigate risk by guarding against the possibility of unfavorable events. ("Dual Focus of the Integration Effort")

2. Timely execution of the integration is predicated on having the plan complete and ready to go before closing. In order to facilitate rapid implementation of the plan, the acquirer should give early, serious consideration to the integration team. ("Early Formation")

3. The integration plan should map out its first three months in great detail, immediately engaging all members of the team. Beyond this initial period, the plan should emphasize goals and milestones rather than detailed steps, keeping the team focused on attaining its target, yet allowing some leeway to make midcourse corrections. ("First 90 Days vs. Longer Term")

4. Team reporting should foster timely updates and facilitate rapid decisions, objectives that argue against requiring voluminous reports. Instead, the teams should meet frequently, provide information and

feedback, and quickly and decisively make any necessary adjustments. ("Reporting and Decision Making")

5. We believe that the team's more focused risk-mitigation measures should be supplemented with a contingency plan, which takes a broader, enterprise-wide approach to identifying and managing risks. ("Broader View of Risks")

6. Cultural integration refers to the meshing of two entities' organizations, attitudes and behaviors, with the characteristics most relevant to acquisitions being each organization makes business decisions. While some level of conflict may be inevitable, the challenge for the integration leader is to prevent cultural conflict from becoming debilitating. ("Culture")

7. A lot of hard-won, specialized knowledge is gained by the individuals working on the acquisition and its integration. Active acquirers should consider creating processes to capture and share this knowledge so that future transaction teams will benefit, as well as increase their organizational capacity to do future deals. ("Knowledge Transfer")

What Is the Premerger
Notification Program

An Overview*

The Hart-Scott-Rodino Antitrust Improvements Act of 1976 (HSR) established a premerger program requiring those engaged in certain mergers and acquisitions to notify the Federal Trade Commission (FTC) and the Department of Justice (DOJ) of an impending transaction. The HSR thresholds that trigger notification are quite low and, as a result, affect a significant percentage of M&A transactions. Because of its pervasive impact and the complex nature of its requirements, the text of the FTC's *Introductory Guide "What Is the Premerger Notification Program"* has been provided in this Appendix. This document is meant to alert those engaged in M&A transactions of the requirements of the Act and *is not a substitute for legal guidance.* If a given transaction appears to fall within the parameters of the Act, advice of counsel with the appropriate regulatory expertise should be sought.

INTRODUCTION

The Act requires that parties to certain mergers or acquisitions notify the Federal Trade Commission and the Department of Justice (the "enforcement

---

*This material is reprinted from the Hart-Scott-Rodino-Rodino Premerger Notification Program, *Introductory Guide I, What Is the Premerger Notification Program: An Overview*, revised September 2008, FTC Premerger Notification Office. Available at http://www.ftc.gov/bc/hsr/introguides/introguides.shtm.

agencies") before consummating the proposed acquisition. The parties must wait a specific period of time while the enforcement agencies review the proposed transaction. The Program became effective September 5, 1978, after final promulgation of the Rules.[1]

The Program was established to avoid some of the difficulties and expense that the enforcement agencies encounter when they challenge anticompetitive acquisitions after they have occurred. In the past, the enforcement agencies found that it is often impossible to restore competition fully once a merger takes place. Furthermore, any attempt to reestablish competition after the fact is usually very costly for the parties and the public. Prior review under the Program enables the Federal Trade Commission ("FTC" or the "Commission") and the Department of Justice ("DOJ") to determine which acquisitions are likely to be anticompetitive and to challenge them at a time when remedial action is most effective.

In general, the Act requires that certain proposed acquisitions of voting securities, non-corporate interests ("NCI") or assets be reported to the FTC and the DOJ prior to consummation. The parties must then wait a specified period, usually 30 days (15 days in the case of a cash tender offer or a bankruptcy sale), before they may complete the transaction. Much of the information needed for a preliminary antitrust evaluation is included in the notification filed with the agencies by the parties to proposed transactions and thus is immediately available for review during the waiting period.

Whether a particular acquisition is subject to these requirements depends upon the value of the acquisition and the size of the parties, as measured by their sales and assets. Small acquisitions, acquisitions involving small parties, and other classes of acquisitions that are less likely to raise antitrust concerns are excluded from the Act's coverage.

If either agency determines during the waiting period that further inquiry is necessary, it is authorized by Section 7A(e) of the Clayton Act to request additional information or documentary materials from the parties to a reported transaction (a "second request"). A second request extends

---

[1] The Premerger Notification Rules are found at 16 C.F.R. Parts 801, 802 and 803. The Rules also are identified by number, and each Rule beginning with Rule 801.1 corresponds directly with the section number in the C.F.R. (so that Rule 801.40 would be found in 16 C.F.R. § 801.40). In this Guide, the Rules are cited by Rule number.

the waiting period for a specified period, usually 30 days (ten days in the case of a cash tender offer or a bankruptcy sale), after all parties have complied with the request (or, in the case of a tender offer or a bankruptcy sale, after the acquiring person complies). This additional time provides the reviewing agency with the opportunity to analyze the submitted information and to take appropriate action before the transaction is consummated. If the reviewing agency believes that a proposed transaction may violate the antitrust laws, it may seek an injunction in federal district court to prohibit consummation of the transaction.

The Program has been a success. Compliance with the Act's notification requirements has been excellent, and has minimized the number of postmerger challenges the enforcement agencies have had to pursue. In addition, although the agencies retain the power to challenge mergers post-consummation, and will do so under appropriate circumstances, the fact that they rarely do has led many members of the private bar to view the Program as a helpful tool in advising their clients about particular acquisition proposals.

The Rules, which govern compliance with the Program, are necessarily technical and complex. We have prepared Guide I to introduce some of the Program's specially defined terms and concepts. This should assist you in determining if proposed business transactions are subject to the requirements of the Program.

DETERMINING REPORTABILITY

The Act requires persons contemplating proposed business transactions that satisfy certain size criteria to report their intentions to the enforcement agencies before consummating the transaction. If the proposed transaction is reportable, then both the acquiring person and the person whose business is being acquired must submit information about their respective business operations to the enforcement agencies and wait a specific period of time before consummating the proposed transaction. During that waiting period, the enforcement agencies review the antitrust implications of the proposed transaction. Whether a particular transaction is reportable is determined by application of the Act, the Rules, and formal and informal staff interpretations.

As a general matter, the Act and the Rules require both acquiring and acquired persons to file notifications under the Program if all of the following conditions are met:

1. As a result of the transaction, the acquiring person will hold an aggregate amount of voting securities, NCI, and/or assets of the acquired person valued in excess of $200 million (as adjusted)[2], regardless of the sales or assets of the acquiring and acquired persons[3]; or
2. As a result of the transaction, the acquiring person will hold an aggregate amount of voting securities, NCI, and/or assets of the acquired person valued in excess of $50 million (as adjusted) but at $200 million (as adjusted) or less; and
3. One person has sales or assets of at least $100 million (as adjusted); and
4. The other person has sales or assets of at least $10 million (as adjusted).

Size of Transaction Test

The first step is to determine what voting securities, NCI, assets, or combination thereof are being transferred in the proposed transaction. Then you must determine the value of the voting securities, NCI, and/or assets as well as the percentage of voting securities and NCI that will be "held as a result of the acquisition." Calculating what will be held as a result of the acquisition (referred to as the "size of the transaction") is complicated and requires the application of several rules, including Rules 801.10, 801.12, 801.13, 801.14, and 801.15. Generally, the securities and/or NCI held as a result of the transaction include those that will be acquired in the proposed transaction, as well as any voting securities and/or NCI of the acquired person, or entities within the acquired person, that the acquiring person already holds.

---

[2] The 2000 amendments to the Act require the Commission to revise certain thresholds annually based on the change in the level of gross national product. A parenthetical "(as adjusted)" has been added where necessary throughout the Rules (and in this guide) to indicate where such a change in statutory threshold value occurs. The term "as adjusted" is defined in subsection 801.1 (n) of the Rules and refers to a table of the adjusted values published in the Federal Register notice titled "Revised Jurisdictional Thresholds for Section 7A of the Clayton Act." The notice contains a table showing adjusted values for the rules and is published in January of each year.

[3] See § 7A(a)(2) of the Act.

Assets held as a result of the acquisition include those that will be acquired in the proposed transaction as well as certain assets of the acquired person that the acquiring person has purchased within the time limits outlined in Rule 801.13.[4]

If the value of the voting securities, NCI, assets or combination thereof exceeds $200 million (as adjusted) and no exemption applies, the parties must file notification and observe the waiting period before closing the transaction.

If the value of the voting securities, NCI, assets or combination thereof exceeds $50 million (as adjusted) but is $200 million (as adjusted) or less, the parties must look to the size of person test.

Acquiring and Acquired Persons/Acquired Entity

The first step in determining the size of person is to identify the "acquiring person" and "acquired person." "Person" is defined in Rules 801.1(a)(l) and is the "ultimate parent entity" or "UPE" of the buyer or seller. That is, it is the entity that ultimately controls the buyer or seller.[5] The "acquired entity" is the specific entity whose assets, NCI or voting securities are being acquired. The acquired entity may also be its own UPE or it may be an entity within the acquired person.

Thus, in an asset acquisition, the acquiring person is the UPE of the buyer, and the acquired person is the UPE of the seller. The acquired entity is the entity whose assets are being acquired. In a voting securities acquisition, the acquiring person is the UPE of the buyer, the acquired person is the UPE of the entity whose securities are being bought, and the acquired entity is the issuer of the securities being purchased. In an acquisition of NCI, the acquiring person is the UPE of the buyer, the acquired person is the UPE of the entity whose NCI are being bought, and the acquired entity is the entity whose NCI are being acquired. Oftentimes the acquired person and acquired entity are the same.

In many voting securities acquisitions, the acquiring person proposes to buy voting securities from minority shareholders of the acquired entity,

---

[4] The Rules on when to aggregate the value of previously acquired voting securities and assets with the value of the proposed acquisition are discussed in greater detail in Guide II.

[5] See "control" under 801.1(b).

rather than from the entity itself (tender offers are an example of this type of transaction). These transactions are subject to Rule 801.30, which imposes a reporting obligation on the acquiring person and on the acquired person, despite the fact that the acquired person may have no knowledge of the proposed purchase of its outstanding securities.[6] For this reason, the Rules also require that a person proposing to acquire voting securities directly from shareholders rather than from the issuer itself serve notice on the issuer of the shares to ensure the acquired person knows about its reporting obligation.[7]

Size of Person Test

Once you have determined who the acquiring and acquired persons are, you must determine whether the size of each person meets the Act's minimum size criteria. This "size of person" test generally measures a company based on the person's last regularly prepared annual statement of income and expenses and its last regularly prepared balance sheet.[8] The size of a person includes not only the entity that is making the acquisition or whose assets or securities are being acquired, but also the UPE and any other entities the UPE controls.[9]

If the value of the voting securities, NCI, assets or combination thereof exceeds $50 million (as adjusted) but is $200 million (as adjusted) or less, the size of person test is met. and no exemption applies, the parties must file notification and observe the waiting period before closing the transaction.

Notification Thresholds

An acquisition that will result in a buyer holding more than $50 million (as adjusted) worth of the voting securities of another issuer crosses the first of five staggered "notification thresholds."[9] The rules identify four additional thresholds: voting securities valued at $100 million (as adjusted) or greater but less than $500 million (as adjusted); voting securities valued at $500 million (as adjusted) or greater; 25 percent of the voting securities of an issuer, if the 25 percent (or any amount above 25 percent but less than 50 percent) is valued at greater than $1 billion (as adjusted); and 50 percent of the voting securities of an issuer if valued at greater than $50 million (as adjusted).

---

[6] See Rule 801.1; Rule 801.30.
[7] See Rule 803.5.
[8] See Rule 801.11.
[9] See Rule 801.1(a)(l).

The thresholds are designed to act as exemptions to relieve parties of the burden of making another filing every time additional voting shares of the same person are acquired. As such, when notification is filed, the acquiring person is allowed one year from the end of the waiting period to cross the threshold stated in the filing.[10] If within that year the person reaches the stated threshold (or any lower threshold), it may continue acquiring voting shares up to the next threshold for five years from the end of the waiting period.[11] For example, if you file to acquire $100 million (as adjusted) of the voting securities of Company B and cross that threshold within one year, you would be able to continue to acquire voting securities of Company B for a total of five years without having to file again so long as your total holding of Company B's voting securities did not exceed either $500 million (as adjusted) or 50 percent, i.e., additional notification thresholds. Once an acquiring person holds 50 percent or more of the voting securities of an issuer, all subsequent acquisitions of securities of that issuer are exempt.[12]

These notification thresholds apply only to acquisitions of voting securities. The 50 percent threshold is the highest threshold regardless of the corresponding dollar value.

Exempt Transactions

In some instances, a transaction may not be reportable even if the size of person and the size of transaction tests have been satisfied. The Act and the Rules set forth a number of exemptions, describing particular transactions or classes of transactions that need not be reported despite meeting the threshold criteria.[13] For example, certain acquisitions of assets in the ordinary course of a person's business are exempted, including new goods and current supplies (e.g., an airline purchases new jets from a manufacturer, or a supermarket purchases its inventory from a wholesale distributor).[14] The acquisition of certain types of real property also would not require notification. These include certain new and used facilities, not being acquired with a business, unproductive real property (e.g., raw land), office and residential buildings, hotels (excluding hotel casinos), certain recreational land,

---

[10] See Rule 803.7.
[11] See Rule 802.21.
[12] See § 7A(c)(3) of the Act, 15 U.S.C. § 18a(c)(3).
[13] See § 7A(c) of the Act, 15 U.S.C. § 18a(c), and Part 802 of the Rules, 16 C.F.R. Part 802.
[14] See Rules 802.1(b) and 802.1(c).

agricultural land and retail rental space and warehouses.[15] In addition, the acquisition of foreign assets would be exempt where the sales in or into the U.S. attributable to those assets were $50 million (as adjusted) or less.[16] Once it has been determined that a particular transaction is reportable, each party must submit its notification to the FTC and the DOJ. In addition, each acquiring person must pay a filing fee to the FTC for each transaction that it reports (with a few exceptions, *see* section "The Filing Fee" below).

THE FORM

The Notification and Report Form ("the Form") solicits information that the enforcement agencies use to help evaluate the antitrust implications of the proposed transaction. Copies of the Form, Instructions, and Style Sheet are available from the PNO, (202) 326-3100, as well as the FTC at http://www.ftc.gov/bc/hsr.

Information Reported

In general, a filing party is required to identify the persons involved and the structure of the transaction. The reporting person also must provide certain documents such as balance sheets and other financial data, as well as copies of certain documents that have been filed with the Securities and Exchange Commission. In addition, the parties are required to submit certain planning and evaluation documents that pertain to the proposed transaction.

The Form also requires the parties to disclose whether the acquiring person and acquired entity currently derive revenue from businesses that fall within any of the same industry and product North American Industry Classification System ("NAICS") codes,[17] and, if so, in which geographic areas they operate. Identification of overlapping codes may indicate whether

---

[15] See Rules 802.2(c)–(h).

[16] See Rules 802.50 and 802.51.

[17] For information concerning NAICS codes *see* the *North American Industry Classification System, 2002*, published by the Executive Office of the President, Office of Management and Budget and available from the National Technical Information Service, 5285 Port Royal Road, Springfield VA 22161 (Order Number PB 2002-101430) or online at http://www.ntis.gov/search/product.aspx?ABBR=PB2002101430; and the *2002 Economic Census Numerical List of Manufactured and Mineral Products* published by Bureau of the Census, available from the Government

the parties engage in similar lines of business. Acquiring persons must also describe certain previous acquisitions in the last five years of companies or assets engaged in businesses in any of the overlapping codes identified. Please note that an acquiring person must complete the Form for all of its operations; an acquired person, on the other hand, must limit its response in Items 5 through 7 to the business or businesses being sold and does not need to answer Item 8.[18] In addition, the acquired person does not need to respond to Item 6 in a pure asset transaction.

Contact Person

The parties are required to identify an individual (listed in Item 1(g) of the Form) who is a representative of the reporting person and is familiar with the content of the Form. This contact person is, in most cases, either counsel for the party or an officer of the company. This person must be available during the waiting period.

Certification and Affidavits

Rule 803.5 describes the affidavit that must accompany certain Forms. In transactions where the acquiring person is purchasing voting securities from non-controlling shareholders, only the acquiring person must submit an affidavit. The acquiring person must state in the affidavit that it has a good faith intention of completing the proposed transaction and that it has served notice on the acquired person as to its potential reporting obligations.[19] In all other transactions, each of the acquired and acquiring persons must submit an affidavit with their Forms, attesting to the fact that a contract, an agreement in principle, or a letter of intent has been executed and that each person has a good faith intention of completing the proposed transaction. These required statements govern when the parties may make a premerger

---

Printing Office or online at http://www.census.gov/prod/ec02/02numlist/m31r-nl.pdf. Information regarding NAICS also is available at the Bureau of the Census at http://www.census.gov/epcd/www/naics.html.

[18] See 803.2(b).

[19] See Rule 803.5(a)(i)(I) through (vi) for the full requirements of such notice. In tender offers, the acquiring person also must affirm that the intention to make the tender offer has been publicly announced. See Rule 803.5(a)(2).

notification filing. The affidavit is intended to assure that the enforcement agencies will not be presented with hypothetical transactions for review.[20]

Rule 803.6 provides that the Form must be certified and the rule specifies who must make the certification.[21] One of the primary purposes of the certification is to preserve the evidentiary value of the filing. It also is intended to place responsibility on an individual to ensure that information reported is true, correct, and complete. Both the certification and the affidavit must be notarized, or may be signed under penalty of perjury.[22]

Voluntary Information

The rules provide that reporting persons also may submit information that is not required by the Form.[23] If persons voluntarily provide information or documentary material that is helpful to the competitive analysis of the proposed transaction, the enforcement agencies' review of a proposed transaction may be more rapid. However, voluntary submissions do not guarantee a speedy review. Voluntary submissions are included in the confidentiality coverage of the Act and the Rules.

Confidentiality

Neither the information submitted nor the fact that a notification has been filed is made public by the agencies except as part of a legal or administrative action to which one of the agencies is a party or in other narrowly defined circumstances permitted by the Act.[24] However, in response to inquiries from interested parties who wish to approach the agencies with their views

---

[20] See Statement of Basis and Purpose to Rule 803.5, 43 Fed. Reg. 33510-33511 (1978).

[21] The certification may be signed by a general partner of a partnership; an officer or director of a corporation; or, in the case of a natural person, the natural person or his/her legal representative.

[22] 28 U.S.C. § 1746 allows use of the following statement in lieu of a notary's jurat: "I declare (or certify, verify or state) under penalty of perjury *under the laws of the United States of America* that the foregoing is true and correct. Executed on (date) [and] (Signature)." The italicized text is necessary only if signed outside the territorial United States.

[23] See Rule 803.1(b).

[24] See Section 7A(h) of the Act.

about a transaction, the agencies may confirm which agency is handling the investigation of a publicly announced merger.[25] The fact that a transaction is under investigation also may become apparent if the agencies interview third parties during their investigation.

Filing Procedures

The parties should complete and return the original and one copy of the Form, along with one set of documentary attachments, to the Premerger Notification Office, Bureau of Competition, Room 303, Federal Trade Commission, 600 Pennsylvania Avenue, NW, Washington, DC 20580. Three copies of the Form, along with one set of documentary attachments, should be sent to the Department of Justice, Antitrust Division, Office of Operations, Premerger Notification Unit, 950 Pennsylvania Avenue, NW, Room 3335, Washington, DC 20530 (for non-USPS deliveries, use zip code 20004).

THE FILING FEE

In connection with the filing of a Form, Congress also mandated the collection of a fee from each acquiring person. The filing fee is based on a three-tiered system that ties the amount paid to the total value of the voting securities, NCI or assets held as a result of the acquisition:[26]

Value of Voting Securities, NCI, or Assets to Be Held	Fee Amount
Greater than $50 million (as adjusted) but less than $100 million (as adjusted)	$45,000
$100 million (as adjusted) or greater but less than $500 million (as adjusted)	$125,000
$500 million (as adjusted) or greater	$280,000

---

[25] A publicly announced merger is one in which a party to the merger has disclosed the existence of the transaction in a press release or in a public filing with a governmental body.

[26] The filing fee thresholds are adjusted annually for changes in the GNP during the previous year. The fees themselves are not adjusted.

For transactions in which more than one person is deemed to be the acquiring person, each acquiring person must pay the appropriate fee (except in consolidations and in transactions in which there are two acquiring persons that would have exactly the same responses to Item 5 of the Form).[27] In addition, an acquiring person will have to pay multiple filing fees if a series of acquisitions are separately reported.[28]

The filing fee must be paid at the time of filing to "The Federal Trade Commission" by electronic wire transfer, bank cashier's check or certified check. Rule 803.9 contains specific instructions for payment of the filing fee. In addition, information is available at http://www.ftc.gov/bc/hsr/filing2.htm.

THE WAITING PERIOD

After filing, the filing parties must then observe a statutory waiting period during which they may not consummate the transaction. The waiting period is 15 days for reportable acquisitions by means of a cash tender offer, as well as acquisitions subject to certain federal bankruptcy provisions, and 30 days for all other types of reportable transactions.[29] The waiting period may be extended by issuance of a request for additional information and documentary material.[30] Any waiting period that would end on a Saturday, Sunday or legal public holiday will expire on the next regular business day.

Beginning of the Waiting Period

In most cases, the waiting period begins after both the acquiring and acquired persons file completed Forms with both agencies. However, for certain transactions in which a person buys voting securities from persons other than the issuer (third party and open market transactions), the waiting period begins after the acquiring person files a complete Form. In a reportable joint venture

---

[27] For example, if two separate UPEs jointly control an acquisition vehicle and own no other entities, their Item 5 responses would be identical.
[28] See Rule 803.9(a)–(c).
[29] See Rule 803.10; 11 U.S.C. § 363(b)(2), as amended (1994).
[30] See Section VIII(C), *infra*.

formation, the waiting period begins after all acquiring persons required to file submit complete Forms.[31] It is important to note that failure to pay the filing fee or the submission of an incorrect or incomplete filing wiil delay the start of the waiting period.[32]

Early Termination

Any filing person may request that the waiting period be terminated before the statutory period expires. Such a request for "early termination" will be granted only if (1) at least one of the persons specifies it on the Form; (2) all persons have submitted compliant Forms; and (3) both antitrust agencies have completed their review and determined not to take any enforcement action during the waiting period.[33]

The PNO is responsible for informing the parties that early termination has been granted. The Act requires that the FTC publish a notice in the Federal Register of each early termination granted. Moreover, grants of early termination also appear on the FTC's Web site at http://www.ftc.gov/bc/earlyterm/index.html.

When it's requested, early termination is granted for most transactions. On the average, requests for early termination are granted within two weeks from the beginning of the waiting period. In any particular transaction, however, the time that it takes to grant a request for early termination depends on many factors, including the complexity of the proposed transaction, its potential competitive impact, and the number of filings from other parties that the enforcement agencies must review at the same time.

REVIEW OF THE FORM

Once a Form has been filed, the enforcement agencies begin their review. The FTC is responsible for the administration of the Program. As a result, the PNO determines whether the Form complies with the Act and the Rules.

The Form is assigned to a member of the PNO staff to assess whether the transaction was subject to the reporting requirements and whether the

---

[31] The joint venture entity does not file. *See* Rule 802.41.

[32] See Rules 803.3 and 803.10(a).

[33] See Formal Interpretation 13 issued August 20, 1982.

Form was completed accurately. If the filing appears to be deficient, the staff member will notify the contact person as quickly as possible so that errors can be corrected. It is important to correct the errors as soon as possible because the waiting period does not begin to run until the Form is filled out accurately, all required information and documentary material are supplied, and payment of the filing fee is received.[34]

When the PNO determines that the Forms comply with all filing requirements, letters are sent to the parties identifying the beginning and ending of the waiting period, as well as the transaction number assigned to the filing. The conclusion that the parties have complied with the Act and the Rules may be modified later, however, if circumstances warrant.

ANTITRUST REVIEW OF THE TRANSACTION

Initially, both agencies undertake a preliminary substantive review of the proposed transaction. The agencies analyze the filings to determine whether the acquiring and acquired firms are competitors, or are related in any other way such that a combination of the two firms might adversely affect competition. Staff members rely not only on the information included on the Form but also on publicly available information. The individuals analyzing the Form often have experience either with the markets or the companies involved in the particular transaction. As a result, they may have industry expertise to aid in evaluating the likelihood that a merger may be harmful.

If, after preliminary review, either or both agencies decide that a particular transaction warrants closer examination, the agencies decide between themselves which one will be responsible for the investigation. Only one of the enforcement agencies will conduct an investigation of a proposed transaction. Other than members of the PNO, no one at either agency will initiate

---

[34] For transactions in which a person buys voting securities from someone other than the issuer (third party and open market transactions), the waiting period begins after the acquiring person submits a complete and accurate Form. An incorrect or incomplete Form from the acquired person will not stop the running of the waiting period. However, the acquired person still is obligated to correct any deficiencies in its filing.

contact with any of the persons or any third parties until it has been decided which agency will be responsible for investigating the proposed transaction.[35] This clearance procedure is designed to minimize the duplication of effort and the confusion that could result if both agencies contacted individual persons at different times about the same matter. The clearance decision is made pursuant to an agreement that divides the antitrust work between the two agencies.

Of course, any interested person, including either of the parties, is free to present information to either or both agencies at any time. However, if the clearance decision has not yet been resolved, the person must make a presentation, or provide written information or documents, to both agencies. If you are representing a party that wishes to make a presentation, or provide written information or documents, you may inform the PNO of that fact; the PNO will let staff attorneys at both agencies who are reviewing the matter know that persons wish to come in and make a presentation, or provide written information or documents.

SECOND REQUESTS

Once the investigating agency has clearance to proceed, it may ask any or all persons to the transaction to submit additional information or documentary material to the requesting agency. The request for additional information is commonly referred to as a "second request."[36] As discussed above, although both agencies review each Form submitted to them, only one agency will issue second requests to the parties in a particular transaction.

Information Requested

Generally, a second request will solicit information on particular products or services in an attempt to assist the investigative team in examining a

---

[35] Staff at either agency may initiate contact with a person prior to the resolution of which agency will handle the matter by first notifying the other agency and offering the other agency the opportunity to participate.

[36] See Rule 803.20(a)(1) for the identities of persons and individuals that are subject to such request.

variety of legal and economic questions. A typical second request will include interrogatory-type questions as well as requests for the production of documents. A model second request has been produced jointly by the FTC and DOJ for internal use by their attorneys and is contained in *Guide III*. Because every transaction is unique, however, the model second request should be regarded only as an example.

Narrowing the Request

Parties that receive a second request and believe that it is broader than necessary to obtain the information that the enforcement agency needs are encouraged to discuss the possibility of narrowing the request with the staff attorneys reviewing the proposed transaction. Often, the investigative team drafts a second request based only on information contained in the initial filing and other available material. At this point, the investigative team may not have access to specific information about the structure of the company or its products and services. By meeting with staff, representatives of the company have an opportunity to narrow the issues and to limit the required search for documents and other information. If second request modification issues cannot be resolved through discussion with staff, the agencies also have adopted a formal internal appeals process that centralizes in one decision maker in each agency the review of issues relating to the scope of and compliance with second requests.[37]

The enforcement agency issuing the second request may have determined that certain data sought in the request can resolve one or more issues critical to the investigation. In such a situation, the agency's staff may suggest use of the informal "quick look" procedure. Under the quick look, the staff will request the parties to first submit documents and other information, which specifically address the critical issues (e.g., product market definition or ease of entry). If the submitted information resolves the staff's concerns in these areas, the waiting period will be terminated on a *sua sponte* basis and the parties will not have to expend the time and cost of responding to the full second request. Of course, if the submitted information does not resolve the staff's concerns on determinative issues, then the parties will need to respond to the full second request.

---

[37] See 66 Fed. Reg. 8721-8722, February 1, 2001.

Extension of the Waiting Period

The issuance of a second request extends the statutory waiting period until 30 days (or in the case of a cash tender offer or certain bankruptcy filings,[38] 10 days) after both parties are deemed to have complied with the second request (or in the case of a tender offer and bankruptcy, until after the acquiring person has complied).[39] During this time, the attorneys investigating the matter may also be interviewing relevant parties and using other forms of compulsory process to obtain information.

The second request must be issued by the enforcement agency before the waiting period expires. If the waiting period expires and the agencies have not issued a second request to any person to the transaction, then the parties are free to consummate the transaction. The fact that the agencies do not issue second requests does not preclude them from initiating an enforcement action at a later time.[40] All of the agencies' other investigative tools are available to them in such investigations.[41]

AGENCY ACTION

After analyzing all of the information available to them, the investigative staff will make a recommendation to either the Commission or the Assistant Attorney General (depending on which agency has clearance).

No Further Action

If the staff finds no reason to believe competition will be reduced substantially in any market, it will recommend no further action. Assuming that the agency concurs in that recommendation, the parties are then free to consummate their transaction upon expiration of the waiting period. As with a decision not to issue a second request, a decision not to seek injunctive relief at that time does not preclude the enforcement agencies from initiating a postmerger enforcement action at a later time.

---

[38] See 11 U.S.C. § 363(b), as amended (1994).

[39] See § 7A(e) of the Act.

[40] See § 7(A)(i)(1) of the Act.

[41] See § 7(A)(i)(2) of the Act.

Seeking Injunctive Relief

If the investigative staff believes that the transaction is likely to be anticompetitive, it may recommend that the agency initiate injunction proceedings in U.S. district court to halt the acquisition. If the Commission or the Assistant Attorney General concurs in the staff's recommendation, then the agency will file suit in the appropriate district court. If it is a Commission case, the FTC is required to file an administrative complaint within twenty days (or a lesser time if the court so directs) of the granting of its motion for a temporary restraining order or for a preliminary injunction.[42] The administrative complaint initiates the FTC's administrative proceeding that will decide the legality of the transaction. If it is a DOJ case, the legality of the transaction is litigated entirely in district court.

Settlements

During an investigation, the investigative staff may, if appropriate, discuss terms of settlement with the parties. The staff of the FTC is permitted to negotiate a proposed settlement with the parties; however, it must then be presented to the Commission, accepted by a majority vote, and placed on the public record for a notice and comment period before it can be made final. A proposed settlement negotiated by DOJ staff must be approved by the Assistant Attorney General and also placed on the public record for a notice and comment period before it will be entered by a district court pursuant to the provisions of the Antitrust Procedures and Penalties Act, 15 U.S.C. § 16(b)–(h).

FAILURE TO FILE

Civil Penalties

If you consummate a reportable transaction without filing the required prior notification or without waiting until the expiration of the statutory waiting period, you may be subject to civil penalties. The Act provides that "any person, or any officer, director or partner thereof" shall be liable for a penalty of up to $11,000 a day for each day the person is in violation of the Act. The enforcement agencies may also obtain other relief to remedy

---

[42] FTC Act Section 13(b).

violations of the Act, such as an order requiring the person to divest assets or voting securities acquired in violation of the Act.[43]

Reporting Omissions

If you have completed a transaction in violation of the Act, it is important to bring the matter to the attention of the PNO and to file a notification as soon as possible. Even a late filing provides information to the enforcement agencies that assists them in conducting antitrust screening of transactions and antitrust investigations. The parties should include a letter with the notification from an officer or director of the company explaining why the notification was not filed in a timely manner, how and when the failure was discovered, and what steps have been taken to prevent a violation of the Act in the future. The letter should be addressed to the Deputy Director, Bureau of Competition, Federal Trade Commission, 600 Pennsylvania Ave., NW, Washington, DC 20580.

Deliberate Avoidance

The Rules specifically provide that structuring a transaction to avoid the Act does not alter notification obligations if the substance of the transaction is reportable.[44] For example, the agencies will seek penalties where the parties split a transaction into separate parts that are each valued below the current filing threshold in order to avoid reporting the transaction, but the fair market value of the assets being acquired is actually above the threshold.[45]

OTHER GUIDES IN THIS SERIES

Guide I is the first in a series of guides prepared by the PNO. Others include:

Guide II: *To File or Not to File—When You Must File a Premerger Notification Report Form,* which explains certain basic requirements

---

[43] See § 7A(g) of the Act, as amended by the Debt Collection Improvements Act of 1996, Pub. L. No. 104134 (Apr. 26, 1996); 61 Fed. Reg. 54548 (Oct. 21, 1996); 61 Fed. Reg. 55840 (Oct. 29, 1996).

[44] See Rule 801.90.

[45] See, e.g., *United States v. Sara Lee Corp.,* 1996-1 Trade Cas. (CCH) ¶ 71,301 (D.D.C. 1996).

of the program and takes you through a step-by-step analysis for determining whether a particular transaction must be reported.

Guide III: *A Model Request for Additional Information and Documentary Material (Second Request),* which contains materials designed for the attorneys of the antitrust enforcement agencies in preparing requests for additional information. It is included in this series to provide an example of what you might expect if either enforcement agency issues a second request.

OTHER MATERIALS

To make effective use of these guides, you must be aware of their limitations. They are intended to provide only a very general introduction to the Act and Rules and should be used only as a starting point. Because it would be impossible, within the scope of these guides, to explain all of the details and nuances of the premerger requirements, you must not rely on them as a substitute for reading the Act and the Rules themselves. To determine premerger notification requirements, you should consult:

1. Section 7A of the Clayton Act, 15 U.S.C. § 18a, as amended by the Hart-Scott-Rodino Antitrust Improvements Act of 1976, Pub. L. 94-435, 90 Stat. 1390, and amended by Pub. L. No. 106-553, 114 Stat. 2762.
2. The Premerger Notification Rules, 16 C.F.R. Parts 801–803. (2008).
3. The Statement of Basis and Purpose for the Rules, 43 Fed. Reg. 33450 (July 31, 1978); 48 Fed. Reg. 34428 (July 29, 1983); 52 Fed. Reg. 7066 (March 6, 1987); 52 Fed. Reg. 20058 (May 29, 1987); 63 Fed. Reg., 13666 (March 28, 1996); 66 Fed. Reg. 8680 (February 1, 2001); 66 Fed. Reg. 23561 (May 9, 2001); 66 Fed. Reg. 35541 (July 6, 2001); 67 Fed. Reg. 11898 (March 18, 2002); 67 Fed. Reg. 11904 (March 18, 2002); 68 Fed. Reg. 2425 (January 17, 2003); 70 Fed. Reg. 4987 (January 31, 2005); 70 Fed. Reg. 11502 (March 8, 2005); 70 Fed. Reg. 73369 (December 12, 2005); 71 Fed. Reg. 35995 (June 23, 2006).
4. The formal interpretations issued pursuant to the Rules, compiled in 6 Trade Reg. Rep. (CCH) at ¶ 42,475.

It is advisable to check the Federal Register for more recent Rules changes that have not yet been incorporated into the Code of Federal

Regulations or these guides. For an up-to-date list of Federal Register notices related to the Statement of Basis and Purpose, see http://www.ftc.gov/bc/hsr/basispurp.shtm. For other HSR-related rulemakings, see http://www.ftc.gov/bc/hsr/rulemaking.shtm. Amendments and formal interpretations, as well as the other material referenced above, are available on the Premerger Notification Office Web site at http://www.ftc.gov/bc/hsr.

There are also non-governmental publications that, while not officially endorsed by the FTC, contain useful compilations of materials relevant to the Program:

1. Commerce Clearing House's *Trade Regulation Reporter* reprints the Act, the Rules, the Form, and the Formal Interpretations.
2. The American Bar Association's Section of Antitrust Law publishes a *Premerger Notification Practice Manual (2007 Edition)* that provides a collection of informal interpretations of the PNO.
3. A loose-leaf treatise by Axinn, Fogg, Stoll and Prager, *Acquisitions under the Hart-Scott-Rodino Antitrust Improvements Act* (published by Law Journal Seminars Press), explains requirements of the Form, the Rules, and the Act, and includes a discussion of the legislative history of the Act.

Finally, if you have questions about the program or a particular transaction not answered by the Commission's HSR Web site, the staff of the PNO is available to assist you. The PNO answers thousands of inquiries each year and is prepared to provide prompt informal advice concerning the potential reportability of a transaction and completion of the Form. For general questions, contact the PNO at (202) 326-3100.

Index

A

Accountants
role, 94, 142–145
Accounting
considerations, 112–114,
142–145, 199, 229, 237
firm, 95, 112, 142
Acquirer
constraints in sale process, 90–92
decision to proceed, 179
decision to renegotiate, 175–178
decision to withdraw, 170–173
financing transaction, 224
elimination from auction process,
167
perspective on acquisition
process, 79–81
perspective on pricing, 129–130
perspective on relationship-based
preemption, 130–131
role in contract drafting and
revision, 202, 215–220
Acquisitions. *See also* Mergers and
acquisitions
characteristics, 42–44
causes for failure, 10–14
inactionable findings, 13–14
marketplace, 58–59
networking, 61–62
planning, *xv*, 32, 53–54

premium, 18, 129–130, 195–202
rationale, 53–54, 73–74
reactive approach, 11–13
research, 60–61
risk, 7, 12, 23. *See also* Risk
risk mitigation, 14
strategy, 53–54. *See also* Strategic
planning
success factors, 14–16
target. *See* Acquisition candidate
Acquisition candidate
assessment, 57, 73–78
availability, 66
engagement, 56, 67–73
identification, 54–55, 58–59
investigation, *xvi*, 53–54
nature of target, 92
proactive engagement, 68–71
profile, 62–63
pursuit, 58, 78–91
qualification, 56, 64–66
reactive engagement, 71–73
strategic fit, 66
winnowing process, 54–58
Acquisition team
assembling core team, 81–82
external resources, 82
key roles of members, 82–83
leader, 82
internal resources, 82–83

Anti-competitive combination. *See* Hart-Scott-Rodino Antitrust Improvements Act
Approval
  proceeding with transaction, 182–186
  pursuit of acquisition, 73–75
Asset sale, 200–202
Assignability of contracts, 224
Auction process letter, 160–161
Auction
  buyer's perspective, 79–81, 127–128
  description, 126–127
  elimination, 167
  seller's perspective, 9, 79–81
Audit 95, 112, 142
  mentality, 106

B
Back-up planning, 45–46, 166
Business broker, 58, 62, 70, 72, 126
Business development, 3, 30, 62, 70, 93, 95
Business portfolio, 33–34
Buyer. *See* Acquirer
Buyer financing, 224

C
Closing the transaction
  buyer financing, 224
  escrow agreement, 206
  process, 220–221, 224
  purchase agreement, 203–205
  purchase price adjustment, 205–206
  regulatory issues, 221–224
  third-party consent, 224

timing, 205
  working capital adjustment, 206
Combined value, 20
Communication
  among due diligence team members, 154–158
  integration progress, 239–242
  logistical information for due diligence, 108
  responsibility and timing of due diligence report submissions, 108
Compartmentalized behavior, 13
Competition, 33–34
Conditions to close, 211
Confidentiality agreement, 70–71
Consultants, 61, 97, 217
Contingency plan, 188, 245–247
Contingent purchase price, 199–200
Contract drafting, 202–203
Contract negotiation
  commitment to success, 220
  effective and efficient process, 215, 218–219
  empowered leadership, 215–216
  principal-to-principal discussions, 219
  reaching final agreement, 219–220
  role of legal counsel, 216
  role of subject area experts, 217–218
Contract review and feedback, 218
Corporate approval, 73–75
Covenant, 208–209

CPA firm. *See* Accounting: firm
Cultural integration, 140–141, 235, 247–248

D
Data room, 135, 137, 161–164
  review, 135–136
  information listing, 161–164
Deal
  champion. *See* Transaction: sponsor
  structure. *See* Transaction: structure
Department of Justice (DOJ), 221, 253
Disclosure schedules, 213–214
Disclosure schedules, illustrative list, 214
Document review, 135–136
Due diligence
  findings and recommendations, 193–194
  mind-set, 105–106
  objectives, 103, 139–140
  origins, 8
Due diligence checklist
  company background, 109–112
  finance, 112–114
  human resources, 119
  insurance, 119
  legal, 116–119
  marketing and sales, 116
  products, 115–116
  technology, 114–115
Due diligence reporting
  comprehensive report, 180
  contingency plan, 188

  corporate approval to proceed, 182–186
  coordination, 108
  elimination from auction, 168–169
  integration plan, 186
  recommendation to proceed, 179
  renegotiation of major terms, 175–178
  summary due diligence report, 180
  withdrawal decision, 175
Due diligence review. *See also* Holistic due diligence
  assessment by function, 141–153
  business development, 9, 95
  causes of failure, 10–14
  components, 131–137
  constraints, 90–93
  creation of team, 93–97
  cross-functional coordination, 154–159
  definition, 8, 88–89
  document review, 135–136
  facilities, 136–137
  finance and accounting, 9, 94, 142–145
  human resources, 9, 95–96, 145–148
  independent accountants, 95.
    See also Accounting: firm
  information technology, 96, 151–152
  legal counsel, 9, 95, 153–154
  management presentation, 132–134
  management team interview, 134–135

Due diligence review (*Continued*)
  objectives-driven approach,
    138–159
  preparing, 98–99, 106–108
  product management, 96
  production/operations, 9, 96–97,
    152–153
  program development, 99–104,
    106
  research and development,
    150–151
  sales and marketing, 96,
    148–149
  success factors, 14–16
  tax, 97
  technology, 137–137
Due diligence review outcomes
  decision to proceed, 179–188
  elimination from auction,
    167–170
  renegotiation of basic terms,
    175–179
  withdrawal from process,
    170–175
Due diligence review program
  coverage breadth, depth, focus,
    102
  conclusions, 102–103
  development process, 99–100,
    106
  findings, 103–105, 193–202
  key aspects, 100–103
  objectives, 103
  procedures, 101
  recommendations, 103
Due diligence team
  coordination, 107
  creation, 93–97

E
Early alert. *See* Approval
Earn-out, 199–200
Employment matters, 209–210
Environmental factors affecting sale
    process, 90–93
Exclusivity, 69–70

F
Federal Trade Commission (FTC),
    221–222, 253
Finance and accounting functions,
    9, 94, 142–145, 217
Financial
  impact, 74–75
  intermediary, advisor, 58, 62, 70,
    72, 126
  statements, 112–114, 142–145,
    161–162, 207, 214, 229
Financing. *See* Buyer financing

G
Growth
  earnings, 4
  strategy, 15, 32. *See also* Strategic
    planning

H
Hart-Scott-Rodino Antitrust
    Improvements Act, 66–67, 99,
    221–224, 253–273
Hold-back, 200
Holistic due diligence, *xiv*, 14–16,
    25, 107, 227

I
Indemnification, 211–212
Independent accountant. *See*
    Accounting: firm

Information disclosure, 81–82
Infrastructure improvement, 38
Insurance, 119, 153–154
Integration. *See* Postacquisition
    integration
Intermediary. *See* Financial:
    intermediary, advisor
Internal development, 39–42, 53
Investment
    alternatives, 38–45
    bankers, 58, 62, 70, 72, 126
    objectives, 34–35
Investment types
    acquisition, 42–44
    internal development, 39–42
    strategic alliance, 44–45

K
Knowledge transfer, 249–250

L
Leadership. *See also* Purposeful
    behavior
    acquisition team, 82
    due diligence team, 93
    integration team, 232–233
    integrated management, 15
    negotiation team, 215–216
Legal counsel, 3, 9, 94, 116, 153,
    202, 216

M
Management presentation,
    132–134
Management team interview,
    134–135
Market targeting, 33

Market expansion, 35–37
Marketing materials
    management presentation,
        132–134
    offering document (prospectus),
        132
    teaser, 91
Marketplace for acquisitions,
    58–59
Mergers and acquisitions
    nature, 5
    reasons, 4
    results, 6
    size, 5
    volume, 4
Mitigating risk, 7–10, 14, 45,
    154–159, 173–174, 188, 202,
    229–231, 245. *See also* Risk

N
Negotiation. *See* Contract
    negotiation
Networking. *See* Acquisition:
    networking
No-go (transaction withdrawal)
    decision, 170–175
Noncompetion covenant, 209
Nondislosure agreement (NDA).
    See Confidentiality agreement

O
Objectives-driven due diligence,
    87–88
Offering document, 132
Operational integration, 234–235
Organic development. *See* Internal
    development

P

Plan to create value, 16–17, 55–58, 76–79, 87–88, 101–102, 139–143, 165–166

Position paper. *See* Approval

Postacquisition integration
cultural, 141, 158, 235, 247–248
first 90 days, 238
operational, 140–141, 157–158, 234
synergistic, 141, 158, 235

Postacquisition integration
plan outline, 236
planning, 186–187, 234–239
reporting, 242–244
team, 187, 231–234

Postacquisition issues, 194–195

Preacquisition issues, 193–194

Preemptive bid, 128–130

Premerger Notification Program, 253–273. *See also* Hart-Scott-Rodino Act

Price preemption, 129–130

Proactive acquisition prospecting, 68–71

Prospectus. *See* Offering document

Purchase agreement
closing, 205–206
conditions to close, 210
covenants, 208–209
employee matters, 209–210
general provisions, 212–213
illustrative outline, 204
indemnification, 211–212
purchase and sale, 203–205
representations and warranties (buyer), 208

representations and warranties (seller), 206–207
tax matters, 212
termination, 211

Purchase premium preemption, 129

Purchase price, 18–24, 128–130, 195–199

Purposeful behavior, 6, 14, 16, 24, 58

R

Reactive acquisition, 11, 71–73

Regulatory issues, 66–67, 99, 221–224, 253–273

Relationship-based preemption, 130

Renegotiation of major terms, 175–178

Representations and warranties
buyer, 208
seller, 206–207

Research. *See* Acquisitions: research

Retrospective analysis, 249–250

Risk, 7, 12, 23, 77–78, 202, 173–175
mitigation, 7–10, 14, 45, 154–159, 173–174, 188, 202, 229–231, 245
sharing, 202

S

Selling materials. *See* Marketing materials

Selling process, 9, 126–131

Standalone performance, 21–22, 101

Standalone value, 18–19, 195–199

Stock sale, 200–202

Strategic alliance, 44–45, 53

Strategic assessment, 17, 32–33,
    64–65
Strategic fit, 64–66, 171–172
Strategic planning
    acquisition strategy, 53–54
    characteristics, 31–32
    outputs, 46–50
    process management, 30
    process overview, 32
    role, 27
Strategic purpose, 17, 73–74,
    76–78
Synergy, 22–23, 64, 101, 195, 199
Synergy-related integration, 235
Synergy value, 20, 22, 64–66,
    195–198

T
Tax matters, 9, 118–119, 212
Tax structure, 22, 97, 111,
    200–202, 212
Team
    acquisition, 81–83
    due diligence, 93–97, 107
    integration, 232–233
    negotiation, 215–216
Teaser, 91

Top-down due diligence. *See*
        Objectives-driven due diligence
Transaction
    considerations, 75
    sponsor, 53, 72–73, 75, 82, 168,
        175, 177–178
    structure, 22, 79–81, 199
Transition services agreement,
        213–215

U
U.S. Anti-trust considerations, 66,
        221–224, 253–273. *See also*
        Hart-Scott-Rodino Act

V
Valuation, 76, 172–173, 195–199
Value
    creation, 16, 20, 228–229.
        See also Plan to create value
    driver, 20–23, 77–78, 198
    extraction, 228–229
Vertical integration, 37–38

W
Withdrawal decision, 170–175
Working capital adjustment, 206